MASS
COMMUNICATION
THEORY

Denis McQuail

MASS COMMUNICATION THEORY

An Introduction

Second Edition

SAGE Publications

London. Newbury Park. Beverly Hills. New Delhi

P 90
.M35
1987

SAGE Publications Ltd
28 Banner Street
London EC1Y 8QE

SAGE Publications Inc
275 South Beverly Drive
Beverly Hills, California 90212
and
SAGE Publications Inc
2111 West Hillcrest Drive
Newbury Park, California 91320

SAGE Publications India Pvt Ltd
C-236 Defence Colony
New Delhi 110 024

British Library Cataloguing in Publication Data
McQuail, Denis
 Mass communication theory: an introduction.—2nd ed.
 1. Mass media
 I. Title
 302.2'34'01   P90

 ISBN 0–8039–8069–8
 ISBN 0–8039–8070–1 Pbk

Library of Congress Catalogue Card Number 87–061113

ISBN 0–8039–8069–8
ISBN 0–8039–8070–1 Pbk

Phototypeset by Dataset, 35 St Clements, Oxford
Printed in Great Britain by J.W. Arrowsmith Ltd, Bristol

CONTENTS

To fellow members of the Euromedia Research Group — good friends and colleagues since 1982

PREFACE

This new edition replaces a book which was itself a successor to an earlier text — *Towards a Sociology of Mass Communications* (McQuail, 1969) — and it still has the same general purpose, that of providing guidance for students in the branch of study concerned with mass communication. The original textbook was based, implicitly at least, on a view of mass media as an object of enquiry which could be investigated from several different perspectives, rather than as something needing its own 'discipline' or body of theory. In the event, mass media were examined mainly in the light of sociological theory and research.

The first edition of this book and the present volume are different in two main respects from their predecessor: first of all, the intention is not to summarize research (now an impossible task), but to offer a framework of theory, with examples and illustrative support from research and media practice; secondly, there is less emphasis on sociology as the source of theory (although it is still important) and more recognition of the need to treat questions of mass communication within a broader framework of 'communication science'. The latter refers not to a newly claimed academic discipline (an outdated notion) but to the body of knowledge relevant to questions of human communication and information in society.

In this edition, the text has been largely rewritten, with three primary objectives: to update and take account of recent theory and research; enlargement, to reflect the continuing expansion of the field; clarification and improved presentation to make ideas more accessible. In addition, this version offers certain new features which make it in several respects a different book. A good deal more attention is paid to new electronic media and to the implications for theory of changes in communication technologies. These are discussed at several points in the book. Secondly, there are a number of new graphic representations and typologies designed to express or summarize major points of theory. Thirdly, there is more specific attention (in chapter 5) to the working out of normative theories of media in terms of principles for assessing 'media performance'.

Finally, while still a book about mass communication, the present edition is intended as a contribution to the development of a broader framework for the study of communication referred to above. This aim is motivated to a large extent by an acceptance of the fact that communication is changing and becoming more central in society. It is no longer justifiable to deal with it in terms of one institutional manifestation alone or from the viewpoint of one of the social sciences.

The main debt in a book of this kind cannot be properly acknowledged, since it is to the many researchers and writers whose work has been drawn on and referred to. In writing these words, I am reminded of a particular loss to the community of researchers caused by the untimely death in 1983 of Phillip Elliott, whose work was a particular source of stimulus and influence for myself as for many others. Another kind of hidden debt is to students from whom ideas and ways of presentation were first worked out. In this case, I am glad to acknowledge the students of Mass Communication at the University of Amsterdam, as the most recent contributors. I am also indebted to many friends and colleagues in different parts of the world for stimulus and encouragement. Toleration and encouragement from my own family has been another indispensable ingredient to finishing this book. The final preparation of the manuscript was greatly helped by the fast and efficient secretarial support of Carin Mulie-Velgersdijk. The initiative towards a new, and improved, version of this book came from Farrell Burnett of Sage Publications and I am grateful to her for the idea and for the necessary support and well-judged pressure actually to fulfil it.

Schoorl, N.H.
January 1987

CHAPTER I

THE RISE OF MEDIA OF MASS COMMUNICATION

Mass communication as an object of study

The significance of mass media

The mass media themselves — press, television, radio, etc, and the process of mass communication (what they set out to do) have been increasingly subjected to systematic study, the more they have become an important institution in society. That the media are important is a basic assumption of this book and it rests on the following propositions:
- The media are a growing and changing industry providing employment, producing goods and services, and feeding related industries; they also comprise an institution in themselves, developing their own rules and norms which link the institution to society and to other social institutions. The media institution is, in turn, regulated by society.
- The mass media are a power resource — a means of control, management and innovation in society, which can be a substitute for force or other resources.
- They provide a *location* (or arena) where, increasingly, the affairs of public life are played out, both nationally and internationally.
- They are often the location of developments in culture, both in the sense of art and symbolic forms, but also in manners, fashions, styles of life and norms.
- They have become a dominant source of definitions and images of social reality for individuals, but also collectively for groups and societies; they express values and normative judgements inextricably mixed with news and entertainment.

A further set of assumptions underlies the composition and general line of this book, not so much about the media themselves, but about the kinds of society in which mass media have reached the status of a significant social institution. Most fundamentally, societies are structured by differences of power between and within economic classes and are characterized by latent, if not active, conflicts and tensions. These conflicts find expression in competing ideologies, in which media are deeply involved as disseminators and stores, if not as originators. The forces historically at work in societies are, however, more potent than the media or the effects which they can produce. The media are essentially dependent on, or at most instruments for, the exercise of power by others. They are also channels by which social changes are given direction and impetus. These assumptions are, nevertheless, matters for reflection in theory and there are alternative versions available of the kind and degree of part played by mass communication in society, sufficient for the reader to make a choice of his or her own.

It follows from the assumptions named that the study of mass communication cannot avoid dealing in values of a fundamental kind, which may well be inconsistent or in conflict with each other. This is not a unique problem for the social scientist to have to face, but it is posed in an unusually extreme form and most theory about the working of the mass media is value-laden in one way or direction or another. At best, alternative value positions can be offered and the conditions under which normative propositions may hold can be made clear.

Different kinds of theory

If theory is understood, not as a system of law-like propositions, but rather as sets of ideas of varying status and origin which may explain or interpret some phenomenon, then one can distinguish at least four kinds of theory concerning mass communication.

The first kind to be expected in a text like this is *social scientific* theory — general statements about the nature, working and effects of mass communication, derived from systematic and, as far as possible, objective observation and evidence about media and often reliant on other bodies of social scientific theory.

Secondly, there is a body of *normative* theory (a branch of social philosophy in effect) which is more concerned with how media *ought* to operate if certain social values are to be observed or attained, and, of course, with the nature of these social values. This kind of theory is important, because it does play a part in shaping media institutions, and has considerable influence on the expectations from media which are held by the media's own publics and by other social agencies and actors.

Thirdly, there is a body of knowledge, partly also normative, but practical too, developed and maintained by media practitioners themselves. This might be called *working* theory, since it offers guidelines on the purposes of media work, how things ought to be done in line with the more abstract principles of social theory and also on how certain ends *can* be achieved. Some of the ideas involved are matters of technique, some are enshrined in traditions, professional practices, norms of behaviour, rules of thumb, which guide the work of media production and give it consistency over time.

The theory is practical because it helps to answer such questions as: 'What will please the audience?' 'What will be effective?' 'What is newsworthy?' 'What, in a given case, are the responsibilities of the journalist or medium?' Such ideas may not be very consciously raised but they are an indispensable foundation for actually carrying out mass communication and they frequently come to light in studies of media production. Katz (1977) has compared the task of the researcher in this respect to that of theorists of music or philosophers of science who can point to underlying regularities which the practising musician or scientist may not and does not usually need to be aware of.

Finally, there is a kind of knowledge which it seems even less appropriate to dignify with the name of theory, but which is also ubiquitous, influential and often encountered in research into mass communication. This, which we might call *commonsense* theory, refers to the knowledge (and ideas) which everyone has, by virtue of direct experience in an audience. Any newspaper reader or television viewer has an implicit theory in the sense of a set of ideas about the medium in question, what it is, what it is good for, how it fits into daily life, how it should be 'read', what its connotations are and how it may relate to other aspects of social life. Most people will carry an elaborate set of associations and ideas of this kind which enable them to act consistently and satisfactorily in relation to the media.

Such commonsense theories are not usually articulated, but in them are grounded a number of basic definitions of what the media are and how they differ from each other (true also of media genres and formats). It is also in such theory that we find many of the norms and standards governing audience uses of media as well as the opinions about mass media which can influence media planning and the making of public policy for media. While it is not the aim of this book to report directly on the detailed substance of this kind of theory, it makes its inevitable appearance by way of surveys of attitudes to media, in motivations which are expressed for media use and it is often incorporated in observations of the behaviour of communicators and audiences.

The substance of this book is drawn from each of these four sources, most recognizably the first and the second, but no less importantly from the third and the fourth. One answer to the question 'What is mass communication?' is 'What people think it is' and the most influential 'thinkers' in the sense of this answer are not social scientists but mass communicators, their clients and their audiences. It is also these who, by their actions, demands and expectations, largely shape the definitions which all media sooner or later acquire. These definitions are not given, in the first instance, by legislators or media theorists. They only express a version of what everyone in society has first established. The emergence of these definitions is a very complex process and their forms are often variable and hazy. They are dealt with later in this chapter.

Theories of communication and of mass communication

The study of mass communication is located within a much larger field of enquiry concerned with human communication, which is sometimes identified as 'communication science' (for an account see Rogers, 1986, or Chaffee and Berger, 1987). There are alternative ways of dividing up this larger whole, but one way is according to the *level* of social organization at which communication takes place. From this perspective, mass communication can be viewed as at the apex of a pyramidal distribution (See Figure 1).

Figure I Communication processes in society

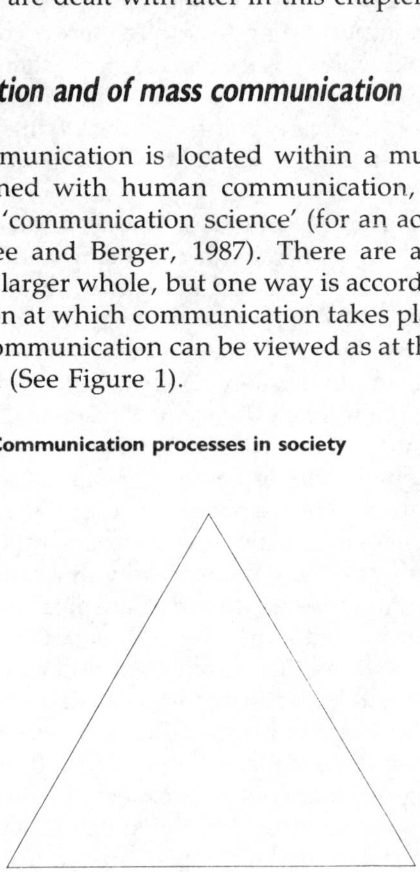

Level of Communication Process:

— Society-wide   Few cases
   (e.g. mass communication)

— Institutional/organizational
   (e.g. political system or
       business firm)

— Intergroup or association
   (e.g. local community)

— Intragroup
   (e.g. family)

— Interpersonal
   (e.g. dyad, couple)

— Intrapersonal
   (e.g. processing information)   Many cases

Each level of communication entails a particular set of problems and priorities and has its own body of evidence and theory. At the intrapersonal level, attention focuses mainly on the processing (e.g. comprehension, recall, interpretation) of information (e.g. media news) and on 'exchanges' with the environment. Here theory deals with mental states and processes. At the interpersonal and intra-group level, the main problems claiming attention concern: forms of discourse, patterns of interaction, questions of affiliation (attachment), control and hierarchy, the setting of norms, the marking of bound-aries, influence and diffusion. Very similar themes, but under more complex conditions they are treated at higher levels. In formal organizations, there is more attention to control and to the efficiency of information transmission. In groups and associations, questions of voluntary attachment, interaction, co-operation and the formation of norms and standards take precedence. Nevertheless, communication science as a whole inclines to identify a set of questions, common to all levels, which theory and research try to answer. These are:

– Who communicates to whom? (sources and receivers)
– Why communicate? (functions and purposes)
– How does communication take place? (channels, languages, codes)
– What about? (content, objects of reference, types of information)
– What are the consequences of communication? (intended or unintended.)

Mass communication (defined below, pp. 31–2) is only one of the processes of communication operating at the society-wide level, readily identified by its institutional characteristics (a mixture of purpose, organization and actual activity). Other processes approach-ing the same status in terms of ubiquity and scope are (or have been) those of government, education and religion. Each has its own institutional network, at times linking large numbers together in the transmission or exchange of information and ideas. Nevertheless, mass communication probably now involves more people for more of the time than any other society-wide process, even if with less intensity.

Because it is so comprehensive, mass communication can involve a consideration of any of the 'lower level' processes named in Figure 1. Individuals receive and handle much information directly from mass media. A good deal of conversation between people is now about the media or their contents. Social relationships, groups and other institutions are frequently portrayed in media and are responded to, or learned about, as much in their media represen-tation as in direct experience. The production and distribution of media is carried out by work organizations with their own communi-cation channels. Many other organizations (e.g. business firms, political parties) use mass media for their ends. It is difficult to see how most other society-wide processes of communication could actually take place without mass media.

The main point of these comments is to emphasize the relevance to the study of mass communication of many kinds of theory, but also to underline the fact that mass communication does also have unique aspects which call for a distinct branch of communication theory. This is likely to be more sociological than psychological and to be more normative than the theory which is relevant to micro-processes of communication (for instance, learning, perception, encoding of texts, patterns of interaction and response), where theory is likely to be more precise, more universal and more reliably predictive. Because mass communication is bound up with the total life of a (national) society, it is strongly influenced by the immediate circumstances of culture and historical events. To study mass communication in a holistic way is to study a complete society (in a global setting) and this has never been satisfactorily achieved. The student of mass communication who wants more certainty should remain at the micro-level, but the temptation to stray to upper slopes is hard to resist and it is the larger questions about mass media and society with which this book is mainly concerned.

The rise of the media: origins of media definitions

The aim of this section is to set out the approximate sequence of development of the present-day set of mass media — to indicate major turning points and to tell briefly something of the circumstances of time and place in which different media acquired their public definitions. These have tended to form early in the history of any given medium and to have become 'fixed' by these circumstances as much as by any intrinsic properties as means of communication. As time has passed, definitions have also changed, especially by becoming more complex and acquiring more 'options', so that it eventually becomes difficult to speak of a single, universally current and consistent definition. Each medium has its own several sub-species, often remarkably variant in form and functions.

In summarizing the history and characteristics of different media, as a step towards typifying mass communication in general, we have assumed a convergence on an original western European form. This does some violence to history, but is justifiable: there is a striking degree of universality about the global phenomena we recognize as mass media, whatever the reasons for the convergence.

In the history of mass media we deal with four main elements: a technology; the political, social, economic and cultural situation of a society; a set of activities, functions or needs; people — especially as formed into groups, classes or interests. These have interacted in different ways and with different orders of primacy for different media, sometimes one seeming to be the driving force or precipitating factor, sometimes another.

Print media

The history of modern media begins with the printed book — certainly a kind of revolution, yet initially only a technical device for reproducing the same or rather similar range of texts that was already being extensively copied. Only gradually does it lead to a change in content — more secular, practical and popular works, especially in the vernacular, political and religious pamphlets and tracts — which played a part in the transformation of the medieval world. Thus there occurred a revolution of society in which the book played an inseparable part.

It was almost two hundred years after the invention of printing before what we now recognize as a prototypical newspaper could be distinguished from the handbills, pamphlets and news books of the late sixteenth and seventeenth centuries. Its chief precursor seems, in fact, to have been the letter rather than the book — the newsletters circulating through the rudimentary postal service, concerned especially with transmitting news of events with a relevance for international trade and commerce. It was thus an extension into the public sphere of an activity which had long taken place in diplomacy and within or for large business houses. The early newspaper is marked by: regular appearance; commercial basis (openly for sale); multiple purpose (for information, record, advertising, diversion, gossip); a public or open character.

The seventeenth-century commercial newspaper was not ident-ified with any single source, but was a compilation made by a printer-publisher. The official variety (as published by Crown or Government) showed some of the same characteristics, but was also a voice of authority and an instrument of state. The commercial paper was the form which has given most shape to the newspaper institution and it can be seen in retrospect as a major turning point in communication history — offering first of all a service to any of its anonymous readers rather than an instrument to propagandists or potentates.

In a sense the newspaper was more of an innovation than the printed book — the invention of a new literary, social and cultural form — even if it might not have been so perceived at the time. Its distinctiveness, compared to other forms of cultural communication, lies in its individualism, reality-orientation, utility, secularity and suitability for the needs of a new class: town-based business and professional people. Its novelty consists not in its technology or manner of distribution, but its functions for a distinct class in a changing and more permissive social-political climate.

The later history of the newspaper can be told either as a series of struggles, advances and reverses in the cause of liberty or as a more continuous history of economic and technological progress. The most important elements in press history which enter into the modern definition of the newspaper are described in the following paragraphs. While separate national histories differ too much to tell a single story, these elements, often intermingling and interacting, have been factors in the development of the press institution, to a greater or lesser degree.

The press as adversary

From its beginning, the newspaper has been an actual or potential adversary of established power, especially in its own self-perception. Potent images in press history refer to the punishment of printers, editors and journalists, the struggle for freedom to publish, the activities of newspapers in the fight for freedom, democracy and working-class rights, and the part played by underground presses under foreign occupation or dictatorial rule. Established authority has usually reciprocated the self-perception of the press and has often found it irritating and inconvenient, although often malleable and in the extreme very vulnerable to power. There has also been a general progression historically towards more freedom for press operations, despite major setbacks. This progress has sometimes taken the form of greater sophistication in the means of control applied to the press. Legal restraint replaced violence, then fiscal burdens were imposed. Now institutionalization of the press within a market system serves as a form of control and the modern newspaper, as a large business enterprise, is vulnerable to more kinds of pressure or intervention than its simple forerunner.

The rise of a newspaper reading public

The extension of newspaper reach beyond the circle of an educated elite or business class to majority availability and use is a familiar feature of press history in many countries. However, there are disputes about the causes of this — whether it was rising literacy, improved technology, reducing costs or popular demand (Williams, 1958). In the end, all of these must have made their contribution and they largely coincided in their timing. Few countries could claim majority penetration by the newspaper until after the First World War and there are still large variations in rates of reading between countries, with the advance of the newspaper seemingly halted by the rise of broadcasting. In assessing the significance of the growth in reading, it is also necessary to distinguish between the growing market penetration of the commercial press (as a vehicle for advertising and entertainment) and the reading of the newspaper for mainly political purposes. The involvement of the newspaper in political movements or at times of national crisis reflects a different aspect of the meaning and function of the newspaper and involves a stimulus to growth with a different dynamic and historical timing.

The growth of the political press

The early history of the printing press makes it unsurprising that the newspaper should later have been used as an instrument for party advantage and political propaganda. The degree to which this happened and the forms it has taken are highly varied. The focus here is not so much on newspapers which express or report political views, or which align themselves with parties, but on newspapers which are founded by political parties and used by them for their own purposes. This phenomenon is now virtually absent from North America and, despite promising beginnings in the nineteenth century (Thompson, 1963; Harrison, 1974), also absent in Britain. It is more common on the European continent (especially in Scandinavia or where political parties receive public funding), although it has also been in general decline for some decades.

As an institutional variant, the party newspaper has lost ground to commercial press forms (as described below), both as an idea and as a viable business enterprise. The commercial newspaper promotes itself as more objective, less manipulative and more fun, and all three have appealed more to more readers more of the time. The idea of a party press, however, still has its place as a component in political democracy and it offers a conceptual bridge to the central and eastern European press arrangements which preserve party newspapers, even if there the presumption of political competition is not met. The party newspaper, where it does survive in western Europe (and there are examples elsewhere), is typically: independent from the state (though possibly subsidized); professionally produced; serious and opinion-forming in purpose. In these aspects it is not far removed from the prestige liberal newspaper, but its uniqueness lies in its special attachment to its readers by way of the party allegiance, its sectionalism and its mobilizing function for party objectives.

The nineteenth-century bourgeois newspaper: origins of the modern prestige press

The reason for singling out the late nineteenth-century newspaper as a high, if not a turning, point in press history is that it has seemed to contribute most to our modern understanding of what a newspaper is or should be. The 'high bourgeois' phase of press history, from about 1850 to the turn of the century, was the product of several events and circumstances: the triumph of liberalism and the ending, except in more benighted quarters of Europe, of direct censorship or fiscal constraint; the establishment of a relatively progressive capitalist class and several emergent professions, thus forging a business-professional establishment; many social and technological changes favouring the operation of a national or regional press of high information quality.

   The chief features of the new 'elite' press which was established in this period were: formal independence from the state and from open vested interests; an acceptance into the structure of society as a major institution of political and social life; a highly-developed sense of social and ethical responsibility; the rise of a journalistic profession dedicated to the objective reporting of events; an adoption, at the same time, of the role of opinion-giver or -former; frequently a tendency to identify with the 'national interest'. Many current expectations about what is a good or 'elite' newspaper reflect several of these ideas and they also provide the basis for criticisms of press forms which deviate from the ideal, either by being too partisan or too 'sensational'.

Commercialization of the newspaper press

Lastly, we should consider the rise of the mass newspaper, often called the 'commercial' newspaper for two reasons: its operation as a profitable business enterprise by monopolistic concerns and its heavy dependence on product advertising revenue. The latter especially made it possible and desirable to establish a mass readership. It has been argued that commercial aims and underpinning have indirectly exerted considerable influence on content, making sections of the press more populist and implicitly more favourable to business, consumerism and free enterprise, if not more favourable to the political right (Curran, 1986). Newspapers which are part of large business empires, and not only mass newspapers, often do seem to display these tendencies (Tunstall, 1982).

For our purpose, it is more relevant to see, as a result of commercialization, the emergence of a new kind of newspaper: lighter and more entertaining, emphasizing human interest, more sensational in its attention to crime, violence, scandals and stars, having a very large readership in which lower income and education groups are over-represented (Schudson, 1978; Hughes, 1940; Curran et al., 1981). While this may now appear to be the dominant newspaper form (in the sense of the most read form) in many countries, it draws its status as a *newspaper* from the 'high bourgeois' form (especially in respect of claiming to give current political and economic information) although it is otherwise most clearly defined by its deviation from the latter.

Film

Film began at the end of the nineteenth century as a technological novelty, but what it offered was scarcely new in content or function. It transferred to a new means of distribution an older tradition of entertainment, offering: stories, spectacles, music, drama, humour and technical tricks for popular consumption. It was partly a response to the 'invention' of leisure — time out of work — and an answer to the demand for economical and (usually) respectable ways of enjoying free time for the whole family. Thus it provided for the working class some of the cultural benefits already enjoyed by their 'betters'. To judge from its phenomenal growth, the latent demand met by film must have been enormous and if we choose from the main formative elements named above, it would not be the technology or the social climate but the needs met by the film for a class (urban lower middle and working) which mattered most — the same elements, although a different need and a different class, which produced the newspaper.

The characterization of the film as show business in a new form for an expanded market is not the whole story. There have been three other significant strands in film history and one or perhaps two major turning points.

First, the use of film for propaganda is noteworthy, especially when applied to national or societal purposes, based on a belief in its great reach, supposed realism, emotional impact and popularity. The practice of combining improving message with entertainment had been long established in literature and drama, but new elements in film were the capacity to reach so many so quickly and to be able to manipulate the seeming reality of the photographic message without loss of credibility. The two other strands in film history were the emergence of several schools of film art (Huaco, 1963) and the rise of the social documentary film movement. Each of these was deviant in, respectively, having a minority appeal and having an orientation to realism. Yet both have a link, partly fortuitous, with the 'film as propaganda' strand of history, in that both tended to develop at times of *social crisis* in several countries.

It is also worth drawing attention to the thinly concealed ideological and implicitly propagandist elements in many popular entertainment films, a phenomenon which seems independent of the presence or absence of societal freedom. This is likely to stem as much from the wish to reflect popular moods as from manipulative intention. A word is due also about the use of film in education, more advocated than practised, based in part on the apparent capacity of film to keep attention and in part on its unique message-carrying capacity. In retrospect, despite the dominance of entertainment uses in film history, there seems to be a unifying thread in its leaning towards didactic-propagandistic applications, in other words towards manipulation. It may be that the film is intrinsically susceptible to manipulative purpose because it requires a much more conscious and artificial construction (i.e. manipulation) than other media, because it is vulnerable to much interference and because so much capital is at risk.

Of the two turning points referred to above, one, the coming of television, is more clearly consequential than the other. The latter development, well chronicled by Tunstall (1977), is the high degree of 'Americanization' of the film industry and film culture in the years after the First World War, partly because of the war itself. The relative decline of nascent, but flourishing, European film industries has probably been responsible for a good many trends in the homogenization of culture and for the dominance of one main definition of what film is about and what the world of film connotes. Television clearly took away a large part of the film-viewing public, especially the general family audience, leaving a much smaller and younger film audience. It also took away or diverted the social documentary stream of film development and gave it a more congenial home. However, it did not do the same for the art film or for film aesthetics, although the art film has probably benefited from the 'demassification' and greater specialization of the film/cinema medium. One last consequence of this turning point is the reduced need for 'respectability'. The film was freer to cater to the demand for violent, horrific or pornographic content. Despite some increase in freedom of this kind, due mainly to changing social norms, the film has not been able to claim the full rights of political and artistic self-expression and many countries retain the apparatus of licensing, censorship and powers of control.

A last concomitant, if not consequence, of film's subordination to television in audience appeal has been its wide integration with other media, especially book publishing, popular music and television itself. It has acquired a certain centrality (Jowett and Linton, 1980), despite its direct audience loss, as a showcase for other media and as a cultural source, out of which come books, strip cartoons, television stars and series, songs. Thus it now contributes as a mass culture creator, instead of merely drawing on other media as it mainly did in its golden days.

Broadcasting

Radio and television have, respectively, a sixty- and thirty-year history as mass media behind them and both grew out of pre-existing technologies — telephone, telegraph, moving and still photography, sound recording. Despite their obvious differences and now wide discrepancies in content and use, radio and television can be treated together. The first point of importance is the extent to which radio seems to have been a technology looking for a use, rather than a response to a demand for a new kind of service or content. According to Raymond Williams (1975), 'Unlike all previous communications technologies, radio and television were systems primarily designed for transmission and reception as abstract processes, with little or no definition of preceding content'. Radio, certainly, was first a technology and only later a service and much the same was true of television, which began more as a toy and novelty than a serious or even popular contribution to social life. Both came to borrow from all existing media and all the most popular content of both is derivative — films, news and sport.

Perhaps the main genre innovation common to both radio and television has been the direct account or observation of events as they happen. However, since many events thought worthy of public notice are planned in advance, the addition of actuality to what writing and film already offered has been somewhat limited. A second main fact of importance in radio/television history has been its high degree of regulation, control or licensing by public authority — initially out of technical necessity, later from a mixture of democratic choice, state self-interest, economic convenience and sheer institutional custom. A third and related historical feature of radio/television has been its centre-periphery pattern of distribution and the association of national television with political life and the power centres of society, as it has become established as both popular and political in its functions. Despite, or perhaps because of, this closeness to power, radio and television have hardly anywhere acquired the same freedom, as of right, to express views and act with political independence as the press enjoys.

New electronic media

Telematic media have been heralded as the product of the latest revolution which will replace broadcast television as we know it. The term covers a set of developments at the core of which is a visual display unit (television screen) linked to a computer network. What are sometimes referred to as the 'new media' which have gradually begun to put in an appearance during the 1980s are in fact a set of different electronic technologies with varied applications and which have yet to be widely taken up as *mass* media or to acquire a clear definition of their function.

Several technologies are involved: of transmission (by cable or satellite); of miniaturization; of storage and retrieval; of display (using flexible combinations of text and graphics); of control (by computer). The main features, by contrast with the 'old media' described, are: decentralization — supply and choice are no longer predominantly in the hands of the supplier of communication; high capacity — cable or satellite delivery overcomes the severe restrictions imposed by surface broadcasting; inter-activity — the receiver can select, answer back, exchange and be linked to other receivers directly; flexibility of form, content and use.

Aside from the further impetus to the distribution of existing radio and television, new telematic media have been offered to the public in two main forms, one known as teletext, the other as videotex. The former makes available much additional textual information by way of over-air broadcasting to supplement normal television programming on adapted receivers and it can be called up at the viewer's initiative. The second provides, via cable, a much larger and more

varied supply of computer-stored information which can be consulted and/or interrogated by users equipped with a terminal and
television screen. It also offers a wide range of interactive services,
including a form of visual communication between centres and
peripherals and in principle between all those connected on the same
(usually telephone) network. Videotex can also be used by the
suitably equipped receiver to obtain a supply of printed material.

Among other new media, one telematic, the other not, are
computer video games and video programmes (or recorded films) for
home replay. The former offers a new leisure service to individuals
with computers, the second is essentially a new way of distributing
familiar content (mainly feature films) to individuals with replay
equipment. It may also be considered as an extension of television,
adding recording and replay possibilities, and loosening the time
constraint which now applies. It is thus a hybrid medium (like
television itself), borrowing essential features from film and television
for content and forms and from the book and music industries for
means of distribution (separate items of content rented or sold).
Much could be said of another innovation, the *videodisc* which uses
laser technology and is characterized by very high definition and
flexibility of use and access. While not yet a mass medium its entry is
significant and illustrates the uncertainty over the future pattern of
media use.

In general, new media have bridged differences between media,
but also between public and private definitions of communication
activities. The same medium can be used interchangeably for public
and private uses and content. In the long run this has implications
not only for definitions of separate media but also for the boundaries
of the media institution.

Although the new media have, in their initial stages, been taken
up mainly as extensions of existing audiovisual media, they represent
a challenge to the production, distribution and basic forms of the
latter. Production needs much less to be concentrated in large
centrally located organizations (typical of film and television) nor
linked integrally with distribution (as with most television and radio)
nor so centrally controlled (see pp. 40–1). Nor are print media immune
to fundamental change, the more direct electronic delivery to
households becomes a reality, and the more the organization of
production and the work of journalists and authors is computerized
(Weaver and Wilhoit, 1986).

Public definitions of the media

As already remarked, the commonsense knowledge which we have from personal experience underlines and gives substance to the concept of a public definition, although it is shaped more directly by the media themselves, by social and cultural circumstances, and by the intrinsic attributes of the different technologies. Each medium tends to be located in our 'mental maps', with a distinctive profile, a set of associations and of expectations about its function or utility. A public definition as used here is thus an abstract construct, an attempt to put together key features which together provide a general and summary description of an otherwise very diffuse set of things, acts and experiences. It represents an idea of what is possible, normal and acceptable and to that extent sets informal limits to what a medium can hope to achieve. Attempts to change the function or form of distribution of media meet resistance insofar as they depart from established definitions and new media have to acquire a definition before they are able to develop fully. Often this process is achieved by borrowing from existing definitions.

The definitions or images which can be reconstructed or inferred are often fragile, internally incoherent, often untrue to any one particular reality. They are vulnerable to historical and cultural change; there are sub-cultural differences within national societies as well as differences between countries; definitions are always multi-faceted and the reality which they summarize is complex. Sometimes a definition is imposed 'from above', or one inherited from the past is in conflict with an image formed in common use 'from below'. This might be said of the tension between the serious and the popular newspaper or between the version of broadcasting's functions institutionalized in many public broadcasting systems and the widespread perception of television as, primarily, a home entertainer.

The media definition as described has affinities with the Weberian 'ideal type', which also involves the selection and accentuation of key features of a complex and variable phenomenon as it exists in empirical reality. Something of the kind has been imaginatively used by writers on mass communication — for instance McLuhan (1962, 1964), Carey (1969), Williams (1975) and Tunstall (1977) — in trying to capture some institutional and cultural essence of one medium or another. A similar approach is more recently exemplified in Ellis' (1982) attempt to contrast the essential features of film and broadcast television as they have been institutionalized. The differences between the media which translate eventually into audience experience and perceptions are, according to Ellis, much less due to technical differences than to differences of social and cultural convention, professional and organizational custom, and methods of distribution. Historical accident also plays a large part. A few of the key contrasts described by Ellis can be summarized (see Figure 2).

Figure 2 Differences between television and film (based on Ellis, 1982)

BROADCAST TELEVISION:	CINEMA FILM:
On content and form	
– Identifies narrator	– No narrator
– Distinguishes fact from fiction	– Only fiction or unclear
– Realistic	– Dreamlike
– Domestic, familial	– Exotic, out of home
– Open-ended, disjointed narrative	– Logical, cause-effect sequence
On dominant tone	
– Sense of being live, in real time	– Not live, in 'historic present'
– Takes a neutral attitude	– Takes sides
– Air of normality and safety	– Air of tension, anxiety
On relationship with the audience	
– Has a permanent audience	– Each item newly marketed
– Requires low engagement	– Rapt attention, self-loss
– Intimacy	– Detachment, voyeurism
On organization	
– Has personalities	– Has stars

The components of media images (public definitions)

The choice of component dimensions which follows is inevitably somewhat subjective, but it is guided by the need to take account of the main features of mass communication around which this book as a whole is structured. In particular, these have to do with: relations of media to state, society and culture; organizational circumstances of production and distribution; variations of type of content; the manner of use by audiences; relations between audiences and communicators; the location of media use in its social context. In using the idea of a *dimension*, the key feature is the variability of the factors identified. There is a range of possibilities for the location of any medium in respect of the characteristics, rather than a simple presence or absence or simply a 'high' or 'low' position. The dimensions discussed are summarily listed in Figure 3.

Political dimensions

In connection with relations to society, we can distinguish factors which are *political* (power-related) from those which are essentially *normative* (having to do with social and cultural values). The former relate to variable tendencies of external authority to limit or regulate a medium and to tendencies within media to be either conformist or critical in their disposition to established authority. These two dimensions have some independence from each other, since a medium which is typically subject to much control (like television) might also adopt a critical stance, while another (like music), which is not controlled, might well not do so. The presence or absence of control is usually related to another variable, which is the degree of centrality to state power. In turn this mainly depends on actual or typical functions: the more a medium operates in the political sphere (as with newspapers), the more centrally it is of interest to power holders or contenders. Whether media use their potential for criticism or not is much more related to circumstances and individual choices.

The dimensions named all have to do with the relative freedom of media. Historically, among media, books and newspapers have provided the tests of freedom, with newspapers (in the modern period) more central to state power and more inclined to contest any effort at control. The claim to press freedom is made irrespective of whether the freedom is used for conformist or critical ends. Broadcast media have inherited, or come to share, the same definition as newspapers as central to power, but they have also been much more tightly controlled and even less inclined to non-conformity (for reasons which have often concerned their mass monopoly position). As noted already, film has largely developed as a non-political medium, except in certain unusual circumstances of political change (Huaco, 1963). It has been very easy to control and, in its dominant mass entertainment form, not much inclined to non-conformity.

Normative dimensions

These relate especially to social and cultural values and can be dealt with in terms of three different sets of expectations. One relates to the moral quality and seriousness of content, in the sense that typical content can be 'improving' or 'entertaining', 'heavy' or 'light', according to one's standards and choice of terms, the first term usually carrying positive moral associations and the second connoting, if not the immoral, at best the non-moral. A second dimension has to do with orientation to reality or fantasy, according to whether content is expected to be true in a literal way to the contemporary scene or free to invent and play with reality. Thirdly, there is an aesthetic, or cultural, dimension, which concerns the extent to which either content or form can be considered as art (e.g. following the lines of distinction made below, p. 37, between high culture and mass culture). These three dimensions tend to be closely correlated and also reflect the dominant values of most societies (which favour reality, morality and art, usually in that order).

Because these dimensions relate primarily to content rather than form and because media are usually so diverse or variable in content, it is hard to give each medium a specific location on the dimensions. Even so, experience suggests that according to their typical content there are some approximate differences between media. Print media in general retain some aura of seriousness and high cultural value and are expected to be more true to reality than audiovisual media. On the other hand, television has an image of being more realistic than film, partly because of its capacity to convey the moment, but partly for less logically accountable reasons (see Ellis, 1982).

Organizational and technological components

These are less likely to have entered into audience perceptions, although as public awareness and knowledge of media increase, they are likely to become more important for public definitions and images. Three aspects can be chosen as most essential. First, there is the matter of the location of organizational emphasis: whether on message, or on production, or on distribution. The relative centrality of each strongly affects the form of organization of a medium and its relation to its audience. A second matter has to do with complexity of technology involved — is the reality and image one of high technology? Thirdly, what is the nature of the professional definition of those who work in the medium? Is there a clear core profession or is it ill-defined or multiple?

Some media are likely to have clearer definition than others. The image (and reality) of the oldest medium, the book, seems to be least ambiguous — as a medium it is 'message-centred', low-technology and strongly associated with a single profession, that of writer. The newspaper probably carries a midway position on all three dimensions, since aspects of all three are important, but none predominates. Film has a similar indeterminate position, although by now it probably no longer carries a 'high technology' association, however much techniques have developed. Radio is probably mainly perceived as a distribution medium (its content is neither unique nor durable), low technology (whatever the reality) and lacking any professional definition. By contrast, television appears to be strongly associated with messages (distinctive and remembered), with organization (complex and large), with distribution (a universal source for all), with high technology and with a new profession of television-maker, star or presenter (however unclear or variable the core activity may be).

Dimensions relating to conditions of distribution, reception and use

These refer to the kind of act or experience typically involved, or available, for the user. The main points to bear in mind are: whether content is chosen as an individual unit or as a wider range of items; whether attention is individual or collective; whether content is limited in time and space; whether use is limited in time or space; whether supply is managed and organized at source.

Media with unitary content are still book, film and recorded music, by contrast with media offering a broad package of items, like the newspaper, television and, though less so, radio. The medium which is most collective in use remains the film, followed by television (in the family group) and most individual are book and (often) radio. The book remains the most time- and space-free medium in respect of use, the film (cinema) the least, but changes in the direction of more flexibility are affecting all media. The reasons for giving separate consideration to content and to use as well as to time and space is that some content of some media is more available over time and more retrievable than that of other media. Again the book 'scores' most highly in this respect — crossing barriers of time and geographical space with the message. The newspaper is at the opposite pole in content terms: its content is typically very perishable and localized (if only by constraints of language). Film content crosses frontiers, often survives over time, but is hard to retrieve (now less so).

In respect of management of supply, the most managed or controllable media (i.e. decisions about supply and availability lying outside the hands of the individual user) are likely to be television and the newspaper press. The least managed tend to be book and music which are, not by coincidence, also media of unitary content items and also have content which is typically rather free in time and space terms (both as to content and use). They are also media of rather less direct interest to the state. Even in the case of the book, management is exercised, if more remotely from the point and moment of use by the receiver by: publishers, libraries, distributors, advertisers, book clubs, families, schools, etc.

Dimensions of relations between sender and receiver

We need to distinguish and illustrate four aspects in particular. One overlaps with that of individual versus collective experience in use, but the new question is whether or not the receiver is typically related to the source as an individual (in private) or as a member of a group (in public). Secondly, there is the matter of degree of involvement typically present in the relationship to the source. Thirdly, the location of the sender in respect of the receiver has to be taken into account. This can be distant or close in respect of any or all of space, time and culture. Media may be connected or not with experience in a local community, a region, a nation, or the source may be inter-national or even lacking in any known location. In general, the more local the source, the stronger the potential for a social relationship to exist between sender and receiver. Fourthly, there is the dimension of 'interactivity': the degree to which a medium allows for exchanges between sender and receivers.

Most media offer diverse possibilities on the first three of these variables. Although the book again is typically least likely to belong to the public aspect of audience experience, it is also possible for reader publics to form and be sustained which are based on common tastes, background and culture and even have some form of organization. These matters are often of significance in the public life of society and readership taste can be an outward expression of cultural or social identity. This is even more likely to be the case with newspaper readership. Media which seem to encourage high involvement are film and, again, the book. Television offers some opportunities for audience involvement (Noble, 1975) and for 'loss of self' in the experience but it seems typically a more detached experience, involving little long-term loyalty to sources.

It is increasingly difficult to distinguish whole media according to typical relations of closeness or distance, since this is often an attribute of content items. Newspaper and radio remain the media most likely to be local, with film and music the most distant (especially in the sense of content and place of production). Distance in respect of culture, place or time does not seem to stand in the way of attachment between individual receivers and sources, although it is likely to be inconsistent with attachment on the part of an audience as a social group or public (see pp. 219–20). None of the established mass media have very developed possibilities for interaction. The smaller in scale and slower the communication process the more possible was it for some exchange to take place, e.g. between an author and a small circle of readers. Some media encourage responses in the form of feedback from fans, or by way of telephone links to radio and television. But freely available exchange is largely ruled out by the technology of one-way transmission. Hence the importance of the innovation of electronic systems like teletext and videotex, described elsewhere (see pp. 16–17).

A summary

The dimensions discussed are summarily presented in Figure 3, although the diversity of possible locations for media and the changes which are occurring make it impossible to give a unique location to any given medium.

As already remarked, definitions and images change and adjust, the former according to the course of institutional and technological history and choice of functions, the images usually in response to experience of changed reality. There are too many changes to catalogue, but the dimensions in Figure 3 provide a checklist as to general patterns of media image change. In some cases trends may go in opposing directions. For instance, economic developments (especially increases in monopoly and in scale of operations) favour more management of supply, while technology (e.g. video, telematics, cable, satellite) may favour unitization of items which were once only available in larger packages. Technology and institutional change (e.g. the decline of broadcast monopoly) also favour more flexibility as to time and place of content and use.

On political dimensions, control may become more difficult because of the multiplication of supply and the delocalization of use in time and space. In respect of values, lines of differentiation between media are becoming more blurred and the development of an audio-visual aesthetic and a language are challenging the hegemony of the written word. The existence of an agreed hierarchy

Figure 3 Main dimensions of media definitions and images

I Relations of media to state and society

i)	Control by state	versus	Independence
ii)	Conformity	versus	Critical tendency
iii)	Centrality to politics	versus	Political marginality

II Social and cultural values

i)	Reality-orientation	versus	Fantasy-orientation
ii)	Serious and moral	versus	Non-moral, entertaining
iii)	Art, high cultural	versus	Non-art, mass-cultural

III Organizational and technological features

i)	Organizational emphasis: message centred: production centred: distribution centred.		
ii)	High technology	versus	Low technology
iii)	Profession defined	versus	Profession ill-defined

IV Conditions of distribution, reception and use

i)	Content unitary	versus	Content multiple
ii)	Content time- and space-bound	versus	Content time- and space-free
iii)	Individual attention & use	versus	Collective (group) attention & use
iv)	Use time- and space-bound	versus	Use time- and space-free
v)	Supply managed	versus	Supply not managed

V Social relationship of sender and receiver

i)	Receiver as private individual	versus	Receiver as member of public
ii)	High involvement or attachment	versus	Low involvement or attachment
iii)	Location of source distant in time, space or culture	versus	Location of source close in time, space or culture
iv)	Interactive	versus	Non-interactive

of cultural values is also less certain. In matters of organization, the general tendency has been towards more high technology as a component of image and reality and there is more organization-centredness. As to social relations, the general trend seems to be towards more privatization and more 'distance' between senders and receivers in the symbolic senses mentioned earlier, although computer-based media allow genuine interaction, for the first time.

Definition and image of new media

New technologies of distribution and recording are rapidly changing many features of existing definitions. They especially affect: the possibilities for control by central authority; the counter-possibilities for more freedom and access; the freedom of receivers to choose and use media according to individual circumstances of time and place; the opportunities for sender-receiver interaction; the older definitions of media and the boundaries between them; the present localization and containment of media within political and geographical boundaries. That much is happening is certain, but it is more difficult to say whether the 'new media' have yet been given any definition or have acquired an image. This is partly because they come in several forms, partly because their coming has often been slow and still low in penetration (McQuail and Siune, 1986; Rogers, 1986). But we may consider the telematic media as exemplified by videotex systems as prototypical of new media and as incorporating the most important features of new communication technology (especially computerization and interactive potential).

If videotex is characterized briefly according to the dimensions described above, the following picture begins to emerge. On the 'political' dimensions, telematic media are carriers rather than broadcasters (Pool, 1983) and lack the central editorializing function which would form a focus for state control. However, they are very open to surveillance by an interested and properly equipped central authority (see p. 41) and there is no doubt of the interest of the state in sponsoring the development of telematic networks. Even if this is initially for economic/industrial reasons, it reflects the centrality of political concern and indicates a future interest in supervision.

In normative terms, content so far seems to belong very much to the 'reality' and 'serious' poles indicated, but certain interactive uses also belong to the entertainment sphere. Organizational and technological facts put the emphasis on message and distribution rather than production, and relegate questions of individual authorship and of professionalism (so far there is no profession clearly involved, although information experts are likely to emerge). Content selection is unitary within a multiple supply package — a divergence from known patterns. Supply is managed unpurposefully and at a distance. The receiver has much freedom of choice and is much less limited by time and space barriers. Social relations of reception are private in the extreme, but powerfully modified by the interactive potential, which many regard as establishing quite a new type of relation. Despite this interaction possibility, high involvement with sources does not seem typical of videotex, although this depends on the source.

These are some of the potentials built into early forms of telematic media provision but the eventual formation of a clear definition and image will depend on changes which occur between now and the arrival of telematics as a mass medium.

CHAPTER 2

CONCEPTS AND DEFINITIONS

The 'mass': an ambivalent concept

The key word 'mass', already much used in this book, is almost impossible to elucidate on its own, because of its many connotations, but an essential feature is its ambivalence. In social thought it has had, and retains, both strong negative and positive meanings. Its negative meanings derive historically from its use in referring to the 'mob' or multitude, especially the mass of unruly and ignorant people. In this context, the word often connotes lack of culture, of intelligence and even of rationality (Bramson, 1961). In its positive sense, especially in the socialist tradition, it connotes the strength and solidarity of ordinary working people when organized together for collective ends. In contexts where *quantity* is defined as positive then it is a word of approbation, as in 'mass support', 'mass movement', 'mass action', etc. Apart from the reference to large numbers in both the positive and the negative senses of its use, a bridge is provided by the fact that the acting multitudes may be engaged either in opposition to oppression or to established and legitimate order. The difference of valuation is thus primarily one of standpoint or opinion, now as in the past.

The relevance for mass communication comes mainly from the meaning of multiple or mass production and the large size of the audience which can be reached by mass media. There is also, in one of the original meanings of the word 'mass', the idea of an amorphous collectivity in which the components are hard to distinguish from each other. The shorter *OED* gives a definition of 'mass' as an 'aggregate in which individuality is lost' and this is close to the meaning which sociologists have attached to the word, especially when applied to the media audience.

Types of collectivity

Herbert Blumer (1939) made the original definition of mass by way of a set of contrasts with other kinds of collectivity encountered in social life, especially the 'group', 'crowd' and 'public' (see Figure 4). In the small group, all members know each other, are aware of their common membership, share the same values, have a certain structure of relationships which is stable over time and interact to achieve some purpose. The crowd is larger, but still restricted within observable boundaries in a particular space. It is, however, temporary and rarely re-forms with the same composition. It may possess a high degree of identity and share the same 'mood', but there is usually no structure and order to its moral and social composition. It can act, but its actions are often seen to have an affective and emotional, often irrational, character.

Figure 4 The 'mass' compared with other forms of collectivity

	GROUP	PUBLIC	CROWD	MASS
Degree of interaction:	High within limited boundaries	Moderate — although members dispersed	High	Low
Cause/or object of interest:	Common purpose + identity + contact	Issue or opinion for discussion and choice	On-going event	Organized objects of attention
Control/ organization	High, but informal + internal	Moderate formal + informal	Low and (if any) external	External + manipulative
Level of consciousness	High	Variable: moderate to high	High, but transient	Low

The third collectivity named by Blumer, the public, is likely to be quite large, widely dispersed and enduring. It tends to form around an issue or cause in public life and its primary purpose is to advance an interest or opinion and to achieve political change. It is an essential element in the institution of democratic politics, based on the ideal of rational discourse within an open political system and often comprising the better informed section of the population. The rise of the public is characteristic of modern liberal democracies and related to the rise of the 'bourgeois', or the political party, newspaper described earlier (p. 12).

The audience as mass

The term 'mass' captured several features of the new audience for cinema and radio which were missing or not linked together by any of the three existing concepts. It was often very large — larger than most groups, crowds or publics. It was very widely dispersed and its members were usually unknown to each other or to whoever brought the audience into existence. It lacked self-awareness and self-identity and was incapable of acting together in an organized way to secure objectives. It was marked by a shifting composition within changing boundaries. It did not act for itself, but was, rather, 'acted upon'. It was heterogeneous, in consisting of large numbers, from all social strata and demographic groups, but hemogeneous in its behaviour in choosing a particular object of interest and according to the perception of those who would like to manipulate it.

The audience for mass media is not the only social formation that can be characterized in this way, since the word is sometimes applied to consumers in mass markets or to large bodies of voters (the mass electorate). It is significant, however, that such entities also often correspond with audiences and that mass media are used to direct or control 'consumer behaviour' and the political behaviour of large numbers of voters. The extension of the idea of the mass to apply to a whole society — the 'mass society' — is discussed in chapter 3.

Mass communication process and relationships

The historical sketch and characterization of the main mass media has already provided the material for formulating in a general way the main features of mass communication, as interpreted by social scientists. This calls for separate remarks about the *institution* of mass media and about *mass culture*, which are dealt with in the following sections. Here we deal with the basic process of mass communication by exaggerating certain of its features and especially by contrasting it with face-to-face communication between persons (interpersonal and intragroup or organizational communication referred to earlier).

Main features of mass communication typified

The source is not a single person but a formal organization, and the 'sender' is often a professional communicator. The message is not unique, variable and unpredictable, but often 'manufactured', standardized, always multiplied in some way. It is also a product of work and a commodity with an exchange value as well as being a symbolic reference with a 'use' value. The relationship between sender and receiver is one-directional and rarely interactional, it is necessarily impersonal and often perhaps 'non-moral' and calculative, in the sense that the sender usually takes no moral responsibility for specific consequences on individuals and trades the message for money or attention.

The impersonality derives partly from the physical and social distance between sender and receiver, but also from the impersonality of the role of being a public communicator, often governed by norms of neutrality and detachment. The social distance involved also implies an asymmetrical relationship, since the sender, while having no formal power over the receiver, does usually have more resources, prestige, expertise and authority. The receiver is part of a large audience, sharing experience with others and reacting in predictable and patterned ways. Mass communication often involves simultaneous contact between one sender and many receivers, allowing an immediate and extensive influence and an immediate response by many at one time. While uniformity of impact cannot be assumed, there is likely to be much less variability of response than occurs with slow and sequential person-to-person diffusion of information.

Alternative modes of communication

This ideal-typical version is already somewhat dated and the main directions of its decline are described later (pp. 39–40) in relation to new media developments. But any close attention to what actually occurs under the heading of mass communication reveals the presence of alternative kinds of communication relationships which co-exist within the whole complex. The alternatives are in part the remaining traces of older networks and purposes which have gradually been incorporated into the single media institution and in part they are an original contribution of mass media.

These alternatives can be summarized in terms of three main *modes of communication relationships* which are relevant for different purposes and contexts. These are:
- The *command* mode. Originating in circumstances of differences in power and authority between senders and receivers, it presumes the latter to be subordinate and dependent. Purposes are likely to be for control or instruction and the relationships are unequal, one-directional and not very voluntary. While it is a 'deviant' mode in mass communication (which presupposes equality and voluntarism), it retains a residual presence and can be activated, for instance at times of crisis when political leaders want to speak to

citizens. But it is also 'shadowed' in more routine circumstances when the voice of authority or expertise is given privileged access by the media in respect of political or cultural events of significance, and it may be adopted for purposes of instruction or religious, commercial or political propaganda, even if the sender has no formal power to command.

– The *service* mode. This is the most normal, frequently occurring form of relationship between senders and receivers in which both parties are united by a mutual interest within a market situation, or its equivalent (supply and demand of a symbolic service). Mass communication either offers information and entertainment in return for payment or attention, or serves to mediate between would-be communicators and their self-selected audiences. Relations are in balance, if not of equality. The main features of the mass communication process summarized above fill out the general character of this mode (impersonality, non-moral character, etc) and it applies most of the time to the most frequent uses of media — for news, entertainment, consumer information and ideas, etc.

– The *associational* mode. Here it is normative ties or shared beliefs which attach a particular group or public to a specific media source. The type deviates from the modal form in the opposite direction to that of the command mode. Attachment and attention by the receiver is voluntary and intrinsically satisfying. It serves primarily the needs of receivers rather than senders (or both equally) and relationships between them tend towards equality and mutuality of regard. Interaction and response are features of the relation insofar as it is practicable. Like the first mode, this has its roots in patterns of communication relationships which preceded, and which remain independent of, mass media.

Models of communication and variants of theory

The three-fold distinction just described derives partly from the work of Etzioni (1961) on complex organizations (see below p. 143). He classified organizations according to the kind of power (and corresponding type of compliance) typically found: physical force; material reward; normative or moral attachment. The communication relationship is generally a weak form of power relationship (usually described in terms of influence) but there are analogies to be found between the exercise of power in (mass) communications and in personal relationships. The 'command' mode is the nearest equivalent to the use of force, the 'service' mode parallels that of material reward, since it involves the offer of a service or gratification in return for attention or payment by the receiver; the 'associational' mode is based on normative or moral ties between sender and receiver. The service type of relationship is the most common and most appropriate for mass communication for a number of reasons, but especially because attention is voluntary and unsupervised and contents belong mainly to the sphere of entertainment or utility.

The distinction can be useful for characterizing differences of organizational goal, communicator intention (see below pp. 143–5) and audience disposition (see p. 220). It is also helpful in considering public policies for mass communication, since these have often involved support for the more 'deviant' modes of communication (command or associational). More recent tendencies of public policy, in Europe at least, have been in the direction of facilitating the service mode (by forms of deregulation) for economic and commercial reasons (McQuail and Siune, 1986; Kleinsteuber et al., 1986). We can further relate the distinction to kinds and themes of theory about mass communication as shown in Figure 5.

Figure 5 Modes of communication and issues of mass communication theory

	I Command mode	II Service mode	III Associational mode
	Propaganda & Ideology	Commercialization Audience behaviour	Participation & Interaction
Issues of theory:	Manipulation Mass society		Social fragmentation Normative media
		Communication markets	theory
	Class dominance	Information Society	Media–audience links

In general, mass communication theory has been most strongly influenced by attention to issues relating to I and III rather than II, despite the predominance in media practice of II. Theorists have tended to be critical of propaganda, manipulation and social fragmentation and advocative of normative ties between senders and receivers. Communication has tended to be regarded in idealistic terms, as if threatened by features built into the mass communication situation (impersonality, large scale, etc) or by interests seeking to gain advantages (of power and money) from new communication possibilities. Issues arising under II have thus often been dealt with according to normative perspectives more appropriate to types I and III – calculative market relations of communication have been treated either as if manipulative or deficient in moral content. A central activity of mass media — the trading of information and other communication satisfactions — has lacked an appropriate theory of its own, which would be non-normative and more akin to theory in other spheres of production and consumption (see below pp. 75–6).

Mass culture

The typical content produced and disseminated by mass media has for decades been described as mass culture (see Rosenberg and White, 1957), although the term applies to a much wider range of artefacts. It too has a largely pejorative connotation, mainly because of its associations with the cultural preferences of the 'uncultivated' or non-discriminating. However, it may, as in the Soviet usage ('culture of the masses'), have a positive connotation for the same reason that the masses can, from a democratic point of view, be seen as the source or agent of progressive social change. However, in such cases the culture referred to is usually rather different from that which is termed mass culture in capitalist societies.

Attempts have been made to define culture, or the culture of mass media, in an objective way. Thus Wilensky (1964, p. 176) contrasts it with the notion of 'high culture', which:

> will refer to two characteristics of the product: (1) it is created by, or under the supervision of, a cultural elite operating within some aesthetic, literary, or scientific tradition: . . . (2) critical standards independent of the consumer of their product are systematically applied to it. . . . 'Mass culture' will refer to cultural *products manufactured solely for the mass market*. Associated characteristics, not intrinsic to the definition, are *standardization* of product and *mass behaviour* in its use.

The comparison would be strengthened by including another cultural form — that of folk culture or culture which does come from the people and may pre-date (or be independent of) mass media and the mass production of culture. Original folk culture was being rediscovered in the nineteenth century at the very time that it was rapidly disappearing. It was originally made unselfconsciously, using traditional designs, themes and materials, and was incorporated into everyday life. It has sometimes been despised by the elite because of its simplicity, lack of fashion, or association with peasant or 'lower-class' life, and official protection usually came rather too late to save it as a living tradition. On the other hand it has also been a source of rejuvenation for cultivated artistic traditions, as in the many varieties of art nouveau of the early twentieth century, when it contributed by way of forms, materials, themes and values. The urban working class, who were the first customers for the new mass culture were probably already cut off from the roots of the folk culture. The mass media have both drawn on some popular culture streams and adapted them to the conditions of urban life, to provide some forms of culture, especially fiction and music, where there was little.

Bauman (1972) describes mass culture, not in evaluative or aesthetic terms, but as an inevitable outcome of some near-universal processes of modern society: the rise of the market; the supremacy of large-scale organization; and the availability of new technology for cultural production. To some extent, the debate about mass culture is simply part of the long process of coming to terms with the consequences, for older conceptions of art, of new possibilities of reproduction (Benjamin, 1977). Yet, despite the increase of relativism about cultural standards and the seeming irrelevance or illogicality of many objections to 'mass culture', what we continue to call culture remains an important element in conceptions of a good society or desirable way of life, and mass media continue to provide workshops where it is made and channels for distributing it.

Types of culture compared

The most commonly cited attributes of mass culture can perhaps best be made clear by a comparison, on essential matters, with the two alternative types of culture referred to — 'high culture' and 'folk culture', shown in Figure 6. According to this presentation, mass culture was made possible by mass media. The media have tended to 'colonize' both high culture and folk culture for content and forms. It is folk culture that has lost most ground since it has lost its audience to mass media and the skills on which it depends have been less resistant than those employed in high culture, which is also institutionally better protected.

Not discussed in this comparison of types of culture is the existence of forms of *popular culture* which do not belong to any of the three categories named. The main defining characteristics would be spontaneous origination and persistence in social life under very varied forms — e.g. in language, dress, music, custom, etc. There is no reason to doubt that living societies continue to produce much popular culture in this sense. It is often drawn on for content and forms by the media, or reflected in media and sometimes also derived in adapted forms *from* the media by people themselves. Its discussion

Figure 6
Mass culture, high culture, folk culture compared

Point of comparison	High Culture	Mass Culture	Folk Culture
Degree and type of institutionalization	Recognized, protected and promoted by formal social organization. High social value.	Left to media and market	Originally neglected. Now often officially protected
Type of organization of production	Not organized, one-off, unique for specialized market	Mass produced for mass market, using technologies in planned and organized ways	Reproduced according to standard, traditional designs by hand. Market not essential.
Content and meaning	Ambiguous, disturbing and timeless	Superficial, unambiguous, pleasing, universal but perishable	Unselfconscious as to meaning and purpose — may be clear or obscure. Decorative or ritualistic. Not universal but persists in time.
Audience	Relatively small, for trained or educated, connoisseurs	Everyone in principle, heterogeneous, consumption-oriented	All members of same culture, but thereby also limited
Purpose of use/ effect	Enlarge/deepen experience. Intellectual satisfaction. Prestige	Immediate gratification, diversion	Continuity, custom solidarity/integration

goes beyond the scope of this book, but it plays quite an important part in the interrelation between media and society.

The media institution

A good part of chapter 1 was devoted to an analytic description of several means of communication (print, film, etc) as they have been *institutionalized* in societies. This means that they have acquired a stable form, structure and set of functions and related public expectations. Here we are concerned with the general characteristics of the media institution which has been jointly shaped by society, the process of mass communication and the audience. While there are important differences between the different media (see above) and between national societies and types of social system, there are also some similarities on which to base a generalization. Any social institution comprises a set of activities, carried out by people occupying certain roles, according to rules and shared understandings. In the case of mass media, we are talking about the activities of cultural and informational production carried out by 'mass communicators' of many kinds and directed to audiences within a framework of regulation and custom.

The special features of the media institution, as it is widely constituted, are as follows:

- It is concerned with producing and distributing 'knowledge' in the form of information, ideas, culture. This is in response to collective social needs as well as the demands of individuals.
- It provides channels for relating certain people to other people: senders to receivers, audience members to other audience members, everyone to their society and its constituent institutions. These are not only the physical channels of the communication network, but also the channels of custom and understanding which define who should, or is likely to, listen to whom.
- The media operate almost exclusively in the public sphere: they comprise an open institution in which all can participate as receivers and, under certain conditions, also as senders. The media institution also has a public character in that mass media deal with matters on which public opinion exists or can properly be formed (i.e. not with personal or private matters or those for expert or scientific judgement).
- Participation in the institution as audience member is essentially voluntary, without compulsion or social obligation, more so than is the case with other institutions concerned with knowledge distribution, such as education, religion or politics. Correlative is the association of media use with leisure and free time and its disassociation from work and duty. Related also is the formal powerlessness of the media institution: it can claim no authority of its own in society nor has it any organization linking 'higher' (message producers) with 'lower' participants (audiences).
- The institution is linked with industry and the market, through its dependence on paid work, technology and the need for finance.
- Although itself without power, the institution is invariably linked with state power through some of its customary uses and through legal mechanisms and legitimating ideas which vary from one state to another (see chapter 5).

These features are not all unique to the media, but their existence in combination gives the mass media their distinctive character and particular significance in a modern society.

The decline of the 'mass' paradigm

Mass experience as a continuum

The terminology and imagery described has always tended to give an exaggerated and somewhat misleading impression of the activities and experiences associated with the technologies of mass communication. Uses of, and responses to, media can be located on a continuum which extends from the case of universal, one-way, domination by powerful and centralized sources of messages to that of the small-scale, local exchange of information and ideas about familiar things. More often than not, we encounter even 'distant' media sources in ways and contexts which are familiar and secure.

We attend by choice to what we like, with others in our familiar social circle and are able to interact with them, if not with the distant senders. Within the general audience for any mass medium are numerous small, selective or local audiences and the possibilities for interaction with, or response to, media 'senders' are greater than the ideal type of mass communication often suggests. The experience of mass media does not necessarily reduce the quality of social life and may contribute to it, since around mass communication there often develop related or fringe activities. It is absorbed into, or shapes, localized or minority cultures. Mass communication also develops out of, and extends, family group and neighbourhood activities and interests. Where experience of mass media does seem to fit the 'ideal type' described, when we are members of an enormous audience, the causes often lie not with the media but in social life itself, which gives rise to some occasions when society exhibits its unity and solidarity and its members unite in common behaviour, interests and sentiments.

Challenge of new media

While the above has always been a necessary qualification to bear in mind, it is true that the technology of mass media has seemed to lend itself to the nightmares sketched by social alarmists. What has changed or is changing, are some features of the technology itself and the possibilities for communication on a society-wide basis. The new (telematic) media described above (pp. 16–17) have features which some now argue to presage a revolutionary change in electronic media as significant as that brought about by the invention of printing. These features include: abundance of supply of culture and information made available at low cost; more real choice and diversity; restored control to the receiver/user; decentralization; interactivity rather than one-way communication. The new media seem to offer the potential of a shift on the balance of power away from the sender and towards the receiver, making much more content of all kinds accessible to users and choosers without dependence on the mediating and controlling systems of mass communication.

New patterns of information traffic

One way of representing and comparing the key features of 'old' and 'new' media flow has been suggested by the work of two Dutch students of telecommunications who have tried to identify the main forms of 'information traffic'. (Note: this section is adapted from an essay, McQuail, 1986, published in Ferguson, 1986.) For them, drawing on the analogy of the computer, the two main features of communication flows are storage of information on the one hand and access to, or use of, information on the other. They locate the key variables which differentiate information systems (not simply human communication) first in terms of the centrality or otherwise of the store of information and, secondly, the centrality or otherwise of control over access — in effect over choice of subject matter to be consulted or received and over the time at which this takes place. Their scheme, given below as Figure 7, assumes a set of participants arranged in the pattern of a wheel around a central hub. Communication flows (traffic) can take place between any set of participants at the rim or between the centre and any one or more of the participants at the rim. By considering each participant (including the centre) as having a store of information which is drawn on (accessed), or added to, in communication, a fuller picture of possible communication patterns can be arrived at.

By cross-tabulating 'Information store' against 'Control over choice of time and subject', in terms of whether each is 'Central' or 'Individual', a set of four categories of communication traffic is arrived at, as in Figure 7. The difference between central and individual information store, while deriving from that between a large data bank and a single person, is also analogous with the

Figure 7 Four patterns of information traffic
(Adapted from J.L. Bordewijk and B. van Kaam, 1986)

	Information store	
	Central	Individual
Control of time & choice of subject: *Central*	ALLOCUTION	REGISTRATION
Control of time & choice of subject: *Individual*	CONSULTATION	CONVERSATION

Key *Allocution* = The simultaneous transmission of a centrally constituted 'offer' of information intended for immediate attention, according to a centrally determined time scheme.
Conversation = An exchange between individuals of information already available to them, according to a mutually convenient time scheme.
Consultation = The selective consultation by individual participants of a central store of information at times determined by each individual.
Registration = The collection in a central store of information, available to, or about, individual participants, according to a centrally determined choice of subject and time.

difference between a mass media organization and a single audience member, or that between a library and a reader. It can also correspond with the difference between 'information-rich' individuals or groups and those which are 'information-poor'. The difference between central and individual control of access to information, while it can be taken literally, also corresponds to that between constraint and freedom and low and high communication potential.

For the most part, the entry labelled 'allocution' (derived from a Latin word meaning direct address from a leader to followers) stands for the typical 'old media' forms of communication — from a central source to many separated receivers and at times and on subjects determined by the sender. This is especially apposite for national broadcasting. The consultation pattern is also long established as a mode of communication (e.g. libraries) and newspapers can be considered as consultation as well as address media. The conversation pattern is currently represented, in media terms, mainly by telephone and postal services and the 'registration' pattern (of which more below) is hardly known as yet in public communication, although it is a long established element in many organizations for record-keeping, control and surveillance.

In brief, the potential of new media is to increase the possibilities for consultation (telematics, multi-channel cable, videodisc and video), for conversation (via interactive cable, radio and linked computers) and for registration (central recording by computer of all uses of information media connected to a system). The general pattern which can be predicted from the potential of new media is of a shift away from the top left cell of Figure 7 and a redistribution of communication 'traffic' to the other three cells. This seems to indicate a general increase in individual freedom to gain information and a reduction in the dominance of centralized sources. There could be a multiplication of allocutive channels for specialist audiences (narrow-casting) stimulated by users (receivers) themselves, by way of their acts of consultation.

Pool (1983) has welcomed the coming of satellite, cable and computer technology and the necessary accompanying 'carrier' model for the organization of media (as opposed to the broadcasting model) as a boost to freedom of communication. This is a defensible position, according to the model presented above, since individuals will have more control over what they receive and consult and limits to freedom are no longer justifiable on technological grounds, as they are with broadcast media. Even so it would be unwise to depend on technology alone and even the new technology has its limitations and darker side. It will still be the case that what is available in central stores has to be decided centrally and diversity of control and management is not secured by technology, but by some form of politics. The range of what is actually available may come to depend on technology (including software) and it will probably not be so visible or open to direct observation, as with print media.

In addition, the registration pattern may be interpreted as significantly increasing the potential for central control, through surveillance, of information and information-related activities of all kinds. Thirdly, the chance of benefiting from the freedoms offered is increasingly dependent on possession of skills and equipment which are bound to be unevenly distributed (Rogers, 1986). The change in communication patterns and potential which is under way should not, for these reasons, be confused with a qualitative shift to 'better' social conditions of communication.

Alternative perspectives on mass communication: the significance of attention

It should be obvious by now that in any society, mass communication involves virtually everyone at one time or another and for many different purposes. Not surprisingly, therefore, it can be viewed from many different perspectives and does encompass very different kinds of process and behaviour. Even so, there has been a tendency on the part of researchers, practitioners and even the general public to deploy one predominant model or image of communication. This model is in the form of a linear process from a sender, by way of a channel, in the form of a message, to a receiver, to achieve some kind of effect, whether intended or unintended. This is a commonsense and robust framework for posing and handling questions about communication, whether practical or theoretical.

When models of communication were being elaborated, especially during the 1950s and 1960s, (McQuail and Windahl, 1982) it was a basic model of this kind which provided the starting point and gave direction to thinking about communication. The refinements added included: that of 'feedback' (response from receiver to sender) and interaction; a recognition of processes of encoding and decoding as separate steps; the incorporation of features of the media organization in which the 'sender' works; the recognition of personal mediation in the diffusion of media messages; and also features of the social context in which the receiver selects from and responds to messages.

One of the most useful models of communication was that of Westley and MacLean (1957), who conceived of the professional mass communicator as occupying a 'channel role' in between those who want to 'speak' in society ('advocates') and the public they want to reach. This role, according to Westley and MacLean, is typically neutral and *purposeless*, although it involves selecting from advocates what is thought to be of interest to the public. The model is helpful in distinguishing a notion of audience feedback, but it still conforms to the general model sketched above in being linear, sequential and characterized by the transfer of messages from point A to point B.

A transmission versus a ritual view of communication

This version of communication has been characterized by James Carey (1975) as a 'transmission' view of communication which

> is the commonest in our culture and . . . is defined by such terms as sending, transmitting or giving information to others. It is formed off a metaphor of geography or transportation . . . The centre of this idea of communication is the transmission of signals or messages over time for the purpose of control.

He points to the existence of an alternative, *ritual*, view, according to which

> communication is linked to such terms as "sharing", participation, association, fellowship and the possession of a common faith . . . A

ritual view is not directed towards the extension of messages in space, but the maintenance of society in time; not the act of imparting information, but the representation of shared beliefs.

This alternative view might equally be called an 'expressive' model of communication, since its emphasis is on the intrinsic satisfaction of the sender rather than some instrumental purpose. These two versions of communication process correspond approximately to the 'command' and the 'associational' modes of communication relationships mentioned above (pp. 32–3), especially if teaching and information-giving are considered under the former heading.

Communication as attention gaining and giving

While both are useful and even necessary alternative conceptions of processes to which mass media lend themselves, they do not exhaust the main possibilities of mass communication or capture its essence. For this a third concept of communication process is required which can be termed an *attention* model. According to this view, the essential communicative activity of mass media is to attract and keep attention rather than to transmit meaning or provide a platform, or increase expressive capacity or promote shared rituals. The business of the media and their primary purpose will be to interest an audience and the skills to be advanced and rewarded in mass communication are to be judged accordingly.

At the core of much dispute about media purpose and effect lies the fact that they (media) may have no other direct purpose beyond that of attracting attention and reaching those they attract with whatever message is being carried in the channel. This is consistent with the Westley/MacLean view sketched above. The point was eloquently encapsulated by Elliott (1972) when he claimed that 'mass communication is liable not to be communication at all' in the sense of the 'ordered transference of meaning'. However, this critical remark depends on the implicit adoption of a transmission model as the appropriate standard and appears to deny the status of genuine communication to attention-gaining and spectatorship.

The three views or models sketched can be summarily compared in the terms of Figure 8, with an indication of what each implies both for sender and for receiver.

The transmission model is largely taken over from other and older institutional contexts — education, religion, government. It is appropriate to certain media activities, those which are instructional, informational or propagandist in purpose (on both sides), but it is

Figure 8 Three versions of the communication process

	Sender's orientation	Receiver's orientation
1. Transmission model:	Transfer of meaning	Cognitive processing
2. Expression or ritual model:	Performance	Gratification/shared experience
3. Attention model:	Display	Attention-spectatorship

misleading if applied to a good many media activities and/or contexts of use. Even the major media task of news provision is not in the first place, or exclusively, purposive information-giving or instructional in nature.

The ritual expression model also captures important elements of the definition, purpose and practice of media performance in both the informational and the cultural/entertainment spheres. However, it reflects more the external interpretation by observers than the stated purpose of senders and receivers.

The significance of the third model (display-attention) lies in the fact that it comes closest to the main goal as defined by the media for themselves (attracting audiences) and also to a common version of the significance of media use held by the audience (escape, involvement, diversion, etc). It also conflicts with, or deviates from, elements in the other two models. A good deal of 'media culture' and media practice is explicable by the wish to maximize audience attention (or the share of a chosen potential audience). This involves initial attraction, then holding and later deepening of attraction. Attention has several measurable dimensions and extends to include the concepts of attachment and involvement, although what counts most is usually simply the time spent with an item or type of content or with a given medium or channel. The *quality* of attention is usually of secondary importance to the media themselves, although the composition of the attenders is of interest, especially for advertisers.

The need to take more account of display-attention as a common, if not most *frequent*, kind of underlying communication process is connected with the comments made above (p. 34) on the relative neglect of theory concerning the 'service' mode and functions of mass communication. 'Attention-display' forms and orientations are strongly related to the service mode, although not exclusively so (for instance, power-seekers or pedagogues also want to gain and keep attention), since the essence of any market is to bring goods and services to the attention of potential consumers, to arouse and keep their interest. Despite this relation, the service mode has, in turn, an independence from this model. The link is nevertheless strong because, in one respect, the mass communication market is essentially about keeping attention before all else. Audience attention is the coin paid by media producers and distributors to advertisers in return for their subsidy to the operation and is thus the basis of profitability. Audience attention is also the key to box-office income or to subscription and thus underlies the other main financial support for media as a service industry. While propagandists and pedagogues on the one hand, and normative organizations on the other, also want attention, they have little use for it except on certain limited terms of their own. Attention alone is not enough and the message cannot easily be adapted to secure attention without risking the defeat of its own ends (consider, for instance, the effect on political communication of using television, p. 289 below).

Going with the idea of communication as a process of *display and attention*, especially in the context of an open, voluntary institution as described, are several noteworthy features which are not associated with the other two models:

- Attention-giving is a *zero-sum* process. The time spent attending to one media object of interest cannot be given to another and time is finite. By contrast, there is no quantifiable limit to the amount of meaning that can be transferred or satisfaction gained from performance.
- Attention is of the present moment. The future does not matter except as continuation or amplification of the present and the past does not matter at all (unlike the case of effect or response).
- Attention-gaining is an end in itself. It has no ulterior or instrumental purpose. In this respect, it may be regarded as *value-neutral*. Technology and form matter rather than content.

These three features can be seen as underlying, respectively, the *competitiveness*, the *actuality/transience*, and the *objectivity/detachment* which are such pronounced features of mass communication, compared to other cultural or knowledge-producing institutions.

Conclusion

The priority given by the media themselves to attention-gaining is reflected in the overwhelming bias of media audience research to audience measurement, rather than effect (which would go with an interest in the transmission model) or with quality of response (which would go with the expression model). The priority is understandable in light of the fact that having an audience at all is the single most necessary condition for continuing in existence and achieving other communicative results. Without appreciating this truism it is not easy to understand many aspects of the professional media culture or of some basic characteristics of the media cultural product (for instance the continuity of successful formulas, the seeming conformity or lack of risk-taking, the dominance of form, appearance, image and presentation over content, etc).

Recognition of this feature of mass communication does not rule out criticism of its content and performance on other grounds, but it helps to explain more of what is to be observed. In particular, it depicts mass communication as, to a large extent, consummatory, an end in itself, enjoyed for the moment, using time and resources but to no particular end. It tends to reduce any expectation of effect, in terms of knowledge, influence or behaviour. It accounts in part for the importance of personalities to the media, for the high value attached to fame, publicity and celebrity independent of any achievement, a value which the media also try to disseminate among their publics. An interesting question arises as to how use of the new media (as characterized earlier) will be adapted to the prevalence of this model, which appears closely linked to the allocutory pattern. It is possible that interactive potentials of new media could be built on to extend the dominance of the display-attention pattern (in the same way as with video games). It is also possible that skills at attracting attention will be applied to manage videotex and teletext uses, so that they are less user-controlled than the theory and technology seem to promise.

CHAPTER 3

THEORY OF MEDIA AND THEORY OF SOCIETY

Mass communication as a society-wide process: the mediation of social relations

The main purpose of this chapter will be to present, in a summary form, the most influential social scientific theories about mass communication and to show how they can be grouped and related to each other. The task is not made easier by the complexity of media activities, the diversity of possible viewpoints and the inconsistency, incompleteness or inadequacy of many of the theories available. There can be no possibility of offering a single agreed theory which will explain what is going on and predict effects, but it does help to begin with a single broad framework within which the essential processes and relationships can be located. This does involve a particular way of looking at mass communication, but does not necessarily prejudge the theoretical alternatives.

The main presuppositions underlying the chosen framework are as follows. First, the media institution is engaged in the production, reproduction and distribution of *knowledge* in the widest sense of sets of symbols which have meaningful reference to experience in the social world. This knowledge enables us to make sense of experience, shapes our perceptions of it and contributes to the store of knowledge of the past and the continuity of current understanding. Collectively, the mass media differ from other knowledge institutions (e.g. art, religion, science, education, etc) in several respects:

- they have a general carrier function for knowledge of all kinds — thus on behalf of other institutions as well;
- they operate in the public sphere, accessible in principle to all members of a society on an open, voluntary, unspecific and low-cost basis;
- in principle, the relationship between sender and receiver is balanced and equal;
- the media reach more people than other institutions and for longer, 'taking over' from early influences of school, parents, religion and so on.

According to this basic assumption, the contours of the symbolic environment (of information, ideas, beliefs, etc) which we inhabit are often known to us by way of the mass media and it is the media which may inter-relate and give coherence to its disparate elements. This symbolic environment tends to be held in common, the more we share the same media sources (and of course, the same social environment). While each individual or group does have a unique world of perception and experience, a precondition of organized social life is a degree of common perception of reality and the mass media contribute to this perhaps more than other institutions on a daily, continuous basis, even if the impact is very gradual and not consciously felt.

A second main presupposition is that mass media have, as one meaning of the word connotes, a *mediating* role, between objective social reality and personal experience. The mass media are inter-mediate and mediating in several senses: they often lie between us (as receivers) and that part of potential experience which is outside our direct perception or contact; they may stand between ourselves and other institutions with which we have dealings – law, industry, the state, etc; they may provide a link between these different insti-tutions; the media are also channels for others to contact us, or us to contact them; they often provide the material for us to form perceptions of other groups, organizations and events. We can know relatively little from direct experience even of our own society and our contact with government and political leaders is largely based on media-derived knowledge. In a similar way, our perception of groups in society to which we do not belong or cannot observe is partly shaped by mass media. It is rare, in any given case, to be entirely dependent on mass media for information and impressions but, in practice and for most people, alternative possibilities are not, or cannot be, used extensively.

The notion of mass media as occupying a place 'between' ourselves and other people and things in space and time is a metaphor which invites the use of other metaphors to characterize the part played by mass media and the possible consequences of that part.

There are different ways in which mediation of the kind referred to can take place, varying especially in terms of degree and kind of activity, purposefulness, interactivity and effectiveness. Mediation can mean many things, ranging from the direct relationship of one to another, through negotiation, to control of one by another. The variations can be captured by the following communication images which express different aspects of the way in which the media connect us to 'reality'. The media are alternatively:

– a *window* on experience, which extends our vision, enables us to see what is going on for ourselves, without interference or bias;

- an *interpreter*, which explains and makes sense of otherwise fragmentary or puzzling events;
- a *platform* or *carrier* for information and opinion;
- an *interactive link* which relates senders to receivers by way of different kinds of feedback;
- a *signpost*, which actively points the way, gives guidance or instruction;
- a *filter*, selecting out parts of experience for special attention and closing off other aspects of experience, whether deliberately and systematically or not;
- a *mirror*, which reflects back an image of society to itself —usually with some distortion by accentuating what people want to see of their own society or sometimes what they want to punish or suppress;
- a *screen* or *barrier* which conceals truth in the service of propagandist purpose or escapism.

While some of these images derive from external analysis of media activity, most can also be found in the media's own self-definition. They do often see themselves as reflecting society, making it more visible, allowing elements within it to speak to the whole society. They also accept some responsibility to engage actively in social interaction and at times to give direction or leadership and contribute to integration and coherence. Even the notion of filtering is recognized, since media apply themselves often to the task of selection and interpretation of what would otherwise be a confusing world of happenings. Not surprisingly, the media reject the negative connotations of filtering and control, and, as will be discussed in chapter 6, there are quite sharp differences of view within media about the extent to which their activity should be neutral and reflective or participant and directive.

A frame of reference for studying mediation

Figure 9 gives graphic expression to the metaphor of mediation. The media institution is placed in the space enclosed by two arcs, one representing what is more remote and powerful, the other locating what is close at hand in the way of things, experience and people. On the first arc are located the main institutions and power centres of society and, beyond these, the world which is relatively hidden or otherwise inaccessible. Social institutions handle the events and eventualities of this more distant reality and sometimes create them. On the second arc, we locate ourselves as members of families, associations, working organizations, communities, observing and experiencing the consequences of institutional activities and environmental changes. Here we also locate the audiences, whose composition is influenced by these other ties and experiences.

Figure 9 Mediation diagram and types of theory

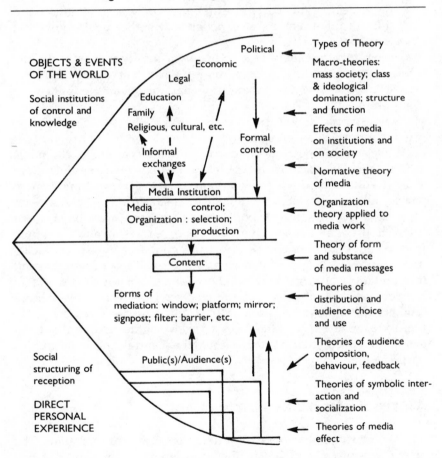

For purposes of the diagram, the media institution has been enlarged and detached from 'society' to show its main component activities and its connections 'back' to society and 'forward' or 'down' to the public. The label 'media institution' refers to the principles, rules, laws, conventions and instruments of control and regulation in the given society and is shown separately from the 'media organizations' which actually perform the production and distribution functions. The separation is artificial, since the media institution is often only open to observation in its actual working, but it is useful for purposes of analysis.

Links between media and other institutions

First, there are general normative and philosophical principles concerning the proper relationship of 'press' to society, which, whether codified or not, are likely to be widely shared by 'elites', media and public. We refer to these as 'normative theories of the press' although they include such general ideological presuppositions as liberty, social responsibility, rationality (see chapter 5). Secondly, there are formal ties in law that put some limits on media freedom and in some cases give positive direction to the media. Thirdly, there are economic links which connect media with financial and work institutions. There may also be formal ties with other social institutions. Fourthly, there are many informal links between media and society which go in both directions and have the character of exchanges. Many things are involved, but especially: attempts to gain access to or to influence the media; the search by the media for sources among societal elites and for information; mutual contacts within the same social milieu. Such informal contacts may either further the control of media by society or facilitate the task of the media in reflecting or revealing what is happening in society. Whichever of these applies, the inevitable result is to place the media 'nearer' to institutional sources and to centres of power in society than to their future audiences.

Links between media organizations and their publics

There are, of course, links other than those represented by the distribution of content which has to be shaped according to certain expectations about the interests and requirements of audiences. It is one aspect of media professional skill to be able to assess these, but there are several 'inputs' from the audience: individual personal contacts initiated by mass communicators; results of audience research; evidence of sales; letters and phone-calls from the public. In principle such linkages can be reciprocal and balanced but in the nature of things — the dispersal and lack of organization of the audience and the decision-making power of media organizations —

the contacts will be mostly controlled and directed by the media. In turn, this strengthens the probability, as Figure 9 implies, that the media are more dependent on, than in control of, institutions in society and the public is more dependent on, than in control of, the media. It should be borne in mind that several institutions, especially that of politics, seek, in various ways, to express or represent the interests of the public. This form of control is not very adequately illustrated, but its consequences will vary from one society to another.

The structure of media publics

The diagram is intended to draw attention to certain other points. The composition of the media public is structured in terms of component social groups and categories and this structuring can be accounted for by different influences. One is the varying interest, relevance and accessibility of different kinds of content, so that selection will be related to differences of taste, life-cycle, education, general social circumstances. Secondly, there are economic influences on audience structure, arising from varying cost of media to the consumer and, more importantly, the financing of media by advertising which makes it essential for media to match messages with appropriate audiences, defined according to income and consumption patterns. Thirdly, there are certain differences in social structures of residence, class, religion, etc, that also account for patterns of availability and media use. In practice, differences of cultural taste, of economic and social position, are too closely inter-related for the separate effect of any one to be clearly identified.

Concluding remarks on mediation

The diagram indicates links, in the sense of channels, relationships and contacts between the main elements of society, media and public. We should recall that the position of the media in this tripartite relationship tends to be 'fixed' in a given society by way of the media definition, described in general terms above. These definitions are themselves an outcome of many influences: history; general social and and political theory; other social institutions; audience expectations and attitudes, based on past experience and current needs; the self-view and chosen activities of the media themselves; technological constraints and possibilities and so forth.

The diagram is drawn to be read vertically, as if it implies that the media are indeed in between a social 'top' and a lower social level, possibly closer and more accessible to the former than the latter. This implication is deliberate even if it pre-empts some theory and seems inconsistent with a feature of the media-audience relationship already remarked on — that of balance and equality. The reasons for the implication lie in the inescapable fact that the media do provide more effective channels 'down' than 'up' and facilitate vertical communication (downwards) rather than lateral or bottom-up flows. They are also inevitably closer to organized political and econmic power (as owners, controllers or sources) than to their audiences. The balance and equality lies only at the point of contact between receiver and media content (the television set or newspaper).

The joining of the arcs on which social institutions and public, respectively, are located in the diagram is also a reminder of the fact that there is a direct as well as mediated contact between ourselves and the main institutions of society, however discontinuous and incomplete. We do also occasionally have personal experience of distant and less accessible events and objects in the world, whether by chance or choice. Thus the media do not monopolize all possibilities of acquiring knowledge and experience. But they do tend to serve as co-ordinator and common point of reference for the various pieces of separate experience and specialist knowledge, and for everything that we do learn or experience for ourselves they provide a massive supplement of vicarious experience and interpretation. Further, it is this supplement which is most widely shared and provides the common ground for social discourse.

Alternative theories of media and society

Social scientific media theory has been developed in order to formulate and provisionally answer a number of central questions about the working of public systems of communication in society. These questions are numerous, but can be reduced to three very fundamental matters, having to do with the exercise of *power* in societies, with *social integration* and with *social change*. Before looking at what theories have to say about each of these (in chapter 4), the most commonly cited varieties of media theory have to be reviewed and related to each other in a systematic way, to show similarities and differences and the choices they offer.

The starting point is the observation that views of how mass media work in society are often fundamentally inconsistent and even opposed, not only because of differences of interpretation of evidence, but because there are fundamental conflicts of value and interest in societies. Such divisions characterize sociology more than other social sciences because they are built into its subject matter and media theory tends to reflect sociology more than other social sciences. A guide to divisions in sociology is provided by Burrell and Morgan (1979), the relevance of which for mass communication was signalled by Rosengren (1983). They suggest that the field of sociology (and, in particular, organizational sociology) has been structured by two major dimensions which, when plotted against each other, locate four main paradigms. Their vertical dimension is (top-down) the 'sociology of radical change' versus the 'sociology of regulation', corresponding with conflict and consensus models of society, respectively. The horizontal dimension (left to right) separates 'subjective' from 'objective' views of the world and modes of enquiry. This latter dimension corresponds with several other fundamental oppositions in the social sciences — nominalism versus realism; antipositivism versus positivism; and voluntarism versus determinism; ideographic versus nomothetic methodologies. The four paradigms are: top left, radical humanism; top right, radical structuralism; bottom left, interpretative schools of sociology; bottom right, functionalism. Rosengren (1983) used much the same scheme to discuss choices of paradigms in communication research.

These materials help us to develop a device for mapping out the field of mass communication theory, substituting new versions of the two main dimensions and adding a third. In place of the vertical dimension mentioned, we substitute a *power* dimension: 'dominance' versus 'pluralism'; in place of the horizontal dimension we place what is for our purposes primarily a *change* dimension (although it is much more, especially in its implications for methods of research) — 'media as mover' versus 'society as mover'; we add a third dimension which, as it were, 'shadows' the vertical, in order to deal especially with *integrn* — 'centrifugal' versus 'centripetal'.

The resulting scheme is presented in Figure 10 and the three main dimensions are further characterized below.

Dominance versus pluralism

Essentially, this dimension separates those who view media as an instrument in the hands of, or service of, a dominant class, elite or power-holding group from those who see them as a response to demand from below, diverse, fragmented and without any inbuilt

Figure 10 Main dimensions and locations of media theory

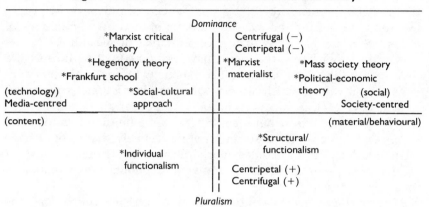

direction. The characteristics of mass media which support the dominance interpretation are: their centralization; their availability for control at source by a few — whether as business or state concerns; their great reach; their unidirectionality; their standardization; their attractiveness and prestige for dependent mass publics. The reverse view is supported by the potential multiplicity of sources and diversity of messages, distributed according to the interests of freely selecting and diverse publics, sub-audiences and individuals. Clearly the choice of position can vary according to objective assessment of a given situation and according to general political and social beliefs.

Centrifugal versus centripetal tendencies of media

This represents a contrast of values and of empirical observation/ prediction as between the notions of change, freedom, diversity and fragmentation (centrifugal tendencies) on the one hand and one of order, control, unity and cohesion (centripetal tendencies) on the other. For theory formulation much depends on whether one takes a positive or negative view of these concepts.

Different theorists have associated the mass media very closely with both tendencies. On the one hand, mass media have, histori- cally, brought messages of what is new, fashionable, and advanced in terms of goods, ideas, techniques, and values from city to country and from the social top to the base, and they have seemed to challenge established ways and value systems. They have also probably motivated people to move in search of better material conditions and stimulated demands for consumption. Beyond that, they have some potential, at least, for weakening the hold of traditional values enforced by group sanctions and have helped to free individuals from the ways of thinking of their own limited social milieu, consequently 'privatizing' certain areas of social life.

On the other hand, the media have been credited with replacing diverse and long-established value systems with new and homogeneous sets of values which are not very complex or constraining, but which, nevertheless, stress conformity and order and, to the extent that they are so widely held, contribute to the binding together of a large-scale, differentiated society more effectively than would have been possible through older mechanisms of religious, family, or group control. Such, at least, might be a functionalist explanation of media tendencies.

The positions seem far apart, the one stressing centrifugal, the other centripetal tendencies, although in fact, as several authors have pointed out, it is not inconsistent to suppose that both forces are at work, the one compensating to some extent for the other (Carey, 1969; McCormack, 1961). Nevertheless, the attempt to hold both views at the same time, or to reconcile them theoretically, can be confusing and it helps to think of both versions of media theory — centrifugal and centripetal — as each having its own dimension of evaluation, so that there are, in effect, four different theoretical positions. In the case of the centripetal proposition about media, there is a positive version which stresses the media as integrative and unifying (essentially the functional view) and a negative version which represents this effect as one of homogenization and manipulative control (critical theory or mass society view).

For the centrifugal proposition, the positive version stresses modernization, freedom, and mobility as the effects to be expected from media (individualism in general), while the negative version points to isolation, alienation, loss of values, and vulnerability (a 'dysfunctional' view of change as social disorder — e.g. Janowitz, 1981). In general, the same characteristics of mass media which have been cited in relation to the power dimension are relevant here. In some circumstances the two dimensions come together and provide two opposed versions of media tendency: towards uniformity and repressive control or towards pluralism and voluntary solidarity.

Media or society as first mover?

The question indicates a choice between a 'media-centred' and a 'society-centred' view of the relationship (see below, pp. 85–6). The former stresses the means of communication as a force for change, either through technology or the typical content carried. The latter emphasizes the dependence of both on other forces in society, especially those of politics and money. From this second point of view, the forms of mass media are an outcome of historical change — a reflection and consequence of political liberalization and industrial-ization and a response to demands for servicing from other social institutions. The media-centred view, which has found its advocates in the work of the 'Toronto School' (Innis, 1951; McLuhan, 1962) and of subsequent writers (e.g. Gouldner, 1976) and its best example in the printing press (Febvre and Martin, 1984; Eisenstein, 1978), allots an independent causal role to the dominant communication tech-nology of the epoch in question.

There are strong and weak versions of media-centred theory and there are also possibilities for attributing causal influence to some media in some cases for some social institutions, without having to reject a general view of media as ultimately dependent on society.

A distinction between technology and content also allows some scope for negotiation between one or other global alternative. For instance, the 'cultivation' theories of Gerbner et al. (1980) seem to involve the view that 'dominant message systems' (i.e. content) owe more to the working of certain institutional forces in society than to the intrinsic properties of television as a medium — hence reconciling a 'sociological' with a 'communicative' perspective. The 'society-centred' view is also open to differentiation, since the forces of 'society' can either be formulated as a matter of class, culture and social structure broadly and collectively conceived, or as individual differences of interest, motive, or social location which account for selective use of, and response to, communication, and subordinate media to the needs of personal and micro-social life. The media are seen as dependent, in much more specific ways, but the same broad conclusion — that people and society are users rather than used — is reached.

The distinction between media and society goes with other relevant theoretical lines of division, which can really only be named: between superstructure and base explanations of social change; between more idealistic and more materialistic approaches; between an emphasis on communication as expression and consummation or a view of it as a means of transmission and an instrument for achieving some end. This last distinction also helps to differentiate 'culturalist' traditions of study from sociological ones, each with its characteristic aims and methods of enquiry. It directs attention also to a major issue which has to be faced in dealing with new media

possibilities — that of weighing cultural against material consequences. In general, media-centred theory is more supportive of a
view of powerful mass media, the power lying either in the
consistency and repetition of messages reaching many people or in
the inevitability of adaptation by social institutions to the opportunities and pressures of communication forms, with consequences
for the messages carried and the relations between senders and
receivers.

A summary of theories

The theories entered under summary labels in Figure 10 may now be
separately described even if, as indicated, they are structured by a set
of similarities and differences and sometimes their tendency is very
close to one or other of the positions already described. They do not
all have an equal status as theories and some are the work of several
hands, while others are associated with a dominant author or school.
Sometimes they can only have unity and identity through their
presuppositions or by the type of problem, approach and method
they indicate.

Mass society theory

This is described first for reasons of historical primacy rather than its
current importance and its elements are built around the concept of
'mass' which was described in chapter 2 (pp. 29–30). There is
an extensive literature to draw on, including Mills (1951; 1956),
Kornhauser (1959; 1968), Bramson (1961), Bell (1961) and Giner
(1976). The theory emphasizes the interdependence of institutions
that exercise power and thus the integration of the media into the
sources of social power and authority. Content is likely to serve the
interests of political and economic power-holders and although the
media cannot be expected to offer a critical or alternative definition of
the world, their tendency will be to assist in the accommodation of
the dependent public to their fate.

   People are likely to be offered some view of their place in the
whole society, the means of relaxation and diversion from their
problems, a culture which is in keeping with the rest of their
existence. This latter is likely to be characterized by routine work and
leisure, subjection to bureaucracies, isolation or family privatization,
competitiveness and lower levels of solidarity and participation. Mass
society theory gives a primacy to the media as cause and maintainer

of mass society and rests very much on the idea that the media offer a view of the world, a substitute or pseudo-environment which is a potent means of manipulation of people but also an aid to their psychic survival under difficult conditions. According to C. Wright Mills (1951, p. 333) 'Between consciousness and existence stand communications, which influence such consciousness as men have of their existence'.

This vision of mass society is pessimistic and not very open to empirical test, since it is already a world view and a total explanation of many of the phenomena in which we are interested. It is more a diagnosis for the sickness of the times, mixing elements of critical thought from the political left with a nostalgia for a golden age of community and democracy. As a theory of the media, it strongly invokes the images of control and filtering and portrays the direction of influence from above downwards.

It also generally conforms to a 'negative centifugalist' view, although the notion of spiritual isolation of the individual is also a central one. Centralized control is achieved through the denial to individuals of the chance or capacity to realize their own collective interests.

Marxism — the classic position

While Marx himself only knew the press before it was effectively a mass medium, it is possible to analyse modern media according to his ideas. The media are a means of production, conforming to a general type of capitalist industrial form, with factors of production and relations of production. They are likely to be in the monopolistic ownership of a capitalist class, nationally or internationally organized and to serve the interests of that class. They do so by materially exploiting cultural workers (extracting surplus labour value) and consumers (making excess profits). They work ideologically by disseminating the ideas and world views of the ruling class, denying alternative ideas which might lead to change or to a growing consciousness by the working class of its interests and by preventing the mobilization of such consciousness into active and organized political opposition. The complexity of these propositions has led to several variants of Marxist-inspired analysis of modern media which can be identified as: *political-economic* theory; *critical theory*; theory of *media hegemony*: the first of these is more true to the materialist Marxist tradition, emphasizing economic (base) factors, the latter two relating more to ideological (superstructural) elements.

Political–economic media theory

Political–economic media theory is an old label that has been revived to identify an approach which focuses more on economic structure than on ideological content of media. It asserts the dependence of ideology on the economic base and directs research attention to the empirical analysis of the structure of ownership and to the way media market forces operate. From this point of view, the media institution has to be considered as part of the economic system though with close links to the political system. The predominant character of the knowledge of and for society produced by the media can be largely accounted for by the exchange value of different kinds of content, under conditions of pressure to expand markets, and by the underlying economic interests of owners and decision makers (Garnham, 1979). These interests relate to the need for profit from media operations and to the profitability of other branches of commerce as a result of monopolistic tendencies and processes of vertical and horizontal integration (e.g. into oil, paper, telecommunications, leisure, tourism, etc).

The consequences are to be observed in the reduction of independent media sources, concentration on the largest markets, avoidance of risk taking, neglect of smaller and poorer sectors of the potential audience. The effects of economic forces are not random, but, according, for instance, to Murdock and Golding (1977, p. 37) work consistently to exclude:

> those voices lacking economic power or resources . . . the underlying logic of cost operates systematically, consolidating the position of groups already established in the main mass-media markets and excluding those groups who lack the capital base required for successful entry. Thus the voices which survive will largely belong to those least likely to criticise the prevailing distribution of wealth and power. Conversely, those most likely to challenge these arrangements are unable to publicise their dissent or opposition because they cannot command resources needed for effective communication to a broad audience.

The main strength of the approach lies in its capacity for making empirically testable propositions about market determinations, although the latter are so numerous and complex that empirical demonstration is not easy. A weakness of the political-economic approach is that elements of media under public control are not so easy to account for in terms of the working of the free market. While the approach centres on media as an economic process leading to the commodity (content), there is an interesting variant of the political-economic approach which suggests that media really produce audiences, in the sense that they deliver audience attention to advertisers and shape the behaviour of media publics in certain distinctive ways (Smythe, 1977).

While Marxism has been the main inspiration for political-economic analysis of media, it does not have a monopoly of critical analysis of media structure and economics, the tools for which are quite widely available in sociology, political science and economics. (See, for instance, Curran and Seaton, 1985; Hirsch and Gordon, 1975; Bagdikian, 1983; Murdock and Golding, 1977; Curran, 1986.)

The Frankfurt School and critical theory

The work of the Frankfurt School, the third Marxist stream, may now be of largely historical interest, but its intellectual inheritance is so important that it cannot be left out of this account. Those critical theorists who now follow what can be called a 'culturalist' approach owe a great deal to the work of members of the school, especially Adorno and Horkheimer (1972) and Marcuse (1964). The Frankfurt theorists began work in Weimar Germany and were dispersed with the coming of Nazi power, mainly to the United States (for a history, see Jay, 1973). They were concerned with the apparent failure of the revolutionary social change predicted by Marx and in explanation of this failure looked to the capacity of the superstructure, especially in the form of mass media, to subvert historical processes of economic change. In a sense, history seemed to have 'gone wrong' because dominant class ideologies had come to condition the economic base by a process of subversion and assimilation of the working class.

The universal, commercialized, mass culture was the chief means by which this success for monopoly capital had been achieved. The whole system of mass production of goods, services and ideas had more or less completely sold the system of capitalism, along with its devotion to technological rationality, consumerism, short-term gratification, and the myth of 'classlessness'. The commodity is the main ideological instrument of this process since it seems that fine art and even critical and oppositional culture can be marketed for profit at the cost of losing critical power. Frankfurt theory asserts the dependency of the person and the class on the definition of images and terms of debate common to the system as a whole. Marcuse gave the name 'one-dimensional' to the society that has been created with the help of the 'culture industry'. The emphasis that the School placed on the media as a powerful mechanism for containment of change has survived and links it with the 'hegemonic' approach described below, but the 'negativism' of the Frankfurt approach, and perhaps its cultural elitism, has been an object of later criticism on the left. The affinity of general thrust and contemporaneity with mass society theory should also be noticed.

Marxist critical theorists and members of the Frankfurt School can be represented as combining a media-centred view with one of class domination. However, they do not neglect social and material forms and their general view of media power is one which emphasizes conservation of the existing order rather than change.

Hegemonic theory of media

A third school of media analysis in the Marxist tradition can, with caution (since it risks confusing the work of different theorists), be given the general label of 'hegemony' theory, using Gramsci's (1971) term for a ruling ideology. This has concentrated less on the economic and structural determinants of a class-biased ideology and more on ideology itself, the forms of its expression, its ways of signification and the mechanisms by which it survives and flourishes with the apparent compliance of its victims (mainly the working class) and succeeds in invading and shaping their consciousness. The difference from the classic Marxist and political-economic approach lies in the recognition of a greater degree of independence of ideology from the economic base.

Ideology, in the form of distorted definition of reality and a picture of class relationships or, in the words of Althusser (1971), 'the imaginary relationships of individuals to their real conditions of existence', is not dominant in the sense of being imposed by force by ruling classes, but is a pervasive and deliberate cultural influence which serves to interpret experience of reality in a covert but consistent manner. According to Hall (1982, p. 95):

> That notion of dominance which meant the direct imposition of one framework, by overt force or ideological compulsion, on a subordi-nate class, was not sophisticated enough to match the complexities of the case. One had also to see that dominance was accomplished at the unconscious as well as the conscious level: to see it as a property of the system of relations involved, rather than as the overt and intentional biases of individuals in the very activity of regulation and exclusion which functioned through language and discourse.

The theoretical work of several Marxist thinkers, especially Poulantzas (1975) and Althusser (1971), has contributed to the grounding of this approach, directing attention to the ways in which the relationships of capitalism have to be reproduced and legitimized according to the more or less voluntary consent of the working class itself. The tools for carrying out such work have largely been provided by developments in semiological and structural analysis which offer methods for the uncovering of covert meaning and underlying structures of meaning. The shift of theoretical attention from economic to ideological causes of the survival of capitalism has raised the priority of mass media amongst other 'ideological state apparatuses' (Althusser's term) and led to some dissension within the Marxist tradition from those who prefer to emphasize structural and economic determinants (see Williams, 1973).

The 'social–cultural' approach

The 'culturalist' or 'social–culturalist' approach which is now increasingly influential in the study of mass media owes a debt to the Frankfurt School as well as to other traditions of humanistic and literary analysis. It is marked by a more positive approach to the products of mass culture and by the wish to understand the meaning and place assigned to popular culture in the experience of particular groups in society — the young, the working class, ethnic minorities and other marginal categories. The 'cultural' approach seeks also to explain how mass culture plays a part in integrating and subordinating potentially deviant or oppositional elements in society. It has led to much work on the products and contexts of use of popular culture and the work carried out, in particular at the Centre for Contemporary Cultural Studies in Birmingham during the 1970s, has led to the identification of the 'Birmingham School' as a locus for the approach. The person most associated with the work of this School, Stuart Hall, has written of the cultural studies approach that it:

> stands opposed to the residual and merely reflective role assigned to the 'cultural'. In its different ways it conceptualises culture as inter-woven with all social practices; and those practices, in turn, as a common form of human activity. . . . It is opposed to the base-superstructure way of formulating the relationship between ideal and material forces, especially where the base is defined by the determination by the 'economic' in any simple sense. . . . It defines 'culture' as both the means and values which arise amongst

distinctive social groups and classes, on the basis of their given historical conditions and relationship, through which they 'handle' and respond to the conditions of existence. . . (quoted in Gurevitch et al., 1982, pp. 26–7).

The social–cultural approach seeks to attend to both messages and public, aiming to account for patterns of choice and response in relation to the media by a careful and critically-directed understanding of the actual social experience of sub-groups within society. The whole enterprise is also usually informed by an appreciation of the efforts of power holders to manage the recurrent crises of legitimacy and economic failure held to be endemic in industrial capitalist society (Hall et al., 1978). While not all who work within this tradition are Marxists, there is shared agreement that to understand culture you must also understand the working of historical material forces, and vice versa.

Structural functionalist approaches

A theoretical approach that can encompass, by description at least, all the elements of the theory map is a version of general sociological theory which explains recurrent and institutionalized activities in terms of the 'needs' of the society (Merton, 1957). As applied to the media institution, the presumed 'needs' have mainly to do with continuity, order, integration, motivation, guidance, adaptation. Society is to be viewed as a system of linked working parts or subsystems, of which media comprise one, each making an essential contribution. Organized social life requires the continued maintenance of a more or less accurate, consistent and complete picture of the parts of society and the social environment. The emphasis is thus on the image of media as connecting in all the senses mentioned above, thus ensuring internal integration and order and the capacity to respond to contingencies on the basis of a common and reasonably accurate picture of reality.

The mechanisms which produce this contribution from media to society are primarily the needs and demands of participants in society, whether as individual members, or collectivities. By responding to each separate demand in consistent ways, the media achieve unintended benefits for the society as a whole. Thus, structural-functional theory requires no assumption of ideological direction from the media (although it does assume ideological congruence) but depicts media as essentially self-directing and self-correcting, within certain politically negotiated institutional rules. It differs from Marxist approaches in a number of ways, but especially in its apparent objectivity and universal application. While apolitical in formulation, it suits pluralist and voluntarist conceptions of the fundamental mechanisms of social life and has a conservative bias to the extent that the media are likely to be seen as a means of maintaining society as it is rather than as a potential source of change.

The functionalist approach has been beset with difficulties, both intellectual (Wright, 1960 and 1974) and political (because of its seeming conservatism). An underlying difficulty is the confusion over the meaning of 'function' as a term (McQuail, 1987). It can be used in the sense of a *purpose*, or a *consequence*, or a *requirement*, or an *expectation*, and it has yet other meanings such as correlate, use (or even social gathering). As applied to mass communication, for instance, the term 'information function' can refer to three quite separate things: that media try to inform people (purpose): that people learn from media (consequence); that media are supposed to inform people (requirement or expectation). There are more possible ambiguities, but the variation in meaning usually depends on the point of view adopted: whether that of sender, receiver, neutral observer, legislator or regulator, etc (see Figure 11 below). A further difficulty arises from the fact that media do not only act on their own behalf but also for other groups or organizations, making it difficult to distinguish the functions of media (in whatever sense) from those of other bodies (governments, parties, firms, etc).

More fundamentally, an agreed version of media functions would require an agreed version of society, since the same media activity (e.g. mass entertainment) can appear in a positive light in one social theory and negatively in another. Much has also been written about the circularity, and, consequently, conservatism of functionalism. Its starting point is an assumption that any recurrent and institutional-ized activity serves some long-term purpose and contribution to the normal working of society (Merton, 1957), yet beyond the fact of occurrence there is no independent way of verifying either the utility or indispensability of the activity. The conservatism stems from the consequent reification of the present — what exists and seems normal is taken as good and necessary. There is so little chance of proving long-term effect from the media that whether they do good or harm can never really be empirically assessed.

Despite the many difficulties, there are some good reasons for retaining a functional approach for certain purposes. First, it offers a language for discussing the relations between mass media and society and a set of concepts which are hard to replace. This language has the advantage of being to a large extent shared by mass communicators themselves, agents of society, the media audience and social scientists, even if the latter have difficulties with it. Secondly, the approach can at least help to describe the main activities of media in relation to other aspects of social structure and process. Thirdly, it provides a link between empirical observation of media institutions and the normative theories about how media ought to work (see chapter 5).

A view of media function as purpose or motive seems to provide most common ground and avoid the worst difficulties described. This version has, consequently, two main components — a particular kind of media activity (a 'task' of the media), which can be more or less objectively named, and a statement of purpose, value, utility or end provided by one or other of the users, or expected beneficiaries. Although there is an objective element in this version of media function, the construct as a whole is essentially subjective. We are speaking of ideas and beliefs, in effect about 'theories' in the various senses outlined at the start of this book. Thus what the audience member thinks he or she derives from media is part of 'commonsense theory' and what media practitioners think of as their purpose is part of 'working theory', while sociologists or social theorists try to render what society expects or receives from the activities of the media.

Principal functions of mass media for society

The frame of reference presented above already indicates some of the possible functions attributable to the media in their role as mediating channels in society. These refer to such activities as 'connecting', 'pointing the way', 'interpreting', etc. There have been a number of attempts to systematize the main functions (purpose or effect, intended or unintended), beginning with Lasswell (1948) who presented a summary statement of the basic communication functions in the following form: surveillance of the environment; correlation of the parts of the society in responding to its environment; the transmission of the cultural heritage. These refer, respectively, to: the provision of information; the giving of comment and interpretation to help make sense of the fragments of information and also the formation of consensus; the expression of cultural values and symbols which are essential to the identity and continuity of society. Wright (1960) developed this basic scheme to describe many of the effects of the media and added 'entertainment' as a fourth key media function. This may be part of the transmitted culture but it has another aspect — that of providing reward, relaxation and reduction of tension, which makes it easier for people to cope with real-life problems and for societies to avoid breakdown (Mendelsohn, 1966).

With these materials we are in a position to specify the main functions (as purposes) of mass media, from the point of view of the society as a whole (the perspective generally adopted by structural functionalism), if we add one more idea — that of the *mobilizing* function of media. Nearly everywhere, the media are expected to advance national interests and promote certain key values and behaviour patterns, but especially so in times of crisis. And in certain developing societies, as well as in many socialist states, a mobilizing role is formally allotted to the media.

The overall result is the following set of basic ideas about media purpose in society:

I Information.
– providing information about events and conditions in society and the world
– indicating relations of power
– facilitating innovation, adaptation and progress.

II Correlation.
– explaining, interpreting and commenting on the meaning of events and information
– providing support for established authority and norms
– socializing
– co-ordinating separate activities
– consensus building
– setting orders of priority and signalling relative status.

III Continuity.
– expressing the dominant culture and recognizing subcultures and new cultural developments
– forging and maintaining commonality of values.

IV Entertainment.
– providing amusement, diversion, the means of relaxation
– reducing social tension.

V Mobilization.
– campaigning for societal objectives in the sphere of politics, war, economic development, work and sometimes religion.

It should be emphasized that we cannot give any general rank order to these items, nor say anything about their relative frequency of occurrence. The correspondence between function (or purpose) and precise content is not exact, for one function overlaps with another, and some purposes extend more widely than others over the range of media activities. In general, entries I and V have to do with 'change' and II, III and IV are associated with stability and 'integration'. To repeat an earlier point, we cannot easily distinguish between what the media do and what other institutions do, using the mass media, and it is partly for this reason that we need to look separately at media from the point of view of an 'advocate' in another institution and from their own point of view as channel or gatekeeper.

In general, it is not difficult to adapt the main functions described to take account of these alternative perceptions. The actual *content* or *activity* representing the functions will also vary a good deal according to whose purpose is being served. For instance, 'correlation' (interpretation) may come in the form of political opinions, product image making, religious views, journalistic comment and so on.

Individual functionalism

The theory which deals in individual functions and dysfunctions looks at media from the point of view of their audiences, and while it is not inconsistent with structural functionalism, it is concerned with different questions and employs different methods and concepts. It focuses on individual human behaviour and on motives of, and consequences for, individuals. The connection with structural functionalism is provided by the fact that individual motives often have their origins in social experience, their expression and satisfaction is shaped by the social context and ultimately the aggregate consequences feed back to the structure of society as a whole. The assumption that broad functions for society are served by the media (which depend on voluntary reception by many individuals) has in turn to presuppose a complex and extensive pattern of individually chosen uses. In other words, it can be argued that there can be no functions served for society except by way of functions served for individuals.

Functions of media for individuals

Individualist functionalist theory mostly finds its further elaboration in the tradition of 'uses and gratifications' research into the media audience (see below pp. 233–5). Over the last fifty years researchers have tried to answer the questions of *why* people should choose to attend to media in general, to particular media channels or types of content, what satisfactions they expect and get, to what uses they put the results of their attention to media. The result has been a growing inventory of gratifications, satisfactions and uses which shows a convincing degree of patterned regularity and predictability. Enough at least to provide a framework for individual (audience member) satisfaction which parallels and complements the set presented above as from the point of view of society. The following is adapted from a typology suggested by McQuail et al. (1972):

I Information.
- finding out about relevant events and conditions in immediate surroundings, society and the world
- seeking advice on practical matters or opinion and decision choices
- satisfying curiosity and general interest
- learning, self-education
- gaining a sense of security through knowledge.

II Personal identity.
- finding reinforcement for personal values
- finding models of behaviour
- identifying with valued other (in the media)
- gaining insight into one's self.

III Integration and social interaction.
- gaining insight into circumstances of others; social empathy
- identifying with others and gaining a sense of belonging
- finding a basis for conversation and social interaction
- having a substitute for real-life companionship
- helping to carry out social roles
- enabling one to connect with family, friends and society.

IV Entertainment.
- escaping, or being diverted, from problems
- relaxing
- getting intrinsic cultural or aesthetic enjoyment
- filling time
- emotional release
- sexual arousal.

It is even more difficult than usual to connect a motive, expectation or use with a specific type of content, since media use in general may be considered to supply at one time or another all the benefits named. It is also less easy to treat the items listed equally as statements of conscious motivation and purpose. A number of the ideas are often recognizable to a media user without being easily expressible. Yet, for each of the ideas named, there is sufficient empirical evidence to indicate that it is one element in the general pattern of motivation which supports audience behaviour. Consequently, they all fit our conception of media function and are relevant to an understanding of the part played by media in relating people to their society.

Functions and dysfunctions

Many of the connections and similarities between functions at different levels will already be apparent, but it is useful to consider briefly the question of degree of correspondence. If the functional description of media is at all valid there should be some measure of correspondence between the different perspectives. Thus, for purposes to be achieved at the level of society, it is necessary that the media and those who communicate through the media should set out to do certain things and that audiences should approach the media in a compatible way. In practice, societies will vary greatly according to whether there is an integrated and stable system for meeting different purposes. If, in a given case, there are sharp discrepancies between purposes at different levels, they are likely to reflect a strain or conflict within the society and perhaps a failure by the media to meet certain demands.

The description of media functions has been confined to overt and positive (from the given viewpoint) uses or applications of media. There may also be latent or unacknowledged processes at work, most especially at the level of society, which change or conceal the true nature of media purpose. There may also be negative consequences, intended or not, which this formulation cannot cope with. Both latent and dysfunctional elements are allowed for in Wright's (1960; 1974) scheme, but they are bound to be hypothetical and we can as easily use the framework presented here as a source of speculation about concealed purposes or unintended effect.

Thus informational purpose can lead to an intended or unintended 'disinformational' effect through bias in selection or misrepresentation. Interpretative activity may in practice be an excessive or partisan form of social control. Advancing cultural continuity may involve a suppression of new forms and of deviant cultural visions. Entertainment may mean systematic trivialization and consciousness control. Under totalitarian conditions, mobilization can be equated with brainwashing and coercion. This either demonstrates emptiness of the functional description or, alternatively, its great flexibility and convenience as a checklist of media activities and these possibilities are not mutually exclusive.

In summary: diversity of perspectives on function and purpose

The seeming confusion, incompatibility and sometimes redundancy of theories about media and society is bound to strike a newcomer to this field of study. It is not easy to explain or justify why it should be so, but the foregoing discussion of possible functions of mass communication should make the situation more understandable. The potential significance of mass media necessarily varies according to the perspective or point of view adopted and according to associated needs and interests. Much of the variation has now been described, but essential points can be summarized by summarily plotting the main perspectives of differently placed groups and interests as in Figure 11.

Figure 11 Alternative perspectives on function and purpose of mass media

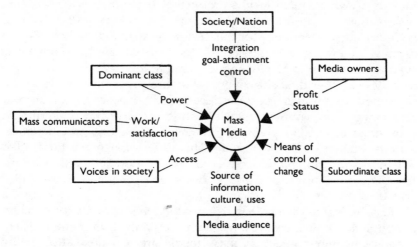

The information society: a new theory of media–society links

Enough has been said in previous chapters (especially pp. 39–43) to call into question the adequacy of the theoretical perspectives just outlined for dealing with the emerging communication situation of modern societies. The theories described here all have their own intrinsic weaknesses and are somewhat time-bound and even dated in formulation. Mass communication has been ·expanding and changing in such a way that it is difficult to retain any consistent theoretical view of it. Societies too are changing and one proposition which has been on the agenda of theorists for decades and can no longer be ignored is that we are entering an 'information society' (Ito, 1981). Its principal features are essentially those of the 'post-industrial' society described by Bell (1973) and its identification belongs to a long tradition of sociological thought about the stages through which societies progress as the basic mode of production changes (especially the transition from agricultural to industrial modes). It is impossible to review the underpinnings, scope and validity of the theory of an information society, but it is based on some observations and propositions that cannot be ignored.

Essentially, the information (or post-industrial) society is one in which information is the most valuable resource, means of production and also the main product, so that a majority of the labour force will consist of information workers and information will also be dominant economically and socially according to other indicators. The category of information worker can be very broadly defined to include all whose main task is producing, processing or distributing information or producing information technology. All advanced societies show a tendency for this sector to expand steadily and quite rapidly. According to Rogers (1986), the United States workforce was predominantly (over 50 percent) engaged in information work by the mid-1980s. Other data show very rapid and progressive increases in the amount of information produced. For purposes of calculation, information can range from scientific papers and government committee reports to personal phone conversations and letters to friends. Pool et al. (1984) provide estimates for Japan and the United States to show an *annual* increase of information production (translated into word units) of 8 and 10 percent respectively between 1960 and 1980.

The share of mass media in this production is not easy to estimate, although, by some measures, it is high. Certainly, information society theorists do not argue that mass media are a major cause in the transformation of society posited, however much they reflect and help to illustrate what is under way. Even so, mass media are sufficiently implicated in the change to be important to the theory of an information society and vice versa. At the very least, it can be said that: mass media are expanding and becoming more efficient at producing and distributing information; they are an important stimulus to the valuation and consumption of information, in its widest meaning; they also stimulate the production and acquisition of communication technology and the development of new technology; they are a growing sector of employment for information workers.

Information society theory involves a break with several of the theories discussed, in holding that the revolutionary potential lies not so much in the *content* of the message as in the *means* of producing and further handling the message, thus affecting the nature of work, of time use, of power relations and of systems of stratification and values in society. As already described, new communication technologies and new media are changing the pattern of mass communication, originally established as a large-scale, one-way, centre-peripheral transfer or address. The question here is whether the changes under way affect the specific issue of media-society linkages as presented above, aside from the question of mutual change in both. It is a question which is not yet easy to answer, since the 'old media' still predominate and the new ones (like video and cable TV) have so far largely been adapted to fit the available institutional forms. It is hard to decide how much credence to attach to what Marjorie Ferguson (1986) has dubbed 'neo-technological determinism'. There is little doubt, as she argues, that a *belief* in technology is now influencing policy (both in its active and reactive forms) and is acting as a self-fulfilling policy in respect of other social changes.

It is also possible to argue that fundamental questions involving matters of power competition within and between national societies, and issues to do with social integration, as discussed above, remain central and much the same in information societies as in industrial societies. The values of freedom, equality and order which structure ideological debate and which are invoked in discussions of mass media are also unlikely to be replaced very soon with alternative and more potent values (McQuail, 1986). Nevertheless, it is quite likely that a number of key aspects of the media-society relationship will have to be re-examined in the light of the changes mentioned, especially because of the following: the increase in individual autonomy of the receiver vis-a-vis the media sender; the changing balance of functions of mass media (more information and self-education); the blurring of boundary lines between mass media (defined as a leisure institution) and communication in other spheres, for instance those of work, learning, and interpersonal relations.

In evaluating the likelihood of the emergence of an information society, its probable character and its typical problems, it is important to bear in mind that the world is still much divided by ideology and level of development, however much the mass media and newer communication systems may seem to show a convergent tendency. In this connection, Salvaggio (1985) has proposed that we think in terms of four main international models: that of competition (the free market model); that of public utility (to be found especially in West Europe and Japan); the communist version; and that of the Third World. In each case, he argues, much the same set of basic factors determine the development of new communication technologies and help to define the social problems associated with each system. However, the relative salience of the factors varies from one model to another although the single factor of ideology is always dominant in each model. Of the other factors, Salvaggio proposes that: *economy* is most influential in the competitive model; *policy-making organizations* in the public utility model; *political party* in the communist model; *external factors* in the case of the Third World. It is the combination of ideology with each of these which accounts for most aspects of new technology development, including the recognition of attendant problems.

CHAPTER 4

MEDIA THEORY APPLIED: POWER, INTEGRATION AND CHANGE

Social scientific theory of media did not develop in a vacuum, but as a response to pressing questions in society or to guide empirical research and help to make sense of its findings. Theory is thus essentially about the posing and solving of problems. As we have seen, little of the relevant theory is exclusively about mass communication, but has a much wider reference. There is little or no social theory which is uniquely applicable to mass media. In this chapter, attention is given to the formulation of propositions and possible responses on the three key aspects of the working of societies named above (p. 57), having to do with *power*, *integration* and *change*. Questions and answers are drawn from three particular theories — mass society theory, Marxism and structural functionalism — chosen because at this particular time they are about all we have in the way of general theory of links between media and society and which also meet the requirements of having reasonable intellectual foundations and some basis in, or record of guiding, empirical research.

As yet there are few alternatives in prospect. There is no worked-out or agreed body of pure communication theory and much of what does exist applies only at the micro-level (see above, p. 6). Media- or channel-centred theories are generally vague or tendentious and as yet there is no elaborated theory appropriate to central features of the 'information society' (see above, pp. 75–8). In the long run we may expect developments in this respect, but so far mass communication has not been very greatly affected by the potential inherent in new technology (Rogers, 1986). The long familiar limitations of the three bodies of theory examined further here lie especially in their respective (sometimes concealed) normative biases.

The question of power

Since media operate in societies in which power is extensively deployed and unevenly distributed between individuals, groups and classes, and since media are invariably related in some way to the prevailing structure of political and economic power, several questions arise as to the nature of this relationship. It is evident, first of all, that media have an economic cost and value, are an object of competition for control and access and are subject to political, economic and legal regulation. Secondly, mass media are very commonly regarded as effective instruments of power on the basis of their capacity to do one or more of the following:

- attract and direct attention
- persuade in matters of opinion and belief
- influence behaviour (e.g. voting, buying)
- confer status and legitimacy
- define and structure perceptions of reality

These propositions give rise to at least the following sub-questions:

- Who controls the media and in whose interest?
- Who has access to the media and on what terms?
- Whose version of the world (social reality) is presented?
- How effective are the media in achieving their chosen ends?
- What variable factors limit or enlarge the power of the media in the respects mentioned?

The following answers are drawn from the three bodies of theory named.

Mass society theory and power

The theory itself (as described above) gives a clear definition of the degree and nature of media power in societies which are characterized by largeness of scale, remoteness of institutions, isolation of individuals and lack of strong local or group integration. It posits that media will be controlled or run in a monopolistic way and will be a principal and effective means of organizing people in masses — as audiences, consumers, markets, electorates. Mass media are usually the voice of authority, the givers of opinion and instruction and also of psychic satisfaction. The media establish a relation of dependence on the part of ordinary citizens, not only in respect of opinion, but also of self-identity and consciousness. The potential created by the media, according to the most influential and articulate theorist of mass society, C.W. Mills (1951; 1956), is for a form of non-democratic control 'from above'. The theory stresses this potential more than any possible limits to the power of the media, mainly because of monopoly tendencies and the difficulty of answering back.

Marxist theory and power

The question of power is also central to Marxism and Marxist interpretations of mass media, while varied, have always emphasized the fact that they are ultimately instruments of control by a ruling capitalist class. The founding text is Marx's *German Ideology* where he states

> The class which has the means of material production has control at the same time over the means of mental production so that, thereby, generally speaking, the ideas of those who lack the means of mental production are subject to it. . . . Insofar, therefore, as they rule as a class and determine the extent and compass of an epoch, it is self-evident that they . . . among other things . . . regulate the production and distribution of the ideas of their age: thus their ideas are the ruling ideas of the epoch (cited in Murdock and Golding, 1977).

Communication media (e.g. newspapers) are likely to be owned by members of a propertied class who can be expected to operate them in the interests of that class. There is a direct link in theory between economic ownership and the dissemination of messages which affirm the legitimacy and the value of a class society. These views are supported in modern times by evidence of tendencies to great concentration of media ownership by capitalist entrepreneurs (e.g. Bagdikian, 1983) and correlative evidence of conservative tendencies in content of media so organized.

Those versions of Marxist media theory which concentrate more on ideas than on material structures emphasize the ideological effects of media in the interests of a ruling class and in 'reproducing' the essentially exploitative relationships and manipulation and legitimate the dominance of capitalism and the subordination of the working class. Louis Althusser (1971) conceived this process to work by way of what he called ideological State Apparatuses (all means of social-ization, in effect) which, by comparison with Repressive State Apparatuses (e.g. army, police, etc), enabled the capitalist state to survive without recourse to direct violence. Gramsci's (1971) concept of hegemony refers to a ubiquitous and internally consistent culture and ideology which is openly or implicitly favourable to a dominant class or elite.

Marcuse (1964) interprets the media, along with other elements of mass production systems, as engaged in 'selling' or imposing a whole social system which is at the same time repressive and desirable. The main contribution of the media is to stimulate, then satisfy, 'false needs', which leads to the assimilation of groups who have no real material interest in common into a 'one-dimensional society'. Enzensberger, a critical thinker whose work is sometimes cited as Marxist, although he addressed his critique against established bureaucracies of socialism as well as capitalism, has seen in the traditional media a mechanism for repression because of their centralization, depoliticization, bureaucratic control and encouragement of passivity by receivers (Enzensberger, 1970).

All in all, the message of Marxist theory is plain, except perhaps on how the power of the media might be encountered or resisted and on how to deal with organized forms of media which are not clearly in capitalist ownership or in the power of the state. For socialist (i.e. mainly eastern European societies), western Marxists offer no clear interpretation or prescription for change and the local Marxists see no reason for change, since for them the media exercise what influence they have in the name of, and on behalf of, the working class or the society in general. For capitalist society, the original Leninist model of the fighting press in the vanguard of revolutionary class struggle seems no longer realistic and Marxist critics of the media either rely on the weapon of disclosure of manipulative tendency or pin their hopes on some form of collective ownership of media as a counter to the media power of the capitalist class. This is not to rule out the possibilities for change (not necessarily in directions endorsed by Marxists) by way of micro- or grass-roots-media, especially under conditions of open repression and denial of legitimate alternative media. The public broadcasting monopolies of western Europe have received their own share of criticism from Marxist theorists for their bureaucratic character and close ties with bourgeois states (Burgelman, 1986) and few would regard them as neutral brokers of power, although that is often their self-chosen model (Kumar, 1975).

Structural functional theory and power

The question of power is not very adequately addressed by such theory, although its exercise is recognized in the emphasis placed on the need for direction, control and internal cohesion of social systems. The means of mass communication, because of their invariable presence in complex modern societies, are presumed to play a necessary part in processes of social guidance and control. What part and how it is performed varies according to the type of society. In authoritarian states, the media are openly used as direct instruments of command, warning and control. In liberal democratic societies, control effects are usually seen as emerging from the competing purposes of organized groups and the needs and choices of individuals. Structural functionalism is thus both flexible and somewhat empty of specific answers to questions posed about media and power. One, essentially functionalist, theory of 'media dependency' formulated by Ball-Rokeach and DeFleur (1976) treats relative dependence by audiences on mass media sources (compared to other information sources) as a variable to be empirically determined. It posits that the more reliant is the audience on mass media for information and the more a society is in a state of crisis or instability, then the more power the media are likely to have (or be credited with).

Alternative models of media power relationships

This discussion can be summarily concluded by using the main vertical dimension of Figure 10 (p. 59) to compare two opposed versions of how the power of the mass media might be exercised. The distinction between Marxists and pluralists which underlies the comparison has been made by Gurevitch et al. (1982, p. 1) as follows: 'pluralists see society as a complex of competing groups and interests, none of them predominant all the time', while Marxists 'view capitalist society as being one of class domination, the media are seen as part of an ideological arena in which various class views are fought out, although within the context of the dominance of certain classes, ultimate power is increasingly concentrated in monopoly capital'. These alternative positions have obvious implications for how the societal 'top' is related to the various publics at the 'base'. In general, mass society theory and Marxism imply the 'dominance' model and structural functionalism the 'pluralist model'. The two models are set side by side for comparison in Figure 12.

Both models are ideal-typical in the sense of accentuating and exaggerating certain features of media and it would obviously be possible to offer intermediate models in which features of both could be found together, as they almost certainly are in reality. Even so, for purposes of description, the polarization is useful and we can express the contrast in terms used in constructing the media theory diagram (see Figure 9).

The 'dominance' model sees the mass media as subservient to other social institutions, which are themselves independent of each other only to a limited degree. The media organizations are likely to be owned or controlled by a small number of powerful interests and to be similar in kind and purpose. They would be characterized by a

Figure 12 Alternative models of media power

	Dominance	Pluralism
Societal source	Ruling class or dominant elite	Competing political, social, cultural interests and groups
Media	Under concentrated ownership and of uniform type	Many and independent of each other
Production	Standardized, routinized, controlled	Creative, free, original
Content and world view	Selective and coherent; decided from 'above'	Diverse and competing views; responsive to audience demand
Audience	Dependent, passive, organized on large scale	Fragmented, selective, reactive and active
Effects	Strong and confirmative of established social order	Numerous, without consistency or predictability of direction, but often 'no effect'

high degree of mass production and mass dissemination of content in which a limited and undifferentiated view of the world, shaped according to the perspective of ruling interests in the society, would be offered. This picture of the world in media content would be received by large audiences, conditioned or constrained to accept a certain kind of culture and information and without much capacity or inclination to make a critical response or to seek alternative sources. The effects would be strong and predictable in direction, both because of the near-monopoly conditions of supply and the dependence and gullibility of the public. They would tend to reinforce both the hold of the media system over its public and that of dominant interests in society. The great power of the media posited in this model would be the power to head off change and challenge by continual legitimation of the present order, by filtering out of alternative voices, by reducing the critical capacity of the public and rewarding their compliance.

The 'pluralist' view is, in almost every respect, the reverse, since diversity and predictability are stressed at every stage, beginning with the concept of a society which is not dominated by any unified elite and is open to change and democratic control. The model stresses in particular the capacity of the differentiated public to make its alternative wishes known, to resist persuasion, to react, to use the media rather than be used by them. The media **respond** more to public demand than vice versa.

This contrast lies at the heart of media theory, deriving from a fundamental difference in perception of the context in which mass communication operates in liberal democracies and of the way in which media work. However, the contrast offered by the two models has a somewhat wider reference than merely to the difference between the self-designated critical researchers (not all Marxist) and those who proclaim liberal values and see critical approaches as ideologically biased. The 'dominance' model could stand not only for a view of commercial media systems, but also for a view of the media contained in mass society theory, or for certain western perceptions of the media in eastern Europe or media under certain authoritarian regimes.

The 'dominance' exercised by the media can thus have different causes. In the case of mass society it may be attributed not only to elite management, but also to the destruction of community by the forces of change. These forces have weakened the capacity of the community to resist authority and act autonomously, so that it is more vulnerable to, and dependent on, control from above. In the case of socialist society (as it is usually seen from outside), dominance is attributable not to commercial and class forces but to political dictatorship and outlawing of dissent as antisocial.

The pluralist model can also suit more than one perception of media and more than one set of values. First, it might represent the libertarian ideal in which there is no control or direction, only the 'hidden hand' of the market working to maximize the satisfaction of changing needs and interests of the customers and clients and eventually the whole society. Secondly, it might stand for a 'social responsibility' view of the media in a liberal democracy, in which media institutions are inclined, and occasionally encouraged, to satisfy the needs of diverse competing interests and to meet the wishes of the public within the limits of their own professional standards. Thirdly, the model tends to emphasize the voluntarism and independence of the audience and could, with some modification, accommodate the concept of 'emancipatory media' developed by Enzensberger (1970).

This concept stresses the potential of media for encouraging interaction, self-expression and self-realization, the raising of consciousness by a people or group and self-mobilization. To correspond to this vision of a possible media future, the directions indicated in the model and relations between content and audience would need to be different, since Enzensberger was indicating a high measure of de-institutionalization, reduction of scale, multiple interaction and self-production of content by means of technologies in the hands of individuals. Perhaps the modification would be too great for the model to cope with: we are now speaking of a version of relationships yet another step further from the notion of dominant media, in which people using small-scale media prevail and large media institutions and undifferentiated content can no longer be found.

The question of integration

A basic issue for many sociologists has long been that of the maintenance of order — especially the question of how it is maintained and why and under what circumstances it breaks down. This same question has also been of interest to students of mass communication. The media were seen to be associated with the problems of rapid urbanization, social mobility and the decline of traditional communities. They were linked, in particular, with social dislocation and a supposed increase in individual immorality, crime and disorder. Mass communication was often typified as predominantly individualistic, impersonal and anomic, thus conducive to loss of social control and solidarity.

At almost the same time, an alternative view of the relation between mass media and social integration was being fashioned. This view was also based on known characteristics of mass communication — especially its capacity to unite scattered individuals within the same large audience, or newcomers into urban communities, and to offer a common set of values, ideas, information and perceptions of the world to everyone. In other words, mass media seem in principle to threaten social integration and also to be an antidote to the threat to integration from other social forces, such as mobility and rapid change.

The main questions for theory and research have, thus, to be grouped according to either an optimistic or a pessimistic expectation and it may be added that this division of perspective seems as much in evidence in relation to new media developments as it was in the early days, when the 'new' media were films and popular comics. Moreover, most questions involve another dimension of valuation or perspective in that integration or fragmentation can, as explained above (pp. 59–60), each appear in a favourable or an unfavourable light. One person's desirable social control is another person's denial of freedom and one person's exercise of individual choice is another's evidence of social fragmentation or privatization.

The following questions for theory and research can now be posed:

- Do mass media increase or decrease the level of social control?
- Do media encourage or discourage the formation and working of intervening institutions, such as family, local community, church, trade union?
- Do mass media tend to offer consensual values, ideas, information?
- Do media help or hinder the formation of diverse groupings based on sub-culture, opinion, social experience, social action, etc?
- Do mass media contribute to 'pro-social' behaviour, in line with other agencies of socialization, or do they tend to encourage disorder?

This complex question area is structured by several dimensions of which the most fundamental (that of integration versus fragmentation) has already been discussed (pp. 59–60). Aside from possible alternative valuations, this discussion introduces two other sub-dimensions: that of level of social organization (whether collective or individual) and that of sphere of effect — whether on behaviour or cognitions (including affective and normative matters). The second distinction can also be summed up by terms which Allen (1977) borrows from Deutsch (1966): 'functional integration' versus 'normative integration'. The former refers to the inter-relation and correlation of activities and relationships to achieve various practical tasks (of work, government, etc), while the second refers to the development and growth of common values and beliefs within a social unit. Mass communication can contribute to both, since it does connect people in networks engaged in certain common projects (e.g. the working of markets and political systems) and it also tends to disseminate and reinforce systems of values. The alternative processes are identified by cross-classifying these dimensions as shown in Figure 13.

Figure 13 Media and integration: basic processes

| | Direction of effect: | | | |
| | *Uniting* (centripetal) | | *Fragmenting* (centrifugal) | |
Type of Integration	Collective	Individual	Collective	Individual
Functional: (task-related)	Interrelation	Interaction	Disjunction	Isolation
Normative:	Consensus	Conformity	Conflict	Deviance

A good deal of theory and research, especially in the early phases of study of mass media and society, focused on questions of integration. To judge from the account by Hanno Hardt (1979), in the late nineteenth and early twentieth centuries, Germany was especially rich in reflections on the integrative role of the press in society, to be found in the works of Knies, Blucher, Tonnies and Weber. Among the functions of the press named in this body of literature are: that of 'binding society together'; giving leadership to the public; helping to establish the 'public sphere'; providing for the exchange of ideas between leaders and masses; satisfying needs for information; providing society with a mirror of itself; acting as the 'conscience of society'.

In the United States, the Chicago School, which pioneered research into mass communication, especially in the person of Robert Park and his pupil, Herbert Blumer, emphasized not only the potentially negative role of mass media, but also its contribution to the assimilation of immigrants into the country (Clark, 1969).

At a more general level, McCormack (1961) has argued that the function fulfilled by the media in modern states is to integrate and to socialize, but not because of the failure of other institutions. In her view, experience in a modern, changing, society is necessarily segmented and the 'unique function of mass media is to provide both to industry and to society a coherence, a synthesis of experience, an awareness of the whole, which does not undermine the specialisation which reality requires'. This argument finds a place for media content, which is not only informational, but also for entertainment and amusement, that can provide a sense of wholeness, continuity and shared experience. There is also some evidence to suggest that media can help to forge minority identities or to engage creatively in situations of social conflict (McCormack, 1980).

Much of the literature on 'modernization', development and nation-building in the post-colonial era has put quite a lot of emphasis on the contribution of media to forging a new national identity (Pye, 1963). Oddly enough, it is the attempt to put this prescription into practice which has often most offended the advocates of a 'free flow of information' and the debate about a 'new world information and communication' order is partly about the right of governments to control media in the interests of national integration and 'cultural integrity' — a cognate term.

Mass society theory and integration

Mass society theory takes as its starting point the proposition that members of such a society are not integrated or not integrated in a 'healthy' way. According to Kornhauser (1968), the very presence of large numbers of only loosely organized and committed people summons efforts of leaders to mobilize and manipulate them. The very concept of mass (see above, p. 29) has a built-in dimension of non-integration — referring to people who are isolated, anonymous to each other and poorly regulated. C.W. Mills (1951, 1956) also pointed to the decline of the genuine public of classic democratic theory and its replacement by shifting aggregates of people who cannot formulate or realize their own aims in political action.

However, the explanation of such a situation is more likely to be found, not in the media, but in historical events and changes which have broken the cohesion of society. The mass media only become relevant as the device used to guide or control the atomized individual from above. They are certainly indispensable to 'functional integration', but their contribution to normative integration (according to mass society theory) is low in quality and reflects the self-interests of rulers, whether these are elites of power or some newly-raised non-elites (like the new class of Djilas or the fascist bureaucrats of Kornhauser). The only way out would seem to be by way of emancipatory uses of media from below, advocated, for instance, by Enzensberger (1970), or by finding salvation in broader world contexts.

According to recent theorizing, the media have contributed to a loss of sense of place in modern society (Meyrowitz, 1985) and the loss of other bases for identity. However, they are sometimes also thought to offer substitutes for what has been lost. The substitute offered may consist of images of community, small town or rural life, with a nostalgic appeal, often set in the past. Aside from such nostalgia, the media have some capacity to replace the symbolic and ritual aspects of real communities, by offering topics of conversation, characters for identification or objects of gossip. Aside from the specific content of what the media offer, they tend in general to provide a common and continuous symbolic environment to individuals who are otherwise dispersed or isolated.

Research has made some contribution to modifying the large claims of mass society theory. It has tended to reassert the resistance of the audience to manipulation and control and the persistence of strong influences from group, class, locality and other beliefs as a limitation on effects from the media. Research has also shown audiences to be more than mere aggregates, but often complex formations with some continuity, cross-cutting ties and internal patterns of reference, influence and self regulation (see below, pp. 226–9). The possibility of direct contact from a medium to many individuals does not substitute for other communication ties, but may supplement or even reinforce them.

Marxist theory and integration

The concept of integration is of considerable interest to Marxist theorists of a 'post-revolutionary' phase when socialism has to be built and new values disseminated. It is, consequently, central to Soviet media theory, despite the emphasis on progressive social change. In capitalist society, split by conflicts of class interest, integration has another aspect in Marxist theory. Either it will refer to the imposition of an ideological consensus (a false consciousness) and to mechanisms of social control favourable to a ruling class or it refers to the ideological cohesion which a class in opposition will have to develop to achieve change. Normally this will require the possession of independent media.

Structural functional theory and integration

Axiomatic to this body of theory is the view that a condition of integration is essential to the working (survival in its current state) of any social system. Without integration there can be no agreement on goals and means and no co-ordinated activity to achieve them. Both 'functional' and 'normative' integration, according to the meanings noted above, are indispensable. However, in a complex society there will be a number of different ways for societies to achieve the control and consensus called for and mass media are only one institution among several with overlapping tasks in this respect.

Media research has frequently been guided by, or has contributed to, the formulation of media effect as an exercise of informal control or the formation of consensus. There are a good many examples at different places in later chapters, but a few central points can be brought together to illustrate the central tenets of functional theory in respect of social integration. The evidence is to be found in research on media institutions and organizations, media content, audiences and effects. The study of media institutions supports the view that a good many devices and pressures operate to ensure that major media conform to a 'national' or 'general public' interest or, at least, operate within limits of what is considered broadly acceptable in terms of criticism of government and society or matters of public morals and behaviour. Often these limits are set by convention rather than law or censorship, as may be the case in illiberal societies.

At the level of media organizations, there is also pressure, reinforced by direct or informal means to ensure that personnel conform to the policy and tradition of the organization concerned (e.g. Breed, 1956; Burns, 1977). Cohesion and loyalty within media are likely to contribute to integration into the society and support for wider effects of social control and cohesion. Often major media take it upon themselves to speak up for and express what they believe to be the dominant values of their own society (Gans, 1979).

Media do not only serve to support the values of society as a whole, but also of segments within it, defined in various ways. For instance, local community media have consistently been portrayed, following the work of Janowitz (1952) as providing some possibilities for the formation of identity and organization within the anonymity of large urban societies. (Stamm, 1985). They generally give strong support for the values of the community and the maintenance of a local order (Jackson, 1971; Cox and Morgan, 1973; Murphy, 1976). An interesting example of a selective integration function is offered by Ferguson (1983) in what is probably the best sociological study of women's magazines. She proposes an analogy between Durkheim's concept of a religious cult and the relationship between magazines and their female readers, based on the notion of a 'cult of femininity', of which the editors are the priestesses and readers the devotees. The cult of femininity is exclusive, has its rites and rituals, its festivals and ceremonies, by way of which the community of members reaffirms its identity and beliefs. It is the women's magazine press which is the mainstay of this cult, giving it legitimacy, defining norms, giving shape and cementing a common culture based on the importance of gender and female solidarity.

The theme of social integration has been equally strong in studies of media content, where a common finding has been that most content with the largest audiences tends to be conformist in tendency and supportive rather than critical of what may be thought of as dominant values. This support takes several forms — avoidance of criticism of key institutions such as business, the community, religion, family (Breed, 1958); symbolic rewards for those who succeed according to the approved paths of virtue and hard work, and symbolic punishment for those who fail or deviate (see below, pp. 193–6). Media are generally found not to offer a reflection of (national or local) society as it is, but deviate in giving disproportionate attention either to those who exemplify the aspirations of the majority or to those who reject the values of society, usually by way of crime or 'extremist' politics. In the latter case, publicity is thought to act as a warning and deterrent. Functionalist analysis of news (Alexander, 1981) indicates that we can expect to find normative frameworks as well as objective information in news.

Early studies of the audience fit into the interpretation of media as a force for integration, confirming that many looked to the media for reinforcement of their own values, for contact with others and the life of society, for security and reassurance (Klapper, 1960). Such findings continue to be replicated and there seems to be a process initiated from 'below', by individuals, which complements the aspirations of those who would like to control society from above, in the interests of social order and cohesion. In one extensive study of the media audience in Israel, Katz et al. (1973) were able to interpret much of the use and significance of media as an outcome of wishes to strengthen (or weaken) a *connection* with others — friends, family, tradition, social and political institutions, etc. A number of the functions, variously attributed to different media, were designated specifically as 'integrative'. The authors emphasize that 'non-media' sources are more significant for the most salient needs, but even so they stress the extent to which the media have encroached on 'older' ways in which social and psychological needs are satisfied.

In recent years a research tradition has developed concerned with the study of media events — major occasions, often with a ceremonial or ritual character (like a coronation, state wedding, papal visit, major sporting event) which are distinguished by high television attention and massive interest on the part of the viewing public. Such events are held to provide social cement for otherwise atomized societies, uniting individuals and forging or renewing collective normative bonds (Katz and Dayan, 1986).

Not surprisingly, in the light of these observations, research on effects has failed to lend much support to the proposition that mass media, for all their attention to crime, sensation, violence and deviant happenings, are a significant cause of social, or even individual, crime and disorganization. The more one holds to a functionalist theory of media, the less logical it is to expect predominantly socially disintegrative effects. In practice, functional theorists are quite prominent among those who investigate the negative consequences of media, perhaps because they place such importance on integration and have more than usually high expectations of the potentially positive contribution of mass media.

Mass communication and social change

The core question concerns the direction and degree of relationship between mass communication and other changes taking place in society — in brief, are media a cause or effect of social change? No simple answer can be expected and different theories offer alternative versions of the relationships. In this case, the particular general theories of society discussed in relation to power and integration are less relevant than those 'media-centred' theories of historical change described in the previous chapter (pp. 60–1). At issue are the alternative ways of relating three basic elements: technology of communication; form and content of media; changes in society (social structure; institutional arrangements; the distribution of opinion, beliefs, values and practices). An attempt is made in the following paragraphs to summarize the main alternative views on how these elements may be inter-related. These views are not necessarily mutually exclusive, even when they seem to offer alternative explanations. We should expect no single theory to apply universally to all aspects of such a complex matter.

Rosengren's typology of culture–society relationships

The complexity of terms and propositions, as well as the variety of time and place involved, makes it essential to simplify. To this end, a very basic typology for handling most of the key elements has been borrowed from Rosengren (1981a). This involves the cross-tabulation of two basic propositions: 'social structure influences culture' and its reverse: 'culture influences social structure'. For our purposes, which are much the same as those of Rosengren, we can read social structure as social change and culture as mass communication. The scheme offers no separate place for the technology, but by implication it is an aspect of the cultural rather than the social. However, its introduction as a separate element is important for some variants of theory about media. The cross-tabulation yields four cells, for which Rosengren has supplied labels as in Figure 14, and these terms can serve as a classification of the main theoretical approaches.

Figure 14 Types of relation between culture (media) and society

		Social structure influences culture	
		YES	NO
Culture influences	YES	Interdependence	Idealism
Social structure	NO	Materialism	Autonomy

Interdependence

Under this heading can be placed the numerous accounts of the media which portray them as interactive with changes in society but do not single out one dominant direction of effect. Thus society produces the demands for information and entertainment to which media respond, the resources of money and time needed for the growth of media industries, the inventions on which they are based, the social-cultural climate in which they are free to operate. Mass communication in turn, and coterminously, stimulates change, accelerates the demands for its own services, contributes to the climate of cultural and political freedom in which media can themselves better operate, and diffuses new ideas and innovations. Clark (1969) reports the views of the French sociologist, Gabriel Tarde, writing about 1900, that he:

> envisaged a constant interweaving of influences between these two levels (the social structural and the technical): technological developments made newspapers possible, newspapers promote the formation of broader publics, and they, by broadening the loyalties of their members, create an extensive network of overlapping and shifting groupings.

The two influences are so bound together that neither mass communication nor modern forms of society is conceivable without the other and each is a necessary but not a sufficient condition for the other. Much use has, for instance, been made of possession of mass media as an index of development or modernization, without reference to which is the cause of the other. In summarizing the interaction perspective, we can say that the media may equally be considered to mould, mirror and follow social change. This covers all possibilities except that of independence.

Idealism

Because of its many connotations and uses, the term is somewhat misleading but translates into the proposition that media (i.e. culture) are primary moulders of society as well as reflectors of it. The main difficulty in using the term comes from the distinction between technology and content and some variants of theory which emphasize the technological (medium and channel) aspects might seem to be more 'materialist' than 'idealist'. However, we distinguish five main versions under this heading: individual value change; media as an 'engine of change'; technological determinism; cultivation theory; cultural imperialism.

Individual value change

The basic view is that media encourage and help to diffuse a personal value system which is favourable to innovation, mobility, achievement and consumption. While it can apply very widely, the theory has been formulated specifically for developing societies. Lerner (1958), for instance, held that media (of any kind, but especially 'western' media) could help to break down the 'traditionalism' which is an obstacle to 'modernity', by raising expectations and aspirations, widening horizons, enabling people to imagine and want a 'better alternative' for themselves and their families. The view is consistent with psycho-sociological explanations of development (e.g. Hagen, 1962; McLelland, 1961) and emphasizes spontaneous, demand-based change, rather than planned change from 'above'.

Media as an 'engine of change'

Here we have the straightforward alternative view that media can best be used in a planned way to bring about change by applying them in large-scale programmes of development. Their task is to extend public education and promote innovation in agriculture, health practice, population control, and other social and economic matters. A principal worker in this sphere and chronicler of the results is Everett Rogers (1962; 1973; 1976), although he has come, over time, to emphasize less the direct impact of media than their involvement with other networks and channels of influence. Nevertheless, the theory is widely applied and not irrelevant for developed countries where media are used in campaigns with social change as an objective, especially in the fields of health and education. It goes with a general belief that education leads to social change. If one counts the adoption of new products as social change, then advertising also provides a striking example of applied cultural determinism.

Technological (medium) determinism

As noted above, the location of such theories under the heading of 'idealism' may be disputed, although technology in this context has usually acquired a cultural meaning and form before it is treated as an independent influence on further developments in society. The most complete and influential variant of media determinism is probably that of the Canadian economic historian, Harold Innis (1950; 1951), especially as elaborated by Marshall McLuhan. Innis attributed the characteristic features of successive ancient civilizations to be prevailing and dominant modes of communication, each of which will have its own 'bias' in terms of societal form. Thus he regarded the change from stone to papyrus as causing a shift from royal to priestly power. In ancient Greece, an oral tradition and a flexible alphabet favoured inventiveness and diversity and prevented the emergence of a priesthood with a monopoly over education. The foundation of the Roman empire was favoured by a written culture on which legal-bureaucratic institutions, capable of administering distant areas, could be based. Printing, in turn, challenged bureaucratic control and encouraged both nationalism and individualism.

There are two main organizing principles in Innis' work. First, as in the economic sphere, communication leads over time to monopolization by a group or class of the means of communication and knowledge. In turn this produces a disequilibrium which either impedes change and expansion or leads to competitive emergence of other forms of communication which tend to correct the disequilibrium. Secondly, the most important dimensions of empire are space and time, and some means of communication are more suitable to one than the other. Thus empires can persist for long in time or extensively in space, depending on the available form of communication. McLuhan's (1962) developments of the theory offered valuable insights into the consequences of print media, but attempts to assess consequences of audiovisual media by a similar method of analysis have been obscure or unconvincing (McLuhan, 1964).

Other writers have cited more historically-bound examples of social effect from forms of communication and there is a large literature on the social consequences of printing (e.g. Eisenstein, 1978). An interpretation of political changes in the modern period, which gives an important place to communication technology, has been offered by Gouldner (1976). He identified the rise and, perhaps, fall, of 'ideology' as a key aspect of change, defining ideology as a special form of rational discourse. He writes (p. 39):

> The culture of discourse that produces ideology was historically grounded in the technology of a specific kind of mass (or public) media and its specific mode of production: privately owned, small scale, widely diffused, competitive and decentralized units . . .

Printing made it possible and necessary to mobilize political support among the masses. Printing could reach the great numbers concentrated in the growing urban areas.

He goes on to attribute the 'age of ideology' of the eighteenth and nineteenth centuries to the wide availability of print material, especially in the form of news which led to a need for processing and interpretation of information. Ideology was a response to the 'communication revolution' — an effort to 'supply meaning' to otherwise fragmented public knowledge. He then portrays the newer media of radio, film and television as having caused an 'attenuation of ideology' by a shift from a 'conceptual to an iconic symbolism', revealing a split between the 'cultural apparatus' (intelligentsia) which produces ideology and the 'consciousness industry' which controls the new mass public. This is the cause of the 'decline of ideology', with a further change in prospect as universal computer-based systems of communication develop.

This thesis draws in part on the numerous critiques of mass culture and the 'consciousness industry' (e.g. Morin, 1962), and clearly much of the thinking of the Frankfurt School (see pp. 65–6) belongs to the 'idealist' category of media theory, however modified by Marxist emphasis on structural determinism. In such theory, there is a general agreement on the power of modern mass communication forms as applied to shape political and social reality, in particular to hold back change.

Cultivation theory

The term derives from a particular approach to the study of media effects developed by Gerbner (and Gross, 1976) (see below, p. 283), out of his assessment of the major historical significance of the rise of mass media. In essence, he argues that this significance comes not from the formation of 'the mass' but from the 'creation of shared ways of selecting and viewing events', by delivering to them 'technologically produced and mediated message systems', thus common ways of seeing and understanding the world. He calls it the 'cultivation of dominant image patterns'. In effect the media tend to offer uniform and relatively consensual versions of social reality and their audiences are 'acculturated' accordingly. Gerbner makes a prediction that media, especially television because of the systematic character of its message and its consistency over time, have powerful effects and he comes down firmly in favour of the media as moulders of society.

Cultural imperialism

The ideas underlying the thesis of 'cultural' or 'media' imperialism are at the same time simple and complex. They have their origin in early theory and evidence concerning the role of media in national development (e.g. Lerner, 1958; Schramm, 1964) and in critical reformulation by writers such as Schiller (1969), Wells (1972), Mattelart (1979) and many others. The correlate of the view that media can help in 'modernization' by introducing 'western' values is that they do so at the cost of a breakdown of traditional values and the loss of 'authentic' local cultures. In the simple view, it can be argued that the values so introduced are those of capitalism and that the process is 'imperialistic' in deliberately, or knowingly and systematically, subordinating smaller and developing countries to the interests of the dominant capitalist powers, especially the United States.

The complexities, which are well discussed in Tunstall (1977), Boyd-Barrett (1977; 1982), or Golding (1977), arise from the great variety of forms and mechanisms of intercultural penetration, the strength and diversity of the forces sustaining media penetration and the difficulty of finding alternatives. Even so, there is a clear proposition which belongs at this point in our review of theories that states that media exert an influence (formulated as negative or regressive) on receiving cultures, by way of actual media products, themes and genres and by professional practices and values. The direction of effect is said to be favourable to the adoption of social forms and personal behaviour consistent with capitalism and to the political institutions and perceptions which predominate in the 'capitalist' world. The thesis is, however, incomplete without its 'materialist' component, which is briefly discussed below under the heading of 'dependency'.

Materialist approaches

Again there is a potential gap between general term and specific theory, but a unifying element is a clear decision in favour of culture (including media) as a reflection and a dependent phenomenon of social structure. Certain main variants worth identifying are; the main sociological tradition; classical Marxism; recent 'political-economic' media theory; dependency theory of development.

The central position of traditional sociology is that individual behaviour is shaped by social forces arising from the structure of relationships and meanings of a society. In general, culture is also seen as dependent on the structure of society and insofar as mass communication is a cultural phenomenon (and it is treated as such here) it will be dependent on society and not itself a cause. There is room for some discussion as to whether or not mass media have become an element of the social structure, but even if so (argue Murdock and Golding, 1978) the fundamental cause remains the division of political and economic power, in effect the class structure. The media can do little independently to change a social world so determined.

Two main schools of Marxist thought can be distinguished under the 'materialist' heading, although all, strictly speaking, should belong here. There is no need to give a detailed account of classical Marxism, since its message about the role of the media in social change is clear and generally known. Since change emerges from the dynamics of struggle between dominant and subordinate classes, the media as a form of property must be an instrument of the dominant, capitalist class of the modern period in Europe. The work of media belongs essentially to the sphere of superstructure (ideas, ideology, consciousness) and is determined essentially by economic forces. Media do play a part in change, having assisted in the gaining and consolidation of bourgeois power. Subsequently they have been and are being used to resist working-class advance, although the instruments of communication are potentially available to this class to achieve change.

The key is always ownership, whether by the capitalist class, the bourgeois state, the working class or the socialist state. In the post-revolution Soviet state, the 'engine of change' theory has come to operate in relation to media formally controlled by the working-class party. Political-economic theory (discussed in chapter 3) has arisen out of Marxist sociology and media critical theory. It does not fundamentally depart from the main lines of Marxist thinking, but has a narrower historical range and concentrates on uncovering, by empirically grounded analysis, just how the economic forces in capitalist media favour resistance to fundamental social change. Those Marxist approaches discussed under the heading of 'hegemonic' theory in the last chapter have an ambiguous position in the present context. Their basic thrust is to emphasize the role of ruling ideas and ideology in the forging of consciousness or 'false' consciousness. As theories of the 'superstructure', they emphasize the influence of culture, even if the culture itself is ultimately shaped by class relations. They might be better entered in the present scheme as 'interactive' approaches to the relation between media and change, but this would dilute their central logic.

This is not the place to expound the theory of dependency (see especially Frank, 1971), but a word needs to be said to remove the impression that the only place assigned to media in development is as changer of personal values or 'engine of change'. Dependency theory portrays the media as frequently part of the system of exploitation by foreign capital and acting to increase and reinforce the state of dependence. The related theory of 'media imperialism' (Boyd-Barrett, 1977) contains both 'materialist' and 'idealist' elements, since it points both to technological and economic dependence on the capitalist world and to cultural penetration by the values favourable to capitalism. The media thus act to hold back change, except within the framework of capitalist growth (seen as ultimately regressive). For media to have a positive role in change would require a major structural change giving ownership and real autonomy to the developing nation and especially to elements at the basis of society. Dependency theory is thus ultimately a theory of structure rather than culture in relation to mass media.

Autonomy

The view that culture and social structure do, or can, vary independently seems empty of predictive or explanatory value, yet it is an important intellectual starting point and may have considerable practical consequences. It tends to undermine both those critical media approaches which suggest that fundamental change in capitalist society is held back by the dominant ideology purveyed through the media and the view that for Third World countries to develop they need modern, secular and free media on the western model. It is always possible to find historical cases of disjunction between sudden or rapid social or political change and what the media are doing, and it is also possible to point to wide variations in cultural (even mass mediated) forms in societies with much the same economic and political base.

The notion of autonomy is also consistent with a view of culture as a somewhat arbitrary or chance outcome of history. In turn, it stands in opposition to many of the theories just discussed and to general ideas of social and cultural 'convergence'. Yet convergence theory tends to be self-fulfilling and the 'autonomy option' helps to protect the freedom of societies to make choices about their media and other cultural forms, to resist, for instance, the insistence on development of secular, 'modern', market-based media institutions. It may thus be liberating as well as intellectually justifiable, giving the low explanatory power of all the other theories which try to connect media systematically to social change.

Conclusion

There is little point in trying to make a choice among the positions on grounds of evidence. According to Rosengren (1981a, p. 254), surveying what scattered evidence he could find, research gives only 'inconclusive, partly even contradictory, evidence about the relationship between social structure, societal values as mediated by the media, and opinions among the public'. A strong possibility exists that each theory may hold under different conditions at some levels of analysis. Thus mass media may contribute concurrently to two conceptually opposed, but empirically reconcilable, kinds of societal change which have been signalled in sociology: one towards fragmentation and individualization of society (a 'centrifugal' efect) and another towards a new kind of integration (a 'centripetal' effect) which can be portrayed in a more positive light as interdependency, or more negatively as a mass society (see McCormack, 1961).

Carey (1969) has summarized these alternative tendencies and suggests that the 'communication revolution' has supported both — facilitating differentiation and at the same time helping to forge a national consensus. Aside from the remarkable range of choice offered by different views of the party played by mass communication in social change, we may also be struck by the ambiguity of the role assigned to media since they are as often cast in 'regressive' as 'progressive' roles. A final point on which there can be little doubt is that the media, whether moulders or reflectors of change, are undoubtedly messengers about change, or seen as such by their producers and their audiences, and it is around this observation that the main perspectives on mass media can best be organized.

Communication, critical theory, commerce and new media

These theoretical formulations of the part played by mass media in wider processes of society have, as noted at the outset, some deficiencies and biases. They are also of limited help in dealing with prospective changes in mass communication referred to above (pp. 39–42) under the heading 'decline of the mass paradigm' and in relation to an emerging 'information society'. Mass communication theory was developed largely as a reaction or response to the large-scale application of media for political and commercial propaganda and as a business activity in its own right — selling information and mass culture. The theorists were mainly academics removed from the sphere of practical involvement and often with some distaste for what they observed. Theory has tended to be more critical than supportive of those using or running the mass media.

The causes of this distance are complex and numerous, but an important reason among them is the ambiguous or mixed character of mass communication, which has a 'sacred' character when it relates to matters of truth, belief, freedom or the advance of knowledge, but a material or worldly aspect when it involves exchanges for short-term benefit, profits for producers and distributors, short-term pleasure for individuals. The communication relationship can be either, or at the same time, 'calculative' and 'normative', in the senses defined above (p. 33). Most theorists are committed to an idealist view of communication as a relationship, which can only be distorted or debased by the market. Most developed mass media, however, are inextricably involved both in doing business and in meeting the informational and cultural needs of their audiences at the same time.

As individuals, theorists find it less easy to be so apparently inconsistent and have more opportunity to be idealistic. In fact there have always been two bodies of theory (and to an extent, theorists). One has been represented in this chapter by a social theory which is on the whole critical of media 'manipulation' (or prostitution) and commercialism, preferring to speak for the believed interests of the audience and the wider good of society. The alternative body of theory is daily put to use in media institutions and related organizations (especially to do with advertising, marketing, PR, media planning, audience and market research) and is largely a mixture of applied psychology, statistics and business theory. It is not normative and has little to say about the issues discussed in this chapter. The division is an aspect of the long-standing divide between 'critical' and 'administrative' researchers which Lazarsfeld (1941) described.

Since this particular distinction was first made by Lazarsfeld, it has also been conventional to distinguish within social theory between those whose theory was explicitly directed against the dominant forms of (capitalist) society and others, variously designated as pluralists or functionalists (see above p. 85). While there is no agreed definition, or single version, of 'critical theory', it corresponds closely enough to Marxist or 'new left' analyses of media and society, several examples of which have been discussed. Its main features are an attention to the unequal division and exercise of power in society and the adoption of the point of view of exploited classes rather than that of media operators or society 'in general'.

It has been suggested that a convergence between critical theory and liberal pluralist theory (even less easy to define) has been taking place. This is hardly likely, even if critical theory does face problems of adaptation to events (Haight, 1983). What is possible, however, is some greater degree of interdependence or cross-reference. According to Rosengren (1983), critical theorists tend to ask the most interesting questions, while the methods for finding answers belong to the camp of functionalist and positivist empirical researchers. Borrowing of ideas and of methods could be possible without theoretical rapprochement. The circumstances of media change may accelerate such cross-fertilization.

Insofar as the current changes in communication involve greater abundance of offers of information and culture, more freedom for receivers to choose according to their own (increased) communication needs, older social theory geared to problems of mass manipulation and monopoly (whether political or commercial) and wedded to idealist versions of communication, may well have reached the limits of its influence. As was evident in the case of earlier media development, social theory tends to offer a choice in relation to new media of either a pessimistic or an optimistic view of changes under way, appealing more to beliefs and values than rooted in evidence.

Currently, pessimistic theorists predict an increase in differentials of power, insofar as power is dependent on knowledge and on access to electronic data bases, a decline in the cultural quality of life because commercial exploitation of new media is not controlled, a reduction in social integration and in the public sphere as the audience becomes more segmented and fragmented according to taste, locality and lifestyle (Golding and Murdock, 1986; Elliot, 1982). Optimistic theorists stress the benefits of receiver choice as a counter to central power and of the positive consequence for integration and participation stemming from the interactivity potential of new media (Rogers, 1986). The world can seem smaller and better connected.

Until the new communication reality takes clearer shape, neither view can be tested. However, one may suspect that it will not be tested (any more than propositions about the old media have been) without more appropriate concepts and frameworks for handling communication situations which differ from the familiar centre-peripheral mass flows. Relevant developments of theory would involve: some rapprochement between social theory and individualist theory of communication uses; a conceptualization of information and culture with possibilities for objective accounting of provision and use (already partly accomplished — Ito, 1981); a more diverse and detailed analysis of communication exchange relations and of conditions affecting balance of supply and demand of communication; a close attention to different technologies of communication and their biases and possibilities in potential and in use; a closer examination of the alternative meanings of commercialism in communicative relations and a recognition that there are qualitatively diverse kinds of 'trading' in information and communication; a rethinking of the 'public interest' in communication and the nature of information as a form of private property and a public good (see Ferguson, 1986). The older broad themes of social theory and their underlying values remain relevant, but the conceptual tools for applying them are somewhat obsolescent, and the themes and values call for some adaptation to new circumstances.

CHAPTER 5

NORMATIVE THEORIES OF MEDIA STRUCTURE AND PERFORMANCE

Media–society linkages

The links between mass media and society have already been approached in several different ways. First, these links form an aspect of the early history of each mass medium in its own society. They are a product and a reflection of that history and may have played a part in it. Despite the common features of the media institution across societies, the media are also by origin, developed practice and convention very much *national* institutions in their specific contents and are constrained by domestic political and social pressures and by the expectations of their audiences. They reflect, express and sometimes actively serve national interests as determined by other more powerful actors and institutions.

In the second place, the portrayal of media as mediating between the ordinary members of society and a more distant and inaccessible world of events and of power involves a concept of linkage, by information, at the very least, on a continuous basis. Thirdly, the main versions of functionalist theory discussed above involve quite specific assumptions of media as *necessary* to the continuity of the kind of social system which is characteristic of the modern large-scale, industrial (or information) society.

Here we turn to another way in which the idea of linkage is very clearly expressed and to another kind of theory, one already referred to as 'normative theory' (p. 4). This deals with ideas of how media *ought* to or are *expected* to operate. While each national society is likely to have a detailed and distinctive version of normative theory, there exist also a set (or sets) of more general principles that can be used to classify different national cases. Such a classification is a part of everyday discourse about media and at this level is not very obscure or problematic. Each of the main 'theories' discussed below is likely to be connected in fairly obvious ways with a particular form of political system and government.

Despite this intimate connection with familiar matters, it is rare to find press theory spelt out in any definitive form. The Soviet-socialist tradition is somewhat exceptional in making very clear what is expected from media as a contribution to the development of society. Elsewhere, there are many conventions, implicit assumptions, bits of ideology, sometimes rules, laws and constitutional provisions from which the main character of the reigning theory has to be distilled. It should be emphasized that virtually no actual media system is governed by any one 'pure' theory of the press, nor does practice always follow what seems the appropriate theory very closely. Most systems reflect the working of different (even inconsistent) elements from different theories.

In recent decades (mainly since the Second World War), the mass media, newly grown to maturity, have developed some features which have been considered problematic for the rest of society and have stimulated guidance or policy-making from governments or supra-national bodies. Examples of perceived problems which have provoked a return to the examination of normative principles and proposals for reform include the following: concentration of press or other media ownership, threatening the diversity and independence of information and opinion; an increase in transnational and multi-media operations which may weaken national cultural integrity or even political sovereignty; the rise of television as a social force, by-passing or supplanting other agencies of socialization and control and often believed to be exceptionally influential.

Examples of challenges which are not necessarily problematic but call for guidelines include the following: the need for control and allocation of frequencies attendant on the rise of broadcasting; the invention and development of new communication technologies with far-reaching implications for society, for relations between states as well as for existing media. Satellite broadcasting, for instance, raises new issues of communication freedom, national sovereignty and property rights.

The response to perceived problems or challenges has taken a wide variety of forms, ranging from the commissioning of social research to new law making, but has, in general, involved much more thought about the possible social purposes of media and the standards against which they would be judged than was given to earlier phases of historical development of media. All this thought has contributed much to a process of reformulating social theory about the position of media in society and the activities they should or should not engage in. In the second half of the chapter some of the more specific standards or criteria which have been developed are reviewed.

Six normative media theories

The first attempt at a comparative statement of major theories of the press dates from 1956 (Siebert et al.) and it remains the major source and point of reference for work of this kind. The four-fold division made by Siebert et al. has been retained, although supplemented by two further types, in recognition of more recent developments in thinking, if not in practice. It may be that the original 'four theories' are still adequate for classifying national media systems, but as the original authors were aware, it can often be that actual media systems exhibit alternative, even inconsistent, philosophical principles. It is thus appropriate to add further theories to the original set, even if they may not correspond to complete media systems, since they have now become part of the discussion of press theory and provide some of the principles for current media policy and practice. The paragraphs below are not summaries but attempts to express the enduring core of truth that they contain. Changes in media have widened the scope of reference from *printed press* alone, but the word 'press' is still conventionally used to refer to other media, especially in their journalistic functions.

Authoritarian theory

The term was given by Siebert and remains an appropriate one, since the theory identifies, first of all, the arrangements for the press which held in societies when and where the press first began, for the most part monarchies in which the press was subordinated to state power and the interests of a ruling class. The name can also refer to a much larger set of contemporary press arrangements, ranging from those in which support or neutrality is expected from the press in respect of government and state, to those in which the press is deliberately and directly used as a vehicle for repressive state power.

Uniting all cases where the theory holds is the lack of any true independence for journalists and their subordination (ultimately by force) to state authority. Authoritarian theory justifies advance censorship and punishment for deviation from externally set guidelines which are especially likely to apply to political matters or any with clear ideological implications. The variety of forms in which authoritarian theory can be expressed or enforced is wide, including: legislation; direct state control of production; enforceable codes of conduct; use of taxation and other kinds of economic sanction;

controlled import of foreign media; government right of appointment of editorial staff; suspension of publication.

It is easy to identify authoritarian theory in pre-democratic societies and in societies that are openly dictatorial or repressive, for instance under conditions of military rule, occupation or martial law. It is unlikely that under such conditions the media can operate under any other principle. However, it would be a mistake to ignore the existence of authoritarian tendencies in relation to the media in societies that are not generally or openly totalitarian. There are cases and occasions when authoritarianism expresses the popular will and, in all societies, there are situations where media freedom may conflict with some interests of the state or society in general, for instance under conditions of terrorist insurgency or threat of war.

It is also the case that elements of authoritarianism linger on in relation to some media rather than to others. Thus in many countries there are more controls on theatre, film, broadcasting. In particular, the way is often kept open in the licensing arrangements for direct access or control under conditions of national need. We should not, in consequence, regard the theory as merely a historical survival or a relatively rare deviation from established norms. It still offers a justification for submitting the media to those who hold power in society, whether legitimately or not. The main principles of the theory can be briefly summarized:

- Media should do nothing which could undermine established authority or disturb order.
- Media should always (or ultimately) be subordinate to established authority.
- Media should avoid offence to majority, or dominant, moral and political values.
- Censorship can be justified to enforce these principles.
- Unacceptable attacks on authority, deviations from official policy or offences against moral codes should be criminal offences.
- Journalists or other media professionals have no independence within their media organization.

Free press theory

This relabelled version of Siebert et al.'s 'libertarian theory' has its origin in the emergence of the printed press from official control in the seventeenth century and is now widely regarded as the main legitimating principle for print media in liberal democracies. Perhaps because of its long history, great potency and high symbolic value, free press theory has attracted a very large literature (useful sources are: Smith, 1973; Curran and Seaton, 1985; Rivers et al., 1980). It is both a simple theory and one that contains or leads to some fundamental inconsistencies. In its most basic form it merely prescribes that an individual should be free to publish what he or she likes and is thus an extension of other rights — to hold opinions freely, to express them, to assemble and organize with others. The underlying principles and values are thus identical with those of the liberal democratic state, a belief in the supremacy of the individual, in reason, truth and progress, and, ultimately, the sovereignty of the popular will.

Complications and potential inconsistencies have arisen only when attempts have been made to account for press freedom as a fundamental right, to set limits to its application and to specify the institutional forms in which it can best find expression and protection in particular societies. As a statement of opposition to authoritarianism and as a pure expression of libertarianism, as from the pen of John Stuart Mill, few such problems arise. Even so, the motives for advancing it have always been somewhat mixed. It has been seen as an expression of opposition to colonialism (first in the American colonies); as a useful safety valve for dissent; as an argument for religious freedom; as a defence against misrule; as an end in itself; as a means of arriving at truth; as a concomitant and component of commercial freedom; as a practical inevitability.

A central and recurring element has been the claim that free and public expression is the best way to arrive at truth and expose error, hence the wide currency of Milton's eloquent denunciation of censorship in Areopagitica and of John Stuart Mill's more liberal restatement two centuries later:

> the peculiar evil of silencing the expression of an opinion is, that it is robbing the human race, posterity as well as the existing generation, those who dissent from the opinion, even more than those who hold it. If the opinion is right, they are deprived of the opportunity of exchanging error for truth; if wrong, they lose what is almost as great a benefit, the clearer perception and livelier impression of truth, produced by its collision with error.

A free press has thus been seen as an essential component of a free and rational society. The nearest approximation to truth will emerge from the competitive exposure of alternative viewpoints and progress for society will depend on the choice of 'right' over 'wrong' solutions. Political theories of the enlightenment posited, in any case, a convergence between the good of society, the general welfare and the good of the individuals composing it, which only they could perceive and express. The advantage of a free press is that it allows this expression and enables 'society' to know what its members aspire to. Truth, welfare and freedom must go together and control of the press can only lead ultimately to irrationality or repression, even if it may seem justifiable in the short term. Aside from its various justifications, free press theory would seem to need no elaboration beyond such a simple statement as is contained in the First Amendment to the American Constitution which states that 'Congress shall make no law . . . abridging the freedom of speech or of the press'. It is thus simply an absolute right of the citizen.

In practice the application of press freedom has been far from straightforward. The question of whether it is an end in itself, a means to an end, or an absolute right has never been settled and there are those, from the time of Milton to the present, who have argued that if freedom is abused to the extent of threatening good morals and the authority of the state, it must be restrained. According to Pool (1973) 'No nation will indefinitely tolerate a freedom of the press that serves to divide the country and to open the floodgates of criticism against the freely chosen government that leads it'.

For the most part, in societies which have recognized press freedom, the solution has been to free the press from advance censorship but to leave it answerable to the law for any consequences of its activities that infringe other individual rights or the legitimate claims of society. The protection (of their reputation, property, privacy and moral development) of individuals, of groups and minorities and the security or even dignity of the state have often taken precedence over the absolute value of freedom to publish.

Much difficulty has also arisen over the institutional forms in which press freedom has become embodied. In many contexts, press freedom has become identified with property rights and has been taken to mean the right to own and use means of publication without restraint or interference from government. The chief justification for this view, aside from the assumption that freedom in general means freedom from the government, has been through the transfer of the analogy of the 'free market of ideas' expressed above to the real free market in which communication is a good to be manufactured and sold.

Freedom to publish is, accordingly, seen as a property right that will safeguard as much diversity as exists and is expressed by free consumers bringing their demands to the marketplace. Press freedom thus becomes identified with private ownership of the media and freedom from interference in the market. Not only have monopoly tendencies in press and other media made this a very doubtful proposition, but the extent of external financial interests in the press seems to many as potent a source of constraint on liberty of expression as does any governmental action. Moreover, under modern conditions, the notion that private ownership guarantees to the individual a realistic possibility as well as the right to publish looks absurd. The pure theory of press freedom presupposes that some tangible benefits of liberty will actually be delivered.

Certain other problems and inconsistencies can also be noted. First, it is very unclear to what extent the theory can be held to apply to public broadcasting, which now accounts for a large part of media activity in many societies which also remain attached to ideals of individual liberty. It is also unclear how far it applies to other important spheres of communication activity where freedom may be equally important — as in education, culture and the arts. Secondly, the theory seems designed to protect opinion and belief and has much less to say on 'information', especially in matters to do with access, privacy and publication, where personal or property interests are involved. Thirdly, the theory has been most frequently formulated to protect the owners of media and cannot give equal expression to the arguable rights of editors and journalists within the press, or the audiences, or other possible beneficiaries, or victims, of free expression. Fourthly, the theory proscribes compulsory control but provides no obvious way of handling the many pressures to which media are subject, especially, but not only, arising from market circumstances (Wintour, 1973). Having said all this, the notion of a free press is unsuppressable and can be expressed in the following principles:

- Publication should be free from any prior censorship by any third party.
- The act of publication and distribution should be open to a person or group without permit or licence.
- Attack on any government, official or political party (as distinct from attacks on private individuals or treason and breaches of security) should not be punishable, even after the event.
- There should be no compulsion to publish anything.
- Publication of 'error' is protected equally with that of truth, in matters of opinion and belief.
- No restriction should be placed on the collection, by legal means, of information for publication.
- There should be no restriction on export or import or sending or receiving 'messages' across national frontiers.

– Journalists should be able to claim a considerable degree of professional autonomy within their organization.

Social responsibility theory

Social responsibility theory owes its origin to an American initiative — the Commission on Freedom of the Press (Hutchins, 1947). Its main impetus was a growing awareness that in some important respects the free market had failed to fulfil the promise of press freedom and to deliver expected benefits to society. In particular, the technological and commercial development of the press was said to have led to lower chances of access for individuals and diverse groups, and lower standards of performance in meeting the informational, social and moral needs of society. It was also thought to have increased the power of a single class. At the same time, the rise of the new and seemingly powerful media of radio and film had demonstrated the need for some kinds of public control and means of accountability additional to those appropriate to the long-established and professionally organized print media.

Social responsibility theory has a wide range of application, since it covers several kinds of private print media and public institutions of broadcasting, which are answerable through various kinds of democratic procedure to the society. The theory has thus to reconcile independence with obligation to society. Its main foundations are: an assumption that the media do serve essential functions in society, especially in relation to democratic politics; a view that the media should accept an obligation to fulfil these functions — mainly in the sphere of information, and the provision of a platform for diverse views, but also in matters of culture; an emphasis on maximum independence of media, consistent with their obligations to society; an acceptance of the view that there are certain standards of performance in media work that can be stated and should be followed. In short, media ownership and control is to be viewed as a kind of public stewardship, not a private franchise, and there is a pronounced shift away from the relativism about ends characteristic of free press theory and from optimism that the 'free marketplace of ideas' will really deliver the individual and social benefits claimed on its behalf. Under conditions of private ownership, the media professional is not only responsible to consumer and shareholder, but also to society at large.

It can be seen that social responsibility theory has to try to reconcile three somewhat divergent principles: of individual freedom and choice; of media freedom; and of media obligation to society. There can be no single way of resolving the potential inconsistencies but the theory has favoured two main kinds of solution. One is the development of public, but independent, institutions for the management of broadcasting, a development which has in turn powerfully advanced the scope and political strength of the social responsibility concept. The second is the further development of professionalism as a means of achieving higher standards of performance, while maintaining self-regulation by the media themselves.

The feature of public institutions for broadcasting that contributes most to reconciling the principles identified above is the emphasis on neutrality and objectivity in relation to government and matters of societal controversy and the incorporation of mechanisms for making the relevant media responsive to the demands of their audiences and accountable to society for their activities. It happens also that the professionalism encouraged by social responsibility theory involves an emphasis not only on high standards of performance but also on some of the virtues of 'balance' and impartiality which have been most developed in broadcast media.

The influence of broadcasting as a practical expression of social responsibility theory on the privately-owned press has been shown by the increasing willingness of governments to contemplate or carry out measures which do formally contravene free press principles. These include various forms of legal and fiscal intervention designed to achieve positive social aims or to limit the effects of market pressures and trends. They have made their appearance in several forms: codes or statutes to protect editorial and journalistic freedom; codes of journalistic practice; regulation of advertising; anti-monopoly legislation; establishment of press councils; periodic reviews by commissions of enquiry; parliamentary scrutiny; systems of press subsidy (Smith, 1977).

The main principles of social responsibility theory can now be stated as follows:

– Media should accept and fulfil certain obligations to society.
– These obligations are mainly to be met by setting high or professional standards of informativeness, truth, accuracy, objectivity and balance.
– In accepting and applying these obligations, media should be self-regulating within the framework of law and established institutions.
– The media should avoid whatever might lead to crime, violence or civil disorder or give offence to minority groups.
– The media as a whole should be pluralist and reflect the diversity of

their society, giving access to various points of view and to rights of reply.
– Society and the public, following the first named principle, have a right to expect high standards of performance and intervention can be justified to secure the, or a, public good.
– Journalists and media professionals should be accountable to society as well as to employers and the market.

Soviet media theory

The Russian press and other media were completely reorganized after the Revolution of 1917 and furnished with a theory deriving from basic postulates of Marx and Engels and rules of application of Lenin. The theory so constituted and gradually furnished with institutional means has continued to provide the main framework for media practice, training and research, and has provided the model for most media forms within the Soviet sphere of influence (Zassoursky, 1974; Mickiewicz, 1981; Hopkins, 1970; Firsov, 1979; Berezhnoi, 1978). The most important ideas are as follows. First, the working class by definition holds power in a socialist society and, to keep power, has to control the means of 'mental production'. Thus all media should be subject to control by agencies of the working class — primarily the Communist Party.

Secondly, socialist societies are, or aspire to be, classless societies and thus lacking in class conflict. The press should consequently not be structured along lines of political conflict. The range of legitimate diversity and debate does not extend to elements believed to be anachronistic, regressive or dangerous to the basic constitution of society along socialist lines. Thirdly, the press has a positive role to play in the formation of society and the movement towards communism and this suggests a number of important functions for the media in socialization, informal social control and mobilization towards planned social and economic goals. In particular, these functions relate to the furtherance of social and economic change. Fourthly, Marxism presupposes objective laws of history and thus an objective reality that the press should reflect. This reduces the scope for personal interpretation and provides a set of consistent news values which are divergent from those holding in liberal press systems. Finally, the general theory of the Soviet state requires the media to submit to ultimate control by organs of the state and to be, in varying degrees, integrated with other instruments of political life.

Within these limits, the media are expected to be self-regulatory, to exercise a certain degree of responsibility, to develop and follow norms of professional conduct, and to be responsible to the needs and wishes of their audiences. Accountability to the public is achieved by research, by institutionalized forms of audience participation, by responding to letters and by taking some note of public demand. It is clear that, according to this body of theory, censorship and punishment for offences by the media against the state are justified, as they could not be under free press or social responsibility theory. There is an overlap between authoritarian theory and Soviet theory, especially in the strong emphasis in both on support for the existing social order. There are also differences. Under Soviet theory, the media are not subject to arbitrary or unpredictable interference, but work within familiar self-imposed limits; they are supposed to serve and be responsible to their publics; they are not usually monolithic (even if the forms of diversity are limited and not allowed to emerge freely); and they express a diversity of interests. The postulates of the theory can be summed as follows:

- Media should serve the interests of, and be in control of, the working class.
- Media should not be privately owned.
- Media should serve positive functions for society by: socialization to desired norms; education; information; motivation; mobilization.
- Within their overall task for society, the media should respond to wishes and needs of their audiences.
- Society has a right to use censorship and other legal measures to prevent, or punish after the event, anti-societal publication.
- Media should provide a complete and objective view of society and the world, according to Marxist-Leninist principles.
- Journalists are responsible professionals whose aims and ideals should coincide with the best interests of the society.
- Media should support progressive movements at home and abroad.

Development media theory

It is not easy to give a short, general statement of an emerging body of opinion and prescription appropriate to the media situation of developing countries, because of the great variety of economic and political conditions and the changing nature of situations. Nevertheless, it is necessary to make an attempt because of the (varying) inapplicability of the four theories already discussed and the great attention now focused on matters to do with Third World communication. No one source for what follows can be cited, but perhaps the best single most recent source of ideas can be found in the report of the Unesco International Commission for the Study of Communication Problems (McBride et al., 1980).

The starting point for a separate 'development theory' of mass media is the fact of some common circumstances of developing countries that limit the application of other theories or that reduce their potential benefits. One circumstance is the absence of some of the conditions necessary for a developed mass communication system: the communication infrastructure; the professional skills; the production and cultural resources; the available audience. Another, related, factor is the dependence on the developed world for what is missing in the way of technology, skills and cultural products. Thirdly, there is (variable) devotion of these societies to economic, political and social development as a primary national task, to which other institutions should submit. Fourthly, it is increasingly the case that developing countries are aware of their similar identity and interests in international politics.

Out of these conditions have come a set of expectations and normative principles about mass media which deviate from those that seem to apply in either the capitalist or communist world. It is, of course, true that in many countries accounted as 'developing', media are operated according to principles deriving from the theories already mentioned – authoritarian, libertarian and less often social responsibility or Soviet. Even so, there is enough coherence in an alternative to deserve provisional statement, especially in view of the fact that the communication needs of developing countries have tended in the past to be stated in terms of existing institutional arrangements, with an especial emphasis on the positive role of commercial media to stimulate development (e.g. Lerner, 1958) or on media campaigns to stimulate economic change in the direction of the model of the industrial society.

The normative elements of emerging development theory are shaped by the circumstances described above and have both negative and positive aspects. They are, especially, opposed to dependency and foreign domination and to arbitrary authoritarianism. They are for positive uses of the media in national development, for the autonomy and cultural identity of the particular national society. To a certain extent they favour democratic, grass-roots involvement, thus participative communication models. This is partly an extension of other principles of autonomy and opposition to authoritarianism and partly a recognition of the need to achieve development objectives by co-operative means.

The one thing which gives most unity to a development theory of the media is the acceptance of economic development itself (thus social change), and often the correlated 'nation-building', as an overriding objective. To this end, certain freedoms of the media and of journalists are subordinated to their responsibility for helping in this purpose. At the same time, collective ends, rather than individual freedoms, are emphasized. One relatively novel element in development media theory has been the emphasis on a 'right to communicate', based on Article 19 of the Universal Declaration of Human Rights: 'Everyone has the right to freedom of opinion and expression; this right includes freedom to hold opinions without interference and to seek, receive and impart information and ideas through any media regardless of frontiers'. The main principles can be stated as follows:

- Media should accept and carry out positive development tasks in line with nationally established policy.
- Freedom of the media should be open to restriction according to (1) economic priorities and (2) development needs of society.
- Media should give priority in their content to the national culture and language.
- Media should give priority in news and information to links with other developing countries which are close geographically, culturally or politically.
- Journalists and other media workers have responsibilities as well as freedoms in their information-gathering and dissemination tasks.
- In the interest of development ends, the state has a right to intervene in, or restrict, media operations, and devices of censorship, subsidy and direct control can be justified.

Democratic–participant media theory

The last entry here and the most recent addition to the body of normative theory of the media is the most difficult to formulate, partly because it lacks full legitimation and incorporation into media institutions and partly because some of its tenets are already to be found in some of the other theories mentioned. Although the case for its independence as a theory may be questioned, it merits separate identification, however provisional, and it represents something of a challenge to reigning theories. Like many theories, it has arisen both as a reaction against other theory and actual experience and as a positive move towards new forms of media institution.

Its location is mainly in developed liberal societies but it joins with some elements present in development media theory, especially its emphasis on the 'basis' of society, on the value of horizontal rather than vertical (top-down) communication. A primary stimulus has been the reaction against the commercialization and monopolization of privately-owned media and against the centralism and bureaucraticization of public broadcasting institutions, established according to the norm of social responsibility.

Thus, public broadcasting raised high expectations of media systems that could assist in the long process of social improvement and democratic change begun with the economic and political revolutions of the nineteenth century. These expectations have been disappointed by the tendency for some public broadcasting organizations to be at times too paternalist, too elitist, too close to the 'establishment' of society, too responsive to political and economic pressures, too monolithic, too professionalized.

The term 'democratic-participant' also expresses a sense of disillusionment with established political parties and with a system of parliamentary democracy which has seemed to become detached from its grass-roots origins, to impede rather than facilitate involvement in political and social life. There is some element here of a continued reaction to a 'mass society' which is over-organized, over-centralized and fails to offer realistic opportunities for individual and minority expression. Free press theory is seen to fail because of its subversion by the market and social responsibility theory to be inadequate because of its complicity in the bureaucratic state (Burgelman, 1986) and in the self-serving of media organizations and professions. Self-regulation by the press and accountability of large broadcasting organizations have not prevented the growth of media institutions which dominate from the power centres of society or which fail in their task of meeting the needs that arise from the daily experience of citizens.

Thus the central point of a democratic-participant theory lies with the needs, interests and aspirations of the active 'receiver' in a political society. It has to do with the right to relevant information, the right to answer back, the right to use the means of communication for interaction in small-scale settings of community, interest group, sub-culture. The theory rejects the necessity of uniform, centralized, high-cost, highly professionalized, neutralized, state-controlled media. It favours multiplicity, smallness of scale, locality, deinstitutionalization, interchange of sender-receiver roles, horizontality of communication links at all levels of society, interaction, commitment (Enzensberger, 1970).

There is a mixture of theoretical elements, including libertarianism, utopianism, socialism, egalitarianism, environmentalism, localism. Media institutions constructed according to the theory would be involved more closely with social life than they are at present and more directly in control of their audiences, offering opportunities for access and participation on terms set by their users rather than by controllers. The practical expressions of the theory are many and varied, including: the underground press; pirate radio; community cable TV; 'samizdat' publication; micro-media in rural settings; street or neighbourhood sheets; political posters. The new communications technology opens more opportunities, via cheaper reproduction and access to electronic media channels, although the impact on established media dominance remains marginal. A summary statement of principles might appear as follows:

– Individual citizens and minority groups have rights of access to media (rights to communicate) and rights to be served by media according to their own determination of need.
– The organization and content of media should not be subject to centralized political or state bureaucratic control.
– Media should exist primarily for their audiences and not for media organizations, professionals or the clients of media.
– Groups, organizations and local communities should have their own media.
– Small scale, interactive and participative media forms are better than large-scale, one-way, professionalized media.
– Certain social needs relating to mass media are not adequately expressed through individual consumer demands, nor through the state and its major institutions.
– Communication is too important to be left to professionals.

Postscript on press theory

There are simpler versions available of the normative frameworks which have been described. One such has been suggested by Altschull (1984), in terms of three basic forms of press system corresponding to the First World (liberal-capitalist), the Second World (Soviet-socialist) and the Third World (developing). He names the three systems as 'market', 'Marxist' and 'advancing', respectively. The first represents a mixture of 'free press' and 'social responsibility' elements, as described, the second corresponds to the Soviet model, the third to 'development theory'. While each of the three have elements in common, Altschull points to different concepts of press freedom and responsibility. On the question of freedom, market theory differs mainly in defining it in negative terms, as absence of control or of any government policy. On responsibility, it differs from the other two (according to Altschull) by having a non-political or politically impartial informative task. Advancing theory is distinctive for its purposefulness and its devotion to unifying a society rather than dividing it. Despite the differences, Altschull concludes by formulating 'seven laws of journalism' which he holds to have a high degree of cross-system application. These are as follows:

– In all press systems, the news media are agents of those who exercise political and economic power. Newspapers, magazines, and broadcasting outlets thus are not independent actors, although they have the potential to exercise independent power.
– The content of the news media always reflects the interests of those who finance the press.
– All press systems are based on belief in free expression; although free expression is defined in different ways.
– All press systems endorse the doctrine of social responsibility, proclaim that they serve the needs and interests of the people, and state their willingness to provide access to the people.
– In each of the three press models, the press of the other models is perceived to be deviant.
– Schools of journalism transmit ideologies and value systems of the society in which they exist and inevitably assist those in power to maintain their control of the news media.
– Press practices always differ from theory.

These 'laws' are not prescriptions about what ought to happen, but summary observations about what *does* happen in practice. As such they provide a useful reminder of the limited value of normative theory for describing the reality even if it does shape the reality and perceptions of it, especially on the part of those who control, or work in, the media.

Criteria of evaluation of media performance

The broad normative theories described all imply a range of ultimately quite specific criteria to guide practice or to help assess how the media actually do their work in practice. The amount of reflection on the media by society has increased during recent decades, because of the problems and challenges mentioned above, and has led to more attempts to assess the quality of media performance according to objective standards. In a number of countries (e.g. Britain, Canada, Sweden, Germany, the Netherlands), the last decade or so has seen commissions and enquiries concerning the condition of the press and other media which have shown considerable agreement on the kind of principles which should be applied. Not only has this kind of enquiry applied existing principles, it has also helped to develop them and they are an important source for the presentation which follows, in which the most important evaluative concepts are sketched. In general, these concepts can be seen as bridging the gap between very broad principles of freedom and responsibility and the specific practices of media.

The choice of evaluative concepts made below is not arbitrary, although their relative importance is a matter for choice according to circumstances and values. They are all to be found in current public debate about the media, but they also derive from basic political and social values in democratic society, which have been intimately associated with the rise of media. The central values, in particular, are those of *freedom*, *equality*, and *order* (especially in the sense of solidarity and integration of society and its component groups). These values have many meanings and possibilities of interpretation and they also encompass dark as well as light sides of social experience, defining problems as well as identifying positive goals or ideals. For instance, the value of freedom (in the sense of lack of restraint) may conflict with that of order and the latter may come to stand for an unacceptable degree of control. The pursuit of equality can be interpreted as contrary to freedom or diversity, or may find expression in what some see as mindless commercial populism. Without going further, it should be appreciated that these three basic values help to map out a field of tension in which criteria of media performance, especially according to concepts of the public welfare or general good, are to be located.

It should also be stressed that different values have different priorities in different societies at different points in time, and no complete or lasting consensus can be expected over what the media should deliver. However, we do have some broad agreement on the main principles to be applied, an agreement which has its basis in: general social and political theory of society; historical experience (e.g. of war, occupation, loss of liberty); ethical conventions of media professionals; expectations of media publics, based on needs and experiences.

The principles in question can also be applied at more than one level: that of the complete media institution or system; that of the specific media organization (e.g. a newspaper); that of the audience, in respect of its composition and choices. In addition, there is an international level of analysis and some of the same principles, with appropriate adaptation, also apply to international communication. The intention is to clarify the meaning of the principles by indicating what they should lead to in practice and how we can recognize whether or not they are being observed.

The discussion which follows is designed to deal only with those aspects of press performance which are of general consequence, belong to the public domain and which can be assessed systematically by social scientific methods. In particular, it does not deal with values and ethics of media professions on such matters as respect (or not) for privacy, protection of sources, techniques for gaining information, etc. These may be of wider public concern but they do not directly relate to the fulfilment of tasks in and for society and are more a matter for the profession itself than for social scientists (except as a matter of report).

Freedom and independence

This principle has a wider range than others and may appear under other guises (diversity, for instance, is closely related). Even so, its presence or absence is open to assessment directly according to several kinds of evidence. At the level of a society it should mean an absence of laws or controls which limit or direct the activities of media. Most commercial press systems are free in this sense, though not in others. There are few societies, whether developed or less developed, where there are no measures which could not also be used to restrain the press (even if these take such 'benign' forms as limits on concentration or cross-media ownership). Public broadcasting systems are, by definition, not free, but they usually have safeguards built in to protect a degree of independence of policy and professionalism and they are designed, in any case, to maximize other values as well as that of freedom (e.g. equality).

At the level of media organization, freedom is usually measured in terms of the degree of control exercised by owners and managers over communicators (editors, producers, etc) and by these over their own subordinates (journalists, writers, artists, etc) in what are often bureaucratic and hierarchical organizations. The most central issues relate to editorial freedom from owners and controllers, internal (journalistic) press freedom and creative freedom.

These matters do not lend themselves to any easy quantitative assessment and are often more likely to require study of institutions and observational case study approaches. Survey evidence from respondents employed in media can also be a useful guide to the degree of freedom, as perceived from within (e.g. Weaver and Wilhoit, 1986).

At the level of content, there are more possibilities for assessing the degree of freedom and independence actually practised by the media, despite the fact that lack of freedom often results simply in omission, the reasons for which are hard to arrive at. The active use of editorial freedom should result at least in: clear differences between editorial content and what is offered by sources, propagandists and vested interests; generally more expression of critical or controversial points of view; more self-production of news and other content by media (see, for instance, Lemert, 1974; Thrift, 1977; Wagenburg and Soderlund, 1975; Martin, 1981). Creative freedom should be recognizable in novelty, experimentation, authenticity, individualism, as opposed to what is routine, predictable, standardized, recycled, stereotyped.

These ideas of what media freedom should mean in practice do not have to presuppose an ideal world in which there are no pressures, but they do presuppose that media will make active attempts to shape and preserve an area of independent operation and to resist externally imposed control or conformity to vested interest. Freedom of the press should lead to recognizable benefits for society and for media audiences and not simply insulate the media and their owners from the pressures and demands of society.

Order and solidarity

Since this principle may be opposed to that of freedom and may connote authoritarianism, it has to be cautiously invoked and applied, remembering in particular the positive meanings of integration and solidarity. The key difference is that between order imposed from *above* and that which is forged from *below* by people themselves or argued for only by particular media as a free choice. Nevertheless most media systems also operate within limits of what is socially permissible and are subject to expectations about what they ought *not* to do which might lead to social disorganization or cause harm to individuals, social groups or society itself. The criterion for activating such prohibitions has usually to be evidence or strong presumption of actual harm caused — thus measurable consequences for individuals or society.

In most liberal societies, the 'order' principle is more likely to be found in proscription rather than prescription. The media are expected to avoid distributing content which might produce any of the following results: bring institutions or groups in society unfairly into disrepute; encourage deviant, violent or aggressive forms of behaviour; threaten national security; encourage the violent over-throw of legitimate governments (the last is usually legislated against in general and applies to media no more or less than to citizens or organizations). The positive expectations from content, according to this principle, are less commonly to be found, but are sometimes referred to as encouraging "prosocial" behaviour.

A difficulty with the concept is that one person's prosocial behaviour is another person's conformity. Nevertheless, the ex-pression of solidaristic tendencies by media can be recognized in a number of different forms: editorial support offered to a group engaged in conflict (e.g. workers in a strike situation); appeals to common interests or for harmony in matters of conflict; invocation of national identity, interest or spirit; support for values associated with a local community, etc. The range of possible indicators of solidarity in media performance is thus varied and wide. If the audience is taken into account, solidarity values also indicate strong or active ties between a medium and its own public.

Diversity and access

Diversity is often regarded either as a desirable consequence of media freedom or as a goal of media activity. The benefits associated with diversity are themselves varied. It is a necessary condition for choice by audiences. It is often considered as essential to democratic systems where alternative political ideas and policy options are offered competitively. Social change has also to flow from the diffusion and competition of new ideas. In many societies there are social and cultural divisions which lead to demands for alternative communi-cation channels based on region, language, religion, type of culture, etc. Because of this, media systems are usually structured to take account of such divisions, either by policy or as a result of a process of supply and demand.

At the level of the society, the amount of media diversity is likely to be measured, first, by the number of separate and independent media. A media system can also be assessed at these levels: taking all media into account (press, television, radio, etc); at the level of a media sector (e.g. the daily newspaper press). In the former case, the more alternative and independent types of media, the better for diversity. Thus monopoly ownership across media is considered harmful for diversity. In the second case, a media sector has to be assessed internally. With the newspaper press, this is usually according to the number of independent titles available (the more titles, the more diversity), but also according to certain dimensions of quality of news coverage or other relevant attributes.

The dimensions most commonly taken into account are those of the political direction of editorial policy, since a key function of the newspaper is the expression of political opinion. The range of opinions effectively offered is a basic indicator of press diversity. Other divisions which may be relevant concern religion, social class, ethnicity and any other principle according to which society can be stratified or divided. An idea essential to diversity is that media should, in some way, reflect or express approximately the same diversity as exists in that particular society.

However, two sub-principles of diversity contend for primacy and they cannot ultimately be fully reconciled. One has to do with *reflective* diversity — media differences should correspond more or less proportionately to social differences. The second has to do with *open access*, according to which all points of view or sectors of society are regarded as in principle of the same value and thus the ideal standard of diversity is one according to which every voice has the same chance of being expressed, whatever the size of the group or the number of followers involved. The idea of reflection goes more with stability and continuity, the open access principle more with social change. Their assessment would call for different research strategies (McQuail and van Cuilenburg, 1983).

Diversity can also be assessed at the level of a single publication, since within the pages of one newspaper we might find represented quite different points of view and information, or, on the other hand, a uniform and consistent approach. The more a medium tries to represent one group, interest or point of view, the more likely is the latter to be the case. The question here is how *internally* diverse a medium is. On the whole, both the modern mass newspaper and the elite newspaper, as well as many television services, aim or claim to be internally diverse. An alternative ideal or standard is that of *external* diversity, in the sense of there being a range of alternative media in the same society which are different from each other, but internally homogenous. In this situation, the system as a whole is diverse, but the experience of a single average audience member is likely to be of uniformity. This model is best represented in the party press in multi-party democracies, but it is very much in decline. The paradox is that the alternative solution of much internal diversity (in fewer, larger, media) is likely to reduce the range of choice, since each medium offers much the same mixture of news and views as all the others.

There are many ramifications to the diversity discussion. Initially a value judgement about the most relevant variable of diversity has to be made — whether this is religion, class, political colour, language, region or whatever. Consideration of the audience is especially relevant to the question of diversity and in two main respects. One is the question of homogeneity or heterogeneity of the public for a given medium in respect of the dimension chosen. The other concerns the actual distribution of the total public against the different media which are available. A condition of highly differentiated media offered may in practice mean no great diversity if a high proportion of the audience is concentrated on a small part of the media spectrum. This circumstance is quite common and needs to be taken into account in coming to some judgement about the reality of the diversity which actually exists.

Objectivity and information quality

As a principle of evaluation, that of objectivity has a narrower range than those already discussed, yet it has an importance which is hard to overestimate, especially in its widest reference to informative qualities. It deals mainly with news and information, whereas diversity applies to all forms of media output. It is a principle which relates almost exclusively to content and cannot be studied directly at the level of a society or a media organization, although the views of media communicators about objectivity are relevant to an assessment.

The significance of the principle derives from several sources: it is a central value for journalists themselves, underlying their own claim to professional expertise; it is widely valued in modern culture beyond the sphere of mass media, especially in connection with science and bureaucratic rationality; it is one correlate of independence; it is especially valued under conditions of declining external diversity — where there are fewer and more uniform sources, thus effectively a more monopolistic situation. Objectivity then becomes necessary to maintain credibility. Finally, one could mention the rise of television itself as a contributing factor, since this tends towards monopoly in its forms. Most European public broadcasting systems either legally require or expect news and information to be neutral (non-evaluative and factual) or balanced, according to various criteria, depending on the particular society.

It is less easy to say precisely what objectivity should consist of, but its different components have been articulated by the Swedish political scientist, J. Westerstahl in the following scheme (Westerstahl, 1983). It was developed specifically in connection with the evaluation of the neutrality or balance of the Swedish public broadcasting system. The scheme, shown in Figure 15, has the merit of recognizing that objective reporting or news-giving has to involve dealing with values as well as facts and that facts also have evaluative implications.

Figure 15 The main components of news objectivity (after Westerstahl, 1983)

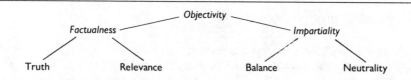

In this scheme, factualness refers to a form of reporting which deals in events and statements which can be checked against sources and are presented free from comment. Impartiality refers, first of all, to the adoption of a neutral attitude by the reporter, in the sense of suspending any personal or subjective preference or judgement for the purpose at hand. Factualness involves several other 'truth' criteria: for instance, completeness of report, accuracy as checked against independent accounts, the lack of intention to mislead or to suppress, all of which contribute to the quality of information. 'Relevance' is more difficult to define or to achieve in an objective way, but ultimately it is as important as truth. It relates to the process of selection rather than to form or presentation and requires that selection take place according to clear and coherent principles of significance for the potential receiver and/or the society (Nordenstreng, 1974). In general that which is more likely to affect people in the short or long term and be most useful for them to know should be considered as more relevant.

It would be very difficult for journalists to achieve relevance so defined, especially given all the pressures and constraints of news production. In practice, judgements about relevance usually come down to informed guesses about what will actually interest the audience and these are incorporated into conventional ideas about news value. According to the scheme, impartiality has to be achieved through a combination of balance (equal or proportionate time/space/emphasis) as between opposing interpretations or points of view and of neutrality in presentation. This mainly refers to avoidance of emotive language or other devices for indicating a preferred response from the audience.

Objectivity remains more a goal than a fully realized ideal of the media and it is not even invariably desirable or sought after. In an externally diverse media system of the kind referred to above, there is a place for partisan presentations of information, although they have to compete with each other and with information sources which do claim to be objective. In any case, there are few, if any, media, whatever their aims and claims, which have been able to completely escape the charge that they are not fully objective.

Cultural quality

While it is widely believed that some kinds of culture are better than others and that some culture is better than none, the criteria for making the necessary distinctions are less easy to agree on and more difficult to turn into specific questions and empirical tests than is the case with any of the principles so far discussed. In general, criteria of cultural quality are not applied to informational content (although they can be), but only to fiction, entertainment and advertising (thus to most of what mass communication is about).

It is possible to mention some common normative expectations about cultural quality, avoiding those matters which might be better dealt with under the heading of 'order' (for instance pornography or sexism). One expectation is that culture should have a quality of truth and authenticity — it should reflect and extend experience and be true to the social conditions of the society in which it is produced and received. A second common expectation is of depth and originality, at least in intention. Thirdly, communicated culture should not try to manipulate audiences for the self-interested ends of the communicators. Fourthly, as argued by the Frankfurt School, among others, culture should have a critical cutting edge in society, or at least be disturbing to set ways of thinking. These requirements are not easy to apply in a systematic or objective way and they incorporate traditional culture values (see above pp. 36–7) or common criticisms made of mass culture. Judgements can, in principle, be made in respect of content by comparing what is offered with 'reality', but authenticity, depth and originality are not easy to assess and qualitative judgements may have to take account of audience experience which is not readily predictable from content (Schroder, 1987).

In the empirical assessment of the cultural quality of media output it is more common to fall back on relatively crude, but reliable, indicators, such as the degree of own production (home-made versus import), the presence or not of accredited items of established cultural traditions (e.g. classical music), the balance of fantasy or reality content. Assessments of cultural quality can then be made either by comparisons between channels or over time or by setting some arbitrary standard of acceptable performance.

One further expectation which can be mentioned is that media should not unduly distort the original message when they act as channels of culture or information, by undue following of 'media logic' (see p. 201). The reference is to devices for attention-gaining, immediate stimulation, subordination of meaning to presentation requirements, etc. This problem was originally identified in the research literature as one of 'sensationalism' (Tannenbaum and Lynch, 1960) but now tends to be formulated in terms of the impact of entertainment forms on news (e.g. Dominick et al., 1975).

Conclusion: new problems for new media?

These evaluative criteria, like the basic values and normative theories in which they are rooted, relate largely to 'old media' situations (even if these still predominate) and to conditions of *mass* communication, where large audiences are dependent on relatively few major channels and their 'gate-keepers', without their having much chance of self-organization or response. These conditions have given rise to perceived problems of monopoly, lack of access, audience dependence, distortion and homogeneity of content, etc. Communication patterns made more possible by technological developments as described above (p. 41) should mean a lessening of these problems, since there should be more channels, access, choice and volume of information available. The media are likely to become more carriers and channels and less editorially responsible for the results of activities, which are in any case less easy to account for (because of variety and volume).

While questions of information quality and interactive potential grow in salience, those concerned with freedom, order, diversity and cultural quality may seem less pressing in the way posed up till now. Nevertheless, changes in media forms do not lessen the extent to which there is a public interest in the overall quality of communication systems and societies and component groups will continue to express demands and seek an accounting of performance. In an 'information society', scrutiny of communication systems is likely to be more rather than less important.

Such a form of society (see pp. 75–8, above) is likely to change the definition of communication 'problems' and bring new criteria into prominence. These changes are still hard to assess, but it seems unlikely that the fundamental values described above are likely to lose their potency and relevance (McQuail, 1986b). We can already point to some emerging issues which relate to freedom and equality, including that of control by central computer registration of many behaviours (see above p. 41) and widening knowledge gaps between the information rich and the information poor. The frequently named problem of 'information overload' (e.g. van Cuilenburg, 1987) is on the agenda of society without yet being clearly translated into normative principles, evaluative criteria or counter-measures.

CHAPTER 6

PRODUCTION OF MEDIA CULTURE: MEDIA INSTITUTION, ORGANIZATION AND ROLE

The context for making media culture

The most essential components for a framework in which to locate questions and answers about media production have already been discussed. At issue are the activities which lie at the core of that frame of reference presented in Figure 9, thus with what specific mass communicators do within specific media organizations, in turn located within a wider institution.

To begin with the last, the *media institution* is likely to embody the spirit of one or more normative press theories and to provide the more general and enduring rules of the game for handling questions of function or purpose in society, the differentiation between media, the scope of media activity vis-a-vis other institutions (e.g. in relation to politics, education, etc) and the degrees of freedom appropriate for media activity in what they make public. These ground rules are rarely codified or laid down in laws or rule books, but embodied in convention, custom, professional practice and in the 'media definitions' described above (pp. 19–25).

The media institution also helps to inter-relate different media and different occupations. This inter-relation occurs by exchange or co-operation and also by way of an ideology, consciousness, or sense of belonging to the same business, if not the same profession. Despite this seeming vagueness and informality, the media institution in many countries strongly influences the activities of those who work in media organizations and it matters to their work whether they belong inside or outside the invisible lines of demarcation.

For instance, the line largely excludes those who work in public relations or in the press offices of governments and large firms, or who produce 'in-house' magazines, even if their specific work tasks are very similar to those of people 'inside' the line working as journalists or film- and programme-makers in public media. There are many instances of demarcation affecting those who work with the techniques of mass communication, but who differ in being subject to different rules, different definitions of purpose and scope of activity and having different professional or craft identities.

The *media organization* is the specific setting in which production takes place, with a more or less self-contained management system, as with a single newspaper, television company, radio channel or station, news agency, publishing house, etc. The concept is not always easy to apply in practice, since organizational lines are often redrawn or unclear. Both may result from amalgamation (integration) into larger, sometimes multi-media or multinational groupings or the functional separation of tasks and new co-operative arrangements. Often an act or process of media production will span several organizational units and require other organizations for distribution to take place. A good deal of media work takes place on a freelance or entrepreneurial basis (e.g. film-making), and many media workers (especially writers, actors, etc) belong to no single production organization, even if they may belong to professional or craft associations.

The term *mass communicator* has been current at least since 1969 (Halmos) to refer in general to those who work in media and the notion of a typical role characterizing those who control or occupy the channels of mass communication has been in use for longer (e.g. Westley and Maclean, 1957). Despite the enormous variety of kinds of work and position encompassed, it is useful to retain the concept to identify an individual level at which to do research or assess findings. These concepts of institution, organization and communicator are related to each other in something approaching hierarchical order, as shown in Figure 16, although the ranking is not only, or necessarily, one of power. It has also to do with precedence in terms of time, scope, status and influence.

There are alternative ways of identifying the levels of analysis for studying the work of media production, for instance that suggested by Dimmick and Coit (1982), who identify nine levels at which influence or power may be exercised. The main ones are: the supra-national (international regulation agencies or businesses); society level (e.g. government); industry level (e.g. competing media firms and their relations with advertisers); the supra-organizational (e.g. chains or conglomerates); community level (e.g. town, local society and business); the intra-organizational formal or informal group (e.g. departments within an organization); that of the individual. This taxonomy helps to indicate the complexity of relationships and is useful for certain kinds of research.

The simpler structure represented by Figure 16 implies several of the points raised by Dimmick and Coit. In particular, the institution not only provides the 'boundaries' around its sphere of jurisdiction, but controls or regulates relations with supra-national agencies, the wider society and the community, especially in terms of the degree of acceptable influence (from outside) and the definition of purpose and

Figure 16 The relationship of media institution, organization and role

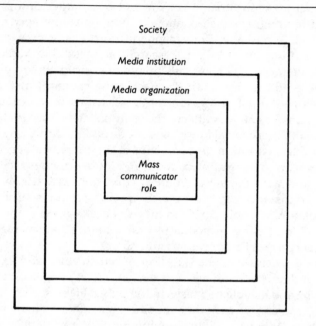

freedom to act. Secondly, Figure 16 shows the mass communicator to be most directly regulated by the organization, and more distantly by the institution. Thirdly, mass communicators are shown to have, as it were, an alternative 'court of appeal', at least to a set of principles which has a wider currency than the decisions or rules of the employing organization.

This is important for establishing some claim to personal freedom and for laying claim to a professional status. A corollary of this possibility of appeal is that 'society' can also make use of the institutional 'rules of the game' to lay complaints against media organizations or individuals (e.g. in matters of publication held to be against the public interest or damaging to morals, or when politicians claim unfair treatment by media which are supposed to be impartial).

Internal diversity of the media institution

The arrangements suggested by Figure 16 far overstate the neatness of the reality. It has already been pointed out that media organizations are often not self-contained units carrying out a complete range of production and distribution tasks, but also often parts in a larger whole (e.g. a local newspaper sharing an editorial control and an infrastructure with other 'titles' owned by a larger group). Alternatively, they might be self-contained units with one very specialized media task (e.g. making music video recordings or managing a local cable network, etc). As yet, research on mass communication has scarcely begun to grapple with this increasing diversity of situation and still tends to deal with the decreasingly typical instance of the large self-contained newspaper or broadcasting bureaucracy.

The same weakness affects research on media occupations, with many of the less central kinds of work receiving hardly any attention. The media institution is also subject to more, rather than less, uncertainty of demarcation as more and more activities are taken over and shared with business, politics, education, etc. It is harder than ever, for instance, to distinguish: public relations and would-be manipulation of opinion from news; entertainment and spectacle from the marketing of goods of brand names displayed; diversion from general public education, and so on.

Most significant is the question of which rules and expectations apply and are dominant — those of the media according to its traditions and established tasks in the public life of society, or those of politics, business or other institutions. Over time, the media institution adapts to its changing environment, but it is often important to know, at any point in time, what the institutional rules are. Total assimilation of media into other institutions would be incompatible with each of the theories of the press which were described in the previous chapter.

The main variants of media institutional definition and the variable application of the 'rules' of the institution have to do primarily with the following factors:

- Type of medium. For reasons, and in ways, explained in chapter 1, there are differing expectations and standards from one established medium to another.
- Scale and range of operation, extending from national and international to local or micro-media. Differences on this dimension relate to degree and kind of professionalism and degrees of freedom and accountability, in complex ways. For instance, local media are both more accompanied by social pressure and less likely to be held accountable for consequences of deviations.
- Work task or function. There are different rules and claims, for instance, for those who produce and create, for those who manage and distribute and for technical personnel.
- Form of ownership, control or management. The most commonly

found differing forms are: general public (or state) ownership and/or accountability; commercial market forms; non-profit, voluntary, autonomous forms, usually with specific 'ideal' goals.

Media work in a field of social forces

It follows from what has been said that any theoretical account of media occupations and organizations has to take accout of a number of different relationships within and across the boundaries of the organization. These relationships are often active negotiations, exchanges and sometimes conflicts, latent or actual. The influential model of mass communication drawn by Westley and MacLean (1957), which has already been mentioned, (p. 43) represents the communicator role as a broker between, on the one hand, would-be 'advocates' in society with messages to convey and, on the other, the public seeking to satisfy its information and other communication needs and interests.

Gerbner (1969) has portrayed mass communicators as operating under pressure from various external 'power roles', including clients (e.g. advertisers), competitors (other media mainly), authorities (especially legal and political), experts, other institutions and the audience. He wrote:

> While analytically distinct, obviously neither power roles nor types of leverage are in reality separate or isolated. On the contrary, they often combine, overlap and telescope . . . the accumulation of power roles and possibilities of leverage gives certain institutions dominant positions in the mass communication of their societies.

Clearly, in the case of government and business, these can represent powerful leverage and at the same time be 'advocates' in the sense used above (self-interested communicators) and also important *sources* for the media themselves. Not only are they often major would-be communicators, they are also *avoiders* of communication attention, except on their own terms. The media have to try to manage the supply of source material in competiton with other would-be managers and in latent competition with some of their own sources.

Using these materials and relying on the wide support for such a view in the research literature (see also Dimmick and Coit, 1982), we can sketch the position of the media organization and those within it as making decisions at the centre of a field of different constraints, demands, or attempted use of power and influence, as in Figure 17.

The picture is based mainly on studies of newspapers, but the newspaper has a range of functions other than news giving and the picture would be much the same for other multi-purpose media organizations, including television. A further refinement of the schema, based partly on the work of Engwall (1978) is the internal division of the media organization into three dominant work cultures which indicate the main sources of tension and lines of demarcation within media organizations (see below p. 165).

Figure 17 The media organization in a field of social force

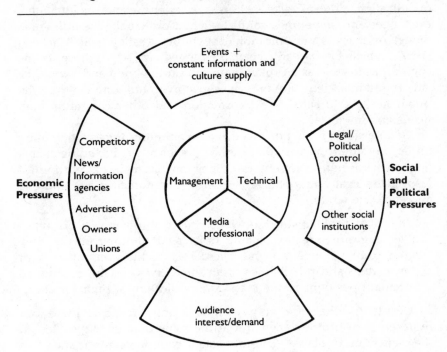

This presentation allows one to identify five main kinds of relationship which need to be examined in order to gain some understanding of the conditions affecting organizational activity and the mass communicator role. These are as follows:

– relations with society
– relations with clients, owners and suppliers
– relations with sources
– relations within the organization between different kinds of role
– relations with the audience.

The remainder of this chapter is structured according to this division of the field. Each set of relations and attendant problems is dealt with in turn, with a conclusion on media tasks divided in respect of activities of selection and of processing.

Relations with society

A good deal has already been said on this matter, especially in the preceding chapter, but the central questions at issue here concern the goals and purposes chosen by a media organization in relation to society and the degree of access which society may claim or expect, given the position of mass communication as a mediator of social reality. Press theories as well as everyday expectation and practice allocate rights to society, embodied in various forms, as well as to media and individual citizens.

Goals of media organizations

Most organizations have alternative goals and rarely are they all openly stated. Mass media are no different and may even be particularly ambiguous in this respect, given the unclear boundaries and internal fragmentation of the media institution. One basic differentiation, developed by Etzioni (1961), distinguishes organizational goals as either coercive, utilitarian or normative (see above, p. 34). The term 'coercive' refers to the use or threat of force for achieving the ends of an organization, as with armies, prisons, etc. The utilitarian organization aims to produce or provide material goods or services and uses financial or material reward and legal contracts for this end (as with the business firm). The normative organization aims to advance some value or achieve a valued condition, based on the voluntary commitment of its participants, as with a religion or a scientific organization. The position of mass media organizations in respect of this typology is ambiguous. The media are never strictly coercive, although as instruments of social power or propaganda, under monopoly conditions, they may take on some coercive aspects, for instance by deliberately causing fear or alarm.

The case of the media organization which is run as a business or public corporation, with paid employees and a public following based on the provision of some valued or useful service, is very common. Equally familiar, though not so common perhaps, is the media organization operated for idealistic purposes with a personal commitment by staff and a moral commitment by the audience to the same purpose. Most media systems in liberal democracies show a mixture of 'utilitarian' and 'normative' components, with corresponding variations in audience commitment, although the modal case is the utilitarian one, given the nature of mass communication (open, voluntary) and the nature of the service provided (useful information, entertainment, etc).

Another suggested basis for organizational classification distinguishes between type of beneficiary (Blau and Scott, 1963). Is it the society as a whole, a particular set of clients, the owners, the audience, or the employees of the organization, whose welfare or good is being served? Again, no single answer can be given for the media as a whole and particular organizations often have several actual or potential beneficiaries. Nevertheless, there is some reason to hold that the general public (not always the direct audience) should be the chief beneficiary. A common element in all the normative press theories discussed is that the media should meet the needs and interests of their audience in the first instance and the interests of clients and the state only secondarily. Since media depend on the voluntary choice of their audiences, this principle has a common-sense basis, but the view that the audience comes first is also often expressed by media personnel themselves.

In a study of newspaper journalists, Tunstall (1971) chose to state the goals of the newspaper in economic terms, distinguishing between revenue goals and non-revenue goals, the latter referring to purposes without a direct financial aspect: gaining prestige, exercising influence or power in society, achieving some moral end. Revenue goals are of two kinds — gaining income from sales and from advertisers. Different kinds of content and press policies go with variation of goals in these terms. While the audience appears to be subordinate in this typology, in practice the satisfaction of advertisers and the gaining of revenue from sales both depend on pleasing the audience, and non-revenue goals are often shaped by some conception of wider public interest. Furthermore, Tunstall indicates that in a case of conflict of goals within the newspaper, the audience revenue goal (increasing the circulation by pleasing the audience) provides the 'coalition-goal', on which most can agree.

The fact that mass media organizations have mixed goals is important for locating the media in their social context, understanding some of the pressures under which they are placed and helping to differentiate the main occupational choices available to employees. It is one essential aspect of a general ambiguity over social role which is discussed a little later (see p. 149). Some further light on this question is shed by the characterization of the newspaper as a 'hybrid organization' (Engwall, 1978), in the sense that it cannot be clearly placed on either of two key organizational dimensions (from Ellis and Child, 1973). These are the manufacture-service dimension and the dimension of variability of product and technology applied. The newspaper organization is both making a product and providing a service. It also uses a wide variety of productive technology, from the simple to the complex.

In varying degrees, this holds true of other mass media organizations, certainly of broadcasting. In such an organization Engwall expects to, and does, find that several different 'work cultures' are flourishing, each justified according to a different goal or work task, namely: the news-oriented culture; the politically-oriented; the economically-oriented; the technically-oriented. The first two named tend to go together and are closer to the Etzioni label 'normative', while the second two are also related and can be thought of as essentially 'utilitarian'. Those holding to the news-oriented culture are likely to be journalists collecting and processing news, while the politically-oriented will generally comprise editorial staff and senior political correspondents. The economic and technically-oriented consist of those involved in financial management and in solving problems of production and they will have much in common with their counterparts in other business organizations.

Insofar as this situation can be generalized, it seems that media organizations are as likely to be internally divided as to purpose as they are different from each other. It is hard to think of another category of organization that is as likely to pursue simultaneously quite such diverse objectives and serve such divergent values. That this should happen without excessive conflict suggests some fairly stable forms of accommodation to the attendant problems. Such an accommodation may be essential in what Tunstall (1971) has characterized by the paradoxical label of 'non-routine bureaucracy'. It may also indicate the presence in media of an above-average degree of compromise, uncertainty and 'displacement of goals' by comparison with other types of complex organization.

Engagement or neutrality?

The fact that media organizations (especially those with an opinion-information purpose) do seek, among other things, to play some part in society is clear enough, but the nature of this role is also open to quite diverse interpretations. It is quite clear that certain kinds of publication, especially prestige or elite newspapers (such as *Le Monde*, *The Times*, *Washington Post*, etc) have set out deliberately to be influential through the quality of their information or the authority of their opinion (Padioleau, 1985), but there are several options for the way in which influence can be exercised and it is not an exclusive property of an internationally-known elite press. Other media can be influential in more restricted spheres and influence can be achieved by publicity and weight of numbers.

There is, nevertheless, a choice to be made by media and journalists between taking a more active and participant, or a more neutral, role in society. Cohen (1963) was one of the first to make the critical distinction between a neutral and participant role when he (p. 191) distinguished two separate self-conceptions of the reporter's role as: that of 'neutral reporter', referring to ideas of the press as informer, interpreter and instrument of government (lending itself as channel or mirror); and that of 'participant', the traditional 'Fourth Estate' notion, covering the ideas of the press as representative of the public, critic of government, advocate of policy and as policy maker. The weight of evidence (e.g. Johnstone et al., 1976) is that the neutral, informative role is most preferred by journalists and it goes with the importance of objectivity as a core value and an element in the new professionalism (Lippman, 1922; Carey, 1969; Schudson, 1978; Tuchman, 1978; Roshco, 1975; Janowitz, 1975; Phillips, 1977).

At the local level, a similar underlying differentiation has been observed. For instance, from a study of regional newspaper journalists in Sweden, Fjaestad and Holmlov (1976) identified two main kinds of purpose each endorsed by over 70 percent of respondents — that of 'watchdog' (e.g. control of local government) and of 'educator' (providing a forum, aid to consumers, social and political information). They also named some secondary or minor functions, recognized by a third or fewer of respondents (especially 'political mobilization', 'entertainment' and 'forging a local consensus'). Studies of journalists and editors in the United States tend to reveal more of a preference for non-engagement and objectivity, but even so Johnstone et al. (1976) found that 76 percent of US journalists thought it extremely important that media should 'investigate claims and statements made by government'. Although the date (1971) when these data were collected was favourable to the adoption of a somewhat critical role by the press, it also corresponds to several elements in the American journalistic tradition — of reformism (Gans, 1979), of an 'adversary role' vis-a-vis government and, more generally, the idea that media should look out for the interests of their public whom they claim to represent. This is different from partisan advocacy of a particular point of view, which still seems to be in decline as a journalistic philosophy.

A replicated survey of American journalists by Weaver and Wilhoit (1986), using the same questions and design as Johnstone et al. (1976) confirmed some enduring features of the situation and extended our understanding of the case. They showed that in 1982–3 there had been some withdrawal from the critical perspective held by journalists of 1971, although they remained somewhat reformist in spirit and, on balance, more left-inclined than right politically. The endorsement of the questionnaire item on the 'extreme importance' that media should investigate claims and statements made by government had dropped to 66 from 76 percent and there was more support for neutral-informative than for participant elements of the journalist's role. Nevertheless, there was also significant minority support of an 'adversary' role.

Perhaps the most useful outcome of this part of the replication study was a reassessment of the neutral versus participant dichotomy. Using similar survey material, Wilhoit and Weaver opt instead for a tripartite division of roles as *interpreter*, *disseminator*, or *adversary*, in that order of prominence. The first of these three involves the same items as were previously used to produce the label 'participant' — analysing and interpreting complex questions, investigating claims made by government and discussing national policy as it happens. The second type — that of disseminator — involves mainly the matter of 'getting information to the public quickly' and 'concentrating on the largest possible audience'. The third, adversary, role (applying to both government and business) was much weaker, but was still recognized in some degree by a majority of journalists. The resulting scheme of role perceptions is reproduced in Figure 18, showing the main overlap between them.

A point also emphasized by the authors is the *plurality* of role conceptions held by journalists. They write (p. 116) 'only about 2 percent of the respondents are exclusively one-role oriented'. They also remind us that, on such matters as role perception and journalistic ethics, there seem to be quite large cross-cultural differences. For instance they quote Donsbach (1983) as showing that British journalists are much more committed to a purely informative role than are German journalists and tend to be much less particular about a range of dubious journalistic practices. Köcher (1986) offers more evidence on this matter, referring to the alternative roles of 'bloodhound' or 'missionary'.

Public broadcasting institutions, like the BBC, are under an especial pressure to meet requirements of neutrality and balance and

Figure 18 Journalists' role perceptions

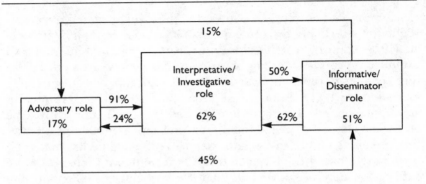

Source: D.H. Weaver and G.C. Wilhoit, *The American Journalist*, Bloomington: Indiana University Press, 1986, p. 116.

the chief aim of BBC decision makers in news and actuality has been described as 'holding the middle ground' (Kumar, 1975), acting as a broker between disputants, rather than being a participant. The question as to whether this lends itself to supporting the established social order has often been discussed. Hall (1977) thinks it does. A more wide-ranging investigation of the BBC by Burns (1977) reached a more cautious conclusion, but spoke nevertheless (p. 209) of a 'collusion thus forged with both the establishment and the "silent (and invisible, perhaps imaginary) majority" . . . against any disturbance of the peace'.

At the heart of Burns' study is a very interesting discussion of 'professionalism' in broadcasting and of alternative orientations to the work task which forms one source of the statement of occupational dilemmas made above. Burns found in the BBC three main attitudes to the occupational task. One was a deep commitment to the traditional goals of public broadcasting as an instrument of cultural and social betterment and for the defence of 'standards'. The second was 'professionalism', sometimes 'television for television's sake', but always involving a deep commitment to the task and the craft of making 'good television'. This concept of media professionalism has several components — standing opposed to 'amateurism' and to external interference, resting ơn the judgement of work by fellow professionals and leading to some insulation from the pressures of both public and management.

For most members of professions, the appropriate wider social role which they perform is usually 'taken care of' by the institution — as in medicine or teaching — leaving individuals to concentrate on the practice of their skills. To a certain extent, this is true of mass communicators, but full professionalization has been held back, perhaps by the internal diversity of media and the recency and flux of some of the occupations involved. There is also a continued uncertainty about what is actually the central professional skill. The sociologist Max Weber (1948) referred to the journalist as belonging to 'a sort of pariah caste' and, like the artist, lacking a fixed social classification. Schudson (1978) aptly characterized journalism as an 'uninsulated profession', because of the lack of clear boundaries.

Weaver and Wilhoit (1986) confirmed from their survey of American journalists the weak 'institutionalization' of the journalistic profession compared, for instance, to law, medicine or accountancy, and little seemed to have changed in this respect since 1971, despite a big increase in the proportion with a professional education in journalism. Success often also depends on unaccountable ups and downs of public taste or on personal and unique qualities which cannot be imitated or transmitted. Apart from skills of performance and other artistic accomplishments, the essential media skill is hard to pin down and may variously be presented as an ability to: attract attention and arouse interest; assess public taste; be understood; 'communicate'; be liked; 'know the media business'. None of these seems comparable to the skills that underlie other professions. Attempts to establish a claim to professional status for journalists have been made, largely resting on the skill of objective news reporting, but without complete success, since the concept of news objectivity is itself very vulnerable. It may be that the freedom, creativity and critical approach that many media personnel still cherish, despite the bureaucratic setting of their work, are ultimately incompatible with full professionalization.

It would, in any case, be very difficult, even allowing for the division of labour in any complex organization, to identify a general occupational type, or archetypal 'mass communicator'. We have to distinguish at least four main kinds of media occupation as follows: managers and controllers; creative workers such as writers, composers, performers, directors; journalists — reporters, editors, correspondents; technicians — design and video experts. The middle two categories are closest to the 'professional core' of media occupations but, in practice, there is considerable movement between them, especially from technical to creative and from creative and journalistic to management. But even the core professions appear to divide according to the way they see their professional task and studies of even apparently homogeneous professional groups reveal some basic lines of cleavage.

There is some general pattern to these divisions, a pattern which connects with a small number of basic oppositions of choice that are built into the media institutional pattern. These choices, in turn, may be thought to stem from the intermediary position of mass communication, as illustrated in chapter 3, between, on the one hand, sources of social power (other institutions) which exert leverage and, on the other, the public who are supposed to be the beneficiaries of mass communication work. The main choices are shown in Figure 19.

Figure 19 Media occupational role dilemmas

Playing an active, participant role in social and political life	vs	Adopting a neutral, informational position
Exercising creative skill and doing independent original work	vs	Meeting the needs of the organization as determined by management
Achieving some communicative purpose with an audience or for society	vs	Satisfying known audience demands for a consumer product

The fundamental dilemma is one of freedom versus constraint in an institution whose own open or implicit ideology places a value on originality and freedom, yet whose organizational setting requires quite strict control.

Characteristics of mass communicators

Many studies of media organizations or occupations include, as a matter of course, an examination of the social background and outlook on society of the group of respondents under study (early examples are Rosten, 1937 and 1941). This is sometimes because of an assumption that the personal characteristics of those most responsible for media production will influence content. It is a hypothesis which accords well with the ideology or mythology of the media themselves and stands opposed to the notion of organizational or technological determinism. Inevitably there are as many descriptions of social background as there are studies and although most concern journalists, there is no single pattern to report.

However, a few general remarks are in order, taking as a starting point the findings of Weaver and Wilhoit concerning the social composition of their sample of American journalists in 1982–3 and using their definition of journalists as 'those who have editorial responsibility for the preparation or transmission of news stories or other information, including fulltime reporters, correspondents, columnists, newsmen and editors'. It is clear that US journalists, however marginal their role in theory, are not marginal in income terms, but belong on average to the middle category, thus within the economically secure sector of society, without being rich. This mirrors the earlier findings of Johnstone et al. (1976) and the data from Britain afforded by Tunstall (1971).

Secondly, there are evidently big variations between the stars of journalism and the ordinary salariat, as in other branches of media business. Weaver and Wilhoit quote a study of 240 elite US news media personnel (by Lichter and Rothman) to the effect that demographically the elite is 'more secular, more white and more male that the country as a whole'. Johnstone et al. are cited as concluding that 'in any society those in charge of mass communication tend to come from the same social strata as those in control of the economic and political systems'. Interestingly, Wilhoit and Weaver themselves find that, since 1971, the composition of the corps of US journalists had changed remarkably in one respect — a much greater representation of women (from 20 to 34 percent), although there were relatively fewer black and Hispanic journalists. There seems little doubt about the general class position of the average media worker — it is a middle-class occupation, but less professionalized or well paid than other established professions (law, medicine, accountancy, etc) and with a small elite of well-paid stars. Peters and Cantor's (1982) account of the acting profession stresses the extreme gap between the powerless and insecure many and the minority at the top.

The theoretical significance of these observations is less easy to interpret. One view, advanced by Gans (1979) is that the middle-class position of the journalistic profession is a guarantee of their ultimate loyalty to the system. Therefore they are free, in the American system, because they can be trusted to see and interpret the world in much the same way as the real holders of power, holding the same basic ideology and values. It is a persuasive view, more so than the alternative idea that they are not only an elite, but a left-leaning one (as US data by Lichter and Rothman do indicate) with subversive motives, or alternatively a conservative elite (as some conspiracy theorists hold). More significant (and not inconsistent) may be the finding that media personnel owe most of their relevant attitudes and tendencies to socialization from the immediate work environment (e.g. Weaver and Wilhoit, 1986, pp. 127–8). This view, while not discounting the influence of social background and personal belief, returns us to the greater probability of organizational rather than individual subjective determination.

Access

The question of access — essentially *to* society as a whole by one (usually institutional) bit of the society has already been raised at several points. The initial frame of reference in chapter 3 (Figure 9) represents the media as creating (or occupying) channels between the main institutions of society and its members. One of the main kinds of pressure shown in Figure 17 is that for access by social and political interests. Much of the normative theory discussed in chapter 5 turns in the end on the question of who in society should have access and on what terms. Even in modern states, claiming to offer a high degree of freedom to their media, there are clear expectations, sometimes backed by considerable pressure, that mass media will make channels available for society-wide communication, especially 'downwards' from leaders or elites to the base of society. Whether this takes place by government command, or purchase of time/space in a free market or by playing the rules of the game (whatever the leader says is news) may not matter much to the eventual outcome, although it matters a good deal to the media, since the freedom to withhold access is an important right.

The situation may be conceptualized in terms of a continuum, at one extreme of which the media are totally 'penetrated' by, or assimilated to, outside interests, whether state or not, and at the other end the media are totally in control and free to exclude or allow in as they will. Pluralistic theory assumes that the diversity of organizations and possibilities for access will ensure an adequate mix of opportunity for 'official' voices of society and for critical, alternative views. 'Access for society' means more, however, than giving a platform for opinions, information, etc. It also relates to the way in which media *portray* what passes for the reality of society. They may do this in ways which alter, distort, or challenge it. In the end, the question of societal access involves a very complex set of conventions over the terms according to which media freedoms and societal claims can be exercised and reconciled. In this matter, much depends on the standardized characteristics of formats and genres and the manner in which they are intended to portray social reality or are understood to do so by their audiences.

This question has been illuminated for the case of television production in one country (Britain) by Philip Elliott, but his proposal could be developed to deal with press media and other national media systems. His typology (Figure 20) shows the variability of competence of the media organization over the giving or withholding of access to other would-be communicators. It portrays an inverse relationship between the degree of freedom of access available to society and the degree of extensiveness of control and action by media personnel. The more extensive the scope of control by the media themselves (scope of production), the more limited the direct access by the society. The reference is to a varying degree of *intervention* or mediation by the media as between the 'voice of society' or social reality on the one hand and the audience on the other.

Figure 20 Typology of production scope and directness of access by society

Scope of production	Production function	Directness of access by society	Type of access	Television example
Limited	1 Technical facilitation	Total	1 Direct	Party broadcast
	2 Facilitation & selection		2 Modified direct	Education
	3 Selection & presentation		3 Filtered	News
	4 Selection & presentation		4 Remade	Documentary
	5 Realization & creation		5 Advisory	Realistic social drama
	6 Imaginative creation	Zero	6 No control by society	Original TV drama
Extensive				

Source: P. Elliott, *The Making of a Television Series* (London, Constable, 1972).

This schema shows the variable degree to which social 'reality' is filtered by the media, with news and documentary falling at a midpoint on the scale, so that the scope of production for selection and shaping is more or less equal to the scope for society to claim direct access to the audience and, correlatively, equal to the scope for the audience to achieve a view of reality. In such 'actuality' material, there is an audience expectation of having a view of reality, but also a recognition of the right of the media to set criteria of selection and presentation. Apart from its other merits, this typology reminds us that news, on which so much study of media selection has been concentrated, is only one of several kinds of messages about reality that have to pass through the 'gates' of the media.

In practice, it is at the intermediate stages of the continuum where most potential conflict exists and where media organizations have to defend their choices in relation both to society and public — thus precisely where information about current reality is likely to be picked up by audiences. This area extends beyond news and documentaries to encompass 'docudramas', historial dramas and many 'realistic' serials which portray police, medicine, the military, etc. The more sensitive and powerful the external representatives of these domains of reality happen to be, the more careful the media have to be and the more obliged they are to avoid sensitive areas or to employ irony, allegory, fantasy and other long-known devices for evading direct accountability. It is not only self-interested authority which exerts constraints, but also the possibility of unintended and unwanted effects on reality itself (e.g. causing panic, crime, suicide, etc).

Relations with clients, owners and suppliers

There is relatively little theory or research to draw on in this area, aside from the prescriptions of normative theory and the voluminous history and actuality of arrangements which bind media organizations to their economic supports. There is much evidence to confirm the view expressed in Altschull's second law of journalism (see p. 124, above) that the piper's paymaster ultimately calls the tune (a law which happens to be entirely consistent with free press theory in its 'market' version). But that can still leave scope for media freedom and there are many kinds of arrangement possible between media and the many different kinds of 'paymaster'.

A simple view of the matter might present two fundamentally opposed options: either media are totally committed to promoting the interests of the state or a capitalist class or they are identified as a set of free professions struggling to achieve ideal communicaton ends in face of material or philistine obstacles set by bureaucratic accountants or moneylenders. Neither situation is very typical.

There is certainly a built-in tension between those who finance and pay for any professional service or economic venture and those who provide the service or carry out the enterprise. One strains for value for money or return on investment and the other usually for satisfaction by professional standards, as well as an income. In the media case, such a situation is modified, or cross-cut by several other factors, which can be summarily put as follows:

- Financial sources, whether public or private, can also have non-profit, or professional, goals.
- Professionals can have profit or career-oriented goals which may cause them to identify with clients, financial backers or employers.
- Media as much (if not more than) other business enterprises involve taking risks and continuous launch of new ventures whose success is hard to calculate, especially ventures of a 'creative'

nature, such as films, new kinds of TV format, etc. New ideas and an oversupply of products are continually needed to match an insatiable demand for products which rapidly become obsolescent (Hirsch, 1973). This situation, paradoxically, increases the freedom of professionals who are the only ones who can originate new products.

– Most market-based media (especially press and broadcast tele-vision) have multiple sources of financing — from investors, advertisers, consumers, sometimes public subsidy. These sources are often both independent of each other and interacting, allowing media organizations some scope for bargaining. One key to potential freedom lies in the most unpredictable of these sources — the audience. If media succeed with the public, they attract other financial benefits and since there is no known way of buying or predicting this success, its attainment and prediction count as professional/organizational secrets, whose possession helps to give leverage in economic bargaining.

– Public media (as, for instance, many television and radio services in Europe and elsewhere) are placed differently, but can acquire leverage through political mechanisms, though usually not without satisfying their audiences to some demonstrable degree.

This list of factors and circumstances which modify the power of external economic agencies does not take away from the fact that, in many circumstances, financial pressure does restrict real freedom and has consequences for quality (Elliot, 1977). Where, as seems to be the case with network television in the United States (Cantor, 1980; Blumler et al., 1986), market considerations penetrate all levels of decision making, the scope for professional freedom seems very restricted. In smaller Third World countries, with no significant production capacity, a dependence on cheap television imports is almost inevitable. There is no public money and little prospect of profit in the market to provide economic conditions for independence and creativity.

Some organizational studies suggest an alternative view — that a competitive commercial environment can possibly have positive effects on creativity and innovation. Ettema and Whitney, for instance (1982) in a study of US public television, report the view that struggling against organizational and financial limits sets puzzles for solution by creative workers. Turow's (1982) comparison of 'unconventional' US TV projects with 'conventional' projects, also concluded that innovation was likely to come not from attempts to meet audience demand but from a series of essentially conflict-laden factors, such as aggressive competition from other media or channels, technical change, enforced internal economy or power struggles between individuals within media organizations.

Relations with sources

The concept of the media as 'gatekeepers' has for long captured the imagination of students of media, since it was first used by White (1950) to describe the activity of the wire editor in a newspaper engaged in choosing a small number of news items from a large inflow of agency telegrams. The process of gate-keeping is examined later as a step in the (news) production process (pp. 162–7). Here a broader view of media organizations is called for, with this aspect of their relationship to their environment in mind. First, it should be said that the idea of a 'gate' as in the boundary surrounding the typical media organization is somewhat misleading, except perhaps for the purpose for which it was originally intended (the wire service gate). The reality is much more complicated. All media have to make selections from a larger range of possible items for placing in channels which have limited capacity, but the nature of selector-source relationships is extremely varied and so consequently are the roles invoved. The following main types of situation can be identified:

- Choice among authors or artists for publication of their work, as in book publishing, magazine editing, theatres, music publishing, etc.
- Regular contacts with informed insiders, experts, of the kind which news or actuality media initiate and maintain in order to secure timely, authoritative or otherwise inaccessible information, especially in advance of competitors.
- Regular contacts similarly initiated by would-be sources themselves, in order to secure favourable access. This applies especially to political actors, large firms, public institutions, show-business personalities, etc.
- Direct observation, information-gathering, reporting on a day-to-day, event-guided, basis by news media in particular.
- Use of services of information suppliers, especially national or international news agencies, film news agencies, television exchange arrangements, but also agencies for writers, authors, artists, etc, which often intervene between individual creators and publishers, as in the first entry above.

Even this does not exhaust the possibilities, especially by leaving out of account the degree to which media serve as sources for each other in unchartable combinations and permutations. Aside from the continuous feeding on each other by press and television, both as sources and objects of information and comment, there are important relations of content provision from the film industry to television and from music to radio.

Research on mass communication has signalled three main features of all this, aside from the inevitable symbiosis which is involved. First, there is the matter of the high degree of planning and predictability which goes with any large-scale continuous media production operation. The media have to have an assured supply for their own needs and thus have to 'order' content in advance, whether of news, fiction or other entertainment. This need is reflected in the growth of secondary organizations such as agencies which provide content regularly. It also implies some inconsistency both with the notion of media as neutral channels carrying the ongoing culture and information of the society and with the ideal of novelty and spontaneity which is sometimes either held to or fostered by the media as an important aspect of their own self-image. If supply has to be planned well in advance according to advance specifications, the reality is very far from this ideal.

Secondly, there is the question of imbalance between suppliers and media takers of information or other content. Some sources are more powerful than others or have more bargaining power because of their status, market dominance or intrinsic market value.

This situation is reflected, for instance, in the privileged access of the more politically and economically powerful and the favoured position of richer media and media systems in the world. Media organizations are far from equal in their degree of access to sources which can further enhance their position. Thirdly, there is the question of 'assimilation' which arises when the second and third types of relation named above (i.e. with informed insiders) tend to coincide when there is a mutual interest on the part of the media and would be communicators. There are obvious examples when political leaders want to address large publics, but less obvious collusion arises in routine news coverage where reporters depend on sources likely to have both inside information and an interest in the volume and the manner of its publication — sources such as politicians, officials, the police, etc.

The process of 'assimilation' has been said to occur (by Gieber and Johnson, 1961) if the degree of collaboration which exists for mutual benefit between reporter and source reaches a point where it conflicts with the 'distributive' role normally expected from those who claim to inform the public. Athough this type of relationship may be justified by its success in meeting the needs of the public as well as those of the media organization, it also conflicts with expectations of critical independence and professional norms, and can lend itself to the suppression or manipulation of information (Murphy, 1976; Chibnall, 1974). There is often a more or less institutionalized collusive relationship between politicians and press which may also serve a range of purposes without necessarily being manipulative in its effect (Whale, 1969; Tunstall, 1970).

Assimilation in the sense used above is also promoted by the activities of professional public relations agencies. A different kind of assimilation occurs in circumstances where commercial advertising or sponsored content becomes attractive in its own right to audiences. Under conditions of extreme commercialism, the distinction between advertising or other paid-for content disappears, the sources and the media become more or less identical. This is most likely to occur in the case of media which are financed entirely by commercial sources (for instance 'free' newspapers or fully sponsored television).

Relations internal to the media organization

The analysis made so far of the relations between the media organization and agencies outside may seem to imply a high degree of unity on the part of the typical organization. It should, however, also have become clear from the discussion of alternative goals and of the ambiguity of the media that they are likely to be internally divided. The sources of division lie in: the diversity of function (e.g. news giving, entertainment, advertising) of many media organizations, with different interests competing for status and finance; the dual (both material and ideal) character of many media; the endemic conflict between creative ends (which have no practical limits) and the need to organize, plan, finance and 'sell' media products. Most accounts of media organizations seek to recognize at least four basic orientations which provide the lines of division internally:

- towards goals of efficiency and economic success set by management;
- towards professional goals, governed by judgements of experts and peers;
- towards the society outside which can be influenced by news, opinion or creative art;
- towards fame and success with a chosen public.

These different tendencies (especially the last) are not mutually incompatible but between them they are a latent source of strain in a type of organization which has also to value the freedom of reporters, writers, opinion formers, creative artists and performers. The main role alternatives for mass communicators which have been indicated by research are as presented in Figure 21.

Figure 21 Alternative communicator role orientations

Object of orientation	*Criteria of success*
1. Own media organization	Management approval Career advancement Economic success
2. Profession or craft	Approval by peers Intrinsic satisfaction
3. Society	Status outside organization Influence (political, social, cultural)
4. The audience	Fame, popularity Influence on behaviour of public

These differences may also be seen as offering solutions to the dilemmas noted above as characteristic of work in mass media (p. 150), insofar as an organization offers some room for choice, but they also tell us about the conflicts to be expected. Muriel Cantor (1971) offers evidence of an unusual kind about a group of producers employed in making films for major television networks. She distinguished three main types. First, there were 'film-makers', mainly younger, well-educated people ambitious to become feature film directors and comparable to the 'professional' category of broadcasters which Burns (1977) singled out. Secondly, there was a group of writer-producers, with a main purpose of making stories with a worthwhile message and of communicating to the public. Thirdly, there were older, less well-educated, career producers, whose main orientation was to the network and their career within it.

Not surprisingly, the last mentioned group was least likely to have conflicts, since their main aim was to reach the biggest possible audience, a goal shared by the networks. The film-makers, for different reasons, were prepared to accept network goals — they wanted to practise their craft, accumulate money and move on to feature films. It was the writer-producers who came most into conflict with the networks (management) because of their different attitude to the content of what they did. Management wanted a saleable, risk-free, product, while the writers still retained some ideals of the craft and wanted to convey a worthwhile message.

The lessons of other research on communicators (mainly journalists) seem to lead to a similar conclusion — that where conflict occurs between media organization and employee, it seems most often to be where the political tendency or economic self-interest of the organization gets in the way of individual freedom of expression (Sigelman, 1973). Studies of newspapers do indicate a strong sense on the part of journalists that editors and publishers have a 'policy', which tends to dictate either the kind of story to be chosen or the manner of treatment. It is less clear how much power lies with owners and chief editors to control the message. Gans' account of several US news media (1979) is somewhat ambiguous about the actual power of corporate executives over reporters. On the one hand, they do make 'policy', conduct frequent and regular briefings, look after the commercial and political interests of the firm and can 'suggest, select and veto news stories whenever they choose'. On the other hand, they do not use their power on a day-to-day basis and there are countervailing powers which lie with TV news producers and editors, if not with individual reporters.

The survey evidence available tends generally to support the view that journalists mainly regard themselves as having a reasonable degree of autonomy, even if the problem of pressure from 'policy' does arise. Weaver and Wilhoit (1986) reported that 60 percent of their journalists thought they had almost complete freedom in selecting stories they wanted to work on and 66 percent in deciding which aspects of a news story to emphasize. It is clear that there are so many considerations in any given case of news selection or treatment, that the issue of influence or autonomy cannot be clearly settled on its own, nor is it easy to separate the issue of internal freedom of expression and reporting from the normal hierarchy of bureaucracy and from the external constraints discussed above.

Relations with the audience

Although the audience is, by conventional wisdom and in reality, the most important of the clients and influences in the environment of any media organization, most research tends to show the audience as having a low salience for many mass communicators, however closely ratings and sales figures are followed by management. Media professionals tend to show a high degree of 'autism' (Burns, 1969), consistent perhaps with the attitude of other professionals, whose very status depends on their knowing better than their clients what is good for them. Burns extended the comparison with that of service occupations, whose members in general 'carry with them a counter-vailing and ordinarily concealed posture of invidious hostility'.

Altheide (1974, p. 59) comments that the pursuit of large audiences by the television stations which he studied 'led to a cynical view of the audience as stupid, incompetent and unappreciative'. Burns (1977), Elliott (1972) and Schlesinger (1978) found something of the same to be true of British television. Schlesinger (p. 111) attributes this partly to the nature of professionalism: 'a tension is set up between the professionalism of the communicator, with its implied autonomy, and the meeting of apparent audience demands and desires, with their implication for limiting autonomy'. Ferguson (1983) also reported a somewhat arrogant attitude to the audience on the part of women's magazine editors. The problem may also stem from the fact that the mass communicator is both offering a professional service and selling a product at the same time, while the dominant criterion applied by the organization is nearly always the ratings (volume of sales). As Ferguson (1983) pointed out, editors in commercial media all agree that professional success has to be demonstrated in terms of rising circulations and advertising revenues.

It is possible that the hostility to the audience is somewhat exaggerated by media respondents themselves, since there is con-trary evidence that media people have quite a strong positive attitude to their audience in the abstract. Ferguson, again, notes that women's magazine editors showed a strong sense of responsibility to their audience and want to provide a helpful service (1983, p. 140). Weaver and Wilhoit (1986) report that the single most important factor contributing to work satisfaction of journalists was the possibility of helping people (endorsed by 61 percent). They also report that the single most frequent source of feedback to journalists is from members of the audience.

On a day-to-day, or item by item, basis, most mass communi-cators in established media do not need to be concerned about the immediate response of the audience and this, coupled with the intrinsic difficulty of 'knowing' a large and very disparate audience, contributes to the relative insulation described above. The most common institutional device for making contact with the audience — that of audience research — serves an important management function and relates media to the surrounding financial and political system, but seems to convey little that is meaningful to the individual mass communicator (Burns, 1977; Gans, 1979). Attitudes to the audience tend to be guided and differentiated according to the role orientations set out in Figure 21 above.

The pragmatic are happy with the ratings, which also satisfy the organization. The craft-oriented are content with the judgements of their fellow-professionals. Those committed to the goals of the organization (for instance, carrying out a cultural mission, or political or commercial propaganda) are content with these goals as internally assessed. Those wishing to have influence in society look to their influential contacts in relevant social contexts. For everyone there are friends, relatives and casual contacts who can provide feedback of a comprehensive kind.

There remains an element of dissatisfaction and uncertainty for those who do want to communicate, who do want to change and influence the general public and use media for this purpose, or who direct themselves at minorities or for minority causes where impact matters. The most likely solution is for such communicators to construct for themselves an abstract image of the kind of people they would like to reach. Nevertheless, mass communication seems unsatisfactory for people in this category and the organized process of mass communication under market conditions does not incorporate many satisfactory devices for relating the message to the active response of an audience. It produces audiences in the sense of spectators, who observe and applaud but do not interact with the senders (Elliott, 1972). Media organizations are to a large extent in the business of producing spectacles as a way of creating audiences and, incidentally, generating profit, employment and various kinds of satisfaction and service. It was for this reason, in particular, that so much emphasis was placed in chapter 2 on the 'display-attention' model as the one most appropriate for mass communication.

Media organizational activities: gate-keeping

Gate-keeping

The first studies of 'gate-keeping' (White, 1950; Gieber, 1956) were restricted in scope to the activity within newsrooms of choosing from among the large number of incoming wire telegrams and pictures from news agencies for the content which makes up or governs the bulk of news in a typical paper. The main purposes of such research have been either to assess the degree of subjective (personal and arbitrary) judgement involved or to learn about the nature of 'news values' as applied in the news media. The second purpose tended to take over, once it was fairly well established that patterns of selection were indeed too consistent to be thought of as subjective (Hirsch, 1977, provides a summary assessment).

Most of the evidence of patterned consistency tends to come from content analysis rather than from studies of news selectors and the latter continue, apparently, to see themselves as exercising a fair degree of personal choice (e.g. Hetherington, 1985). Nevertheless, it is hard to doubt that the same organization tends to follow a similar general pattern over time, or that different organizations behave in a similar way when confronted by the same events and under equivalent conditions (Glasgow Media Group, 1976; McQuail, 1977). There appears to be a stable perception of what is likely to interest an audience and a good deal of consensus among news decision makers.

The gate-keeping concept, despite its usefulness and its potential for dealing with many different media situations, has a built-in limitation in its implication that news arrives in ready-made and unproblematic event-story form at the 'gates' of the media, where it is either admitted or excluded. It is clear that the eventual news content of the media arrives by several different routes and in different forms. It may have to be sought out, ordered in advance, or its discovery systematically planned. At times it also has to be internally manufactured or constructed. Such construction, like the selection of news, is not random and subjective. It takes place largely according to schemes of interpretation and of relevance which are those of the bureaucratic institutions that are either sources of news or which process events (police departments, courts, welfare agencies, government committees, etc). According to Fishman (1982) 'what is known and knowable by the media depends on the information-gathering and information-processing resources' of these agencies.

The main factors which influence eventual choice can be considered under the headings of 'people', 'place' or 'time', usually in one or other combination.

People and selection

The fact that some people and institutions get more attention and privileged access as sources has already been mentioned. News people have their own preferred sources and are also linked to prominent figures by institutional means — press conferences, publicity agents, etc. News is often reports of what prominent people say about events rather than reports of the events themselves and the statements of prominent persons can, under certain conditions, be news events themselves, especially where these statement makers have power to influence future events. Probably the most studied and best-known case is that of the US president — a power figure supported by a large and effective publicity machine. As one study (Grossman and Kumar, 1981) noted, in all the variety of possibilities for reporting the president there is one constant imperative — closeness to senior officials and, if possible, the president in person on as exclusive a basis as possible. This underlies the fact that a great deal of news gathering revolves around persons, especially since persons are more permanently available than events, and can speak.

The significance of personal contacts in any kind of media work involving attention to current social reality has been underlined by research as well as by informal accounts of news producers. What we see of the world through media eyes is often the result of chance encounters or informal communication networks developed by people in the media. Elliott's (1972) study of the making of a documentary about racial prejudice showed the large extent to which the eventual content on screen was determined by ideas and preconceptions held initially within the production team and by the personal contacts they happened to have which could help to realize their ideas. The same study drew attention to the strongly-felt need to personalize the message and to have a well-known television personality as presenter.

Location and selection

The significance of *location* in news gathering was emphasized by Walter Lippman (1922) in his discussion of the routinization of news gathering. He wrote that news consists of events which 'obtrude', above what is normal, and can be anticipated by observation at those places where past newsworthy events have happened or been made public — e.g. courts, police stations, parliaments, airports, hospitals, etc. News media are normally linked to a net which covers the globe, its nodal points marked by the presence of an agency or a correspondent. This net has a very tight weave at places where power is concentrated, like Washington or the triangle of Paris–Bonn–London.

The pre-planning of news coverage in spatial terms thus involves a set of presuppositions about where news is likely to happen, which will have a certain self-fulfilling tendency. This tendency is witnessed by the great continuity of flow of news from regions like the Near East or Southern Africa in recent years, once these have been established as sites for events and foci of political concern. The corollary of this circumstance is that news flow can usually be less easily generated from locations where sudden and unexpected events take place. A further corollary is that the introduction of the means of reporting news in the form of personnel, equipment and communication arrangements stimulates news supply regardless of events and may even stimulate events or shape their course. There are various accounts of the planning of future event coverage having strongly influenced coverage, if not the course of events (e.g. Lang and Lang, 1953; Halloran et al., 1970). The possibility of influence on events has often been canvassed, though not proven, especially in matters of civil disturbance or terrorism (e.g. Paletz and Dunn, 1969; Schmid and de Graaf, 1982). Decisions by authorities to ban media coverage (e.g. in South Africa in 1985), or to manage it, reflect a strong belief in this effect.

Spatial relationships have some obvious and less problematic effects on the flow and selection of news in that these will be governed by physical proximity. The nearer the location of news events is to the city, region, or nation of the intended audience, the more likely it is to be attended to. Nearness may, however, be over-ridden as a factor by other considerations, such as power or the intrinsic character of events (e.g. scale and negativity) (Galtung and Ruge, 1965).

Time and selection

Not surprisingly, since it is built into the definition of news (see pp. 204–5 below), *time* has enormous influence as a consideration on selection. Timeliness means both novelty and relevance, both highly prized, and it also reinforces one of the most significant properties of communication technology — its capacity to overcome barriers of time. The importance of a 'first' or scoop with a newspaper is often more important than any other factor in deciding on selection and prominence. As well as a net to capture space, there is also one for time. Tuchman (1978) has illuminated the nature of this particular 'news net', which underlies the typification of events themselves. The net she describes, distributed in space and time, is designed to maximize the chance of capturing news events when and where they are likely to occur. As she observes, this increases the chance of actually reporting as news those events that fit the predictions of the net and reduces the chance of events that do not do so from being noticed, whatever their intrinsic significance. Further, she reminds us that news people implicitly operate with a typology of news which helps in planning their work.

The main types are 'hard news', dealing with events, and 'soft news', mainly background or time-free news. There are other categories of: 'spot' (very new, immediate, just breaking) news; 'developing' news; and 'continuing' news. There is also a time dimension, according to which news can be classified as 'pre-scheduled', 'unscheduled' or 'non-scheduled'. The first refers to 'diary' events that are known about in advance and for which coverage can be planned; the second to news of events that happen unexpectedly and need to be immediately disseminated — the most difficult for routine handling, but not the largest category of news; the third relates to news (usually soft) that is not tied to any particular time and can be stored and released at the convenience of the news organization. The typification of events in this way narrows the range of uncertainty, but also encourages the tendency to rely on continuing news and pre-scheduled or non-scheduled events, thus telling against uniqueness and novelty.

The extraordinary influence of time in the news operation has been especially remarked in broadcasting and Schlesinger (1978) refers to a 'stop-watch culture'. In his view it goes beyond what is needed for practical purposes: 'It is a form of fetishism in which to be obsessed about time is to be professional in a way which newsmen have made peculiarly their own' (p. 105). Its consequence, in his view, is to do some violence to history and reduce the meaningfulness of news. Molotch and Lester (1974) see more significance in the time dimension of events than the needs of the organization or inclinations of the profession. Time difference is also related to possibilities for news management and intervention by those with more social power. They suggest a four-fold category of events of which the largest is that of 'routine events', the three others being 'accidents', 'scandals' and 'serendipity'. Routine events, however, are divided into: those where 'event promoters have habitual access to the news assemblers'; those where 'event promoters seek to disrupt the routine access of others in order to make events of their own'; and those where 'the access is afforded by the fact that the promoter and news assemblers are identical'. The last category includes normal reporting and the 'pseudo-event'.

Other factors, other media

The strong influence of people, time and place on news selection should not obscure the fact that certain events do have content properties which give them priority in the planning of selection processes, aside from broader questions of news values. According to Galtung and Ruge (1965) modern news organizations are likely to have a preference for events that fit the following criteria: having a short time span (being sudden); having great scale and intensity; being clear and unambiguous; being unexpected; being culturally close to the intended public; having continuity — being already in the news and consistent with past images and expectations. There is also one other important choice. According to Tuchman (1978), reports should carry minimum risk to the news organization and should, consequently, be factual, verifiable and, if possible, directly attributable to authoritative sources.

This account of media selection activity has avoided the question of 'bias', or consistent deviation in a particular direction, which may result from tendencies to ease the organizational task. However, it does look as if the factors discussed do have some consistent and predictable outcomes for the picture of the world conveyed by media. To that extent, organizational/technical causes can have ideological consequences. At the very least, there is likely to be an accentuation of the content characteristics which go with ease of collection. These characteristics include: ready availability and low cost; conformity to expectation and stereotype; closeness to power and authority; quality of interest without disturbance.

Conformity to the pre-definition of the news product is a form of bias when this pre-definition is a somewhat artificial construct of an enclosed and self-supporting professional group. To the extent that the news profession is 'uninsulated' it is also likely to be sensitive to the existence of alternative criteria of newsworthiness. This discussion of selection has been concerned primarily with the question of news, where we have most evidence and where selection is a critical factor (because of what is *not* chosen). The factors which operate in relation to other kinds of content are, however, likely to take the same overall pattern.

Media organizational activity: processing and presentation

It has been argued that not only is there a bias because of patterned selection procedures but also because of what happens within the organization as content is further subject to organizational routines. One aspect is simply a subsequent selection (or reduction) after the initial choice, which is likely to further accentuate the characteristics of the initial bias. This seems to happen not only to news, but to other kinds of content as well, since a high proportion of content acquired or started as projects never reaches distribution (especially true of the film industry which is profligate with creative talent). Another proportion of content (e.g. of television shows in the US) gets a very short or limited distribution, while some media products run for years on television and are resold, remade or imitated. Media organizations tend to reproduce selectively according to criteria which suit their own goals and interests. These may sometimes be professional and craft criteria, but more weight is usually given in commercial media to what sells most or gets highest ratings. Among commercially relevant criteria is that of cheap and easy production according to a proven formula of success.

The evidence is insufficient to be certain about this (except in the case of news — see Bass, 1969), but the probability is that much the same criteria are applied at successive stages of selection, thus reinforcing early tendencies of form and content and diminishing the chances of variety, uniqueness and unpredictability. While bias in this sense may mean no more than an accentuation of characteristics which are easy to reproduce and popular with audiences, they are also likely to reinforce elements of the media culture and increase conformity with organizational policy.

Although mass communication is a form of mass production, the associated standardization relates in the first instance to multiple reproduction and distribution. The individual items of content are not constrained to share all the characteristics of mass-produced products. They can quite easily be original, unique, highly differen-tiated (for instance, the one-off performance of a sports event, a talk show or a news programme, which will never be repeated identically). In practice, however, as many studies of media production reveal, the technology and apparatus of production is not neutral and does tend to exert a standardizing influence. What seems to happen is that the initial diverse and unique content items or ideas are fitted to forms which are both familiar to media producers and thought to be familiar to audiences. These forms are those most suitable for efficient production according to specifications laid down by the organization.

These specifications are of an *economic*, a *technological* and a *cultural* kind. The efficiency/economic pressures come from the need to minimize cost, reduce conflict and ensure continuity and sufficiency of supply. Cost reduction exerts pressure according to different time schemes — in the long run it may lead to the introduction of new technology, in the short run to maximizing output from existing staff resources and equipment and avoiding expensive or loss-making activities. The main pressures on media processors — to save time, use technology, save money, meet deadlines — are so inter-related that it is easier to see them in their combined consequences than in their separate operation.

The *technological* pressures are often quite visible in their effects and they keep changing as a succession of major new inventions has affected different media industries. Film was changed by the coming of sound, the newspaper industry by advances in printing, by the electric telegraph, by computerization, television by the portable video camera and miniaturization of equipment and so on. The pressure is experienced mainly as a result of inventions which set higher technical standards for lower prices and which progressive media organizations conform to. The investment in technical facilities leads to pressure for its maximum use, and prestige as well as utility becomes a factor. New technology often means more speed, flexibility, capacity, but it establishes norms which have to be followed, puts pressure on all media organizations to conform and influences audience expectations about what is most professional or advanced.

The sense in which media organizations exercise a form of *cultural* standardization during the processing of media raw material is not difficult to grasp. It has already been suggested that media are constrained by their 'definitions' and associated expectations as to what they are 'good for' in general and what sort of content they offer. Within the media, the main types of content — news, sports, drama, entertainment, advertising also follow standardized formats which are rooted in traditions (media-made or culturally inherited), ways of work, ideas of audience taste and interest, pressures of time or space. Altheide and Snow (1979) coined the term 'media logic' to capture the systematic nature of pre-existing definitions of what a given type of content should be like. Subsequently, Altheide (1985) advanced the concept of 'media format' to refer to 'the internal organization or logic of any shared symbolic activity' (p. 14).

The idea is of a *dominant form*, to which mass communicators are more or less constrained to conform. Formats not only refer to broad categories of content, but also to unit ideas and representations of reality — akin to stereotypes. They are useful not only to producers but also to audiences who learn to differentiate within the mosaic of what is offered according to formats which they have learned (see below, p. 201). According to Altheide (1985), formats are not only a key to understanding much media production, but also relevant to questions of effect on society, since they shape the perception of reality acquired from media.

In a review of the mechanisms according to which culture is produced in the commercial-industrial world of mass media, Ryan and Peterson (1982) describe five main frameworks for explaining how decisions are made in the media arts (their main interest was in music production).

The first model is that of the *assembly line*, which compares the process to the way in which industrial products are made, with all skills and decisions built into the machinery and with clear procedural rules. Because media cultural products, unlike material goods, have to be marginally different from each other, the answer is overproduction at each stage.

The second model is that of *craft and entrepreneurship*, in which powerful figures, with established reputations for judging talent and putting things together, manage all the creative inputs of artists, musicians, engineers, etc, in innovative ways. This model applies especially to the film business, but could also hold for publications in which editors are personally charismatic and powerful figures.

The third model is that of *convention and formula*, in which members of a relevant 'art world' agree on a 'recipe', a set of widely-held principles which tell workers how to combine elements to produce works in the particular genre.

Fourthly, there is the model of *audience image and conflict*, which sees the creative production process as a matter of fitting production to an image of what the audience will like. It is decisions about the latter which are central and over which powerful competing entrepreneurs come into conflict.

The final model is that of the *product image* and its essence is described as follows:

> Having a product image is to shape a piece of work so that it is most likely to be accepted by decision makers at the next link in the chain. The most common way of doing this is to produce works that are much like the products that have most recently passed through all the links in the decision chain to become commercially successful (p. 25).

This mode does not require a consensus of all involved, or an entrepreneur, or an agreed audience image. It is the model which is said to guide the work of established publishers or the BBC, according to Ryan and Peterson. It is also a model which seems closest to the notion of professionalism defined as the special knowledge of what is a good piece of work — 'good television' or 'good journalism', rather than of what will succeed commercially.

Several studies of media production, such as Elliott (1972), Ferguson (1983), Burns (1977) and Gans (1979), seem to confirm the strong feeling held by established professionals that they know how best to combine all the available factors of production within the inevitable constraints. This may be achieved at the cost of not actually communicating to the audience, but it does secure the integrity of the product.

This typology of frameworks is especially useful in stressing the *diversity* of frameworks within which a degree of regularity and predictability can be achieved in the production of cultural goods (including news). There are different ways of handling uncertainty and reconciling the needs for continuous production with artistic originality or journalistic freedom. The concepts of manufacturing or bureaucracy, often invoked to apply to media production, should be used with caution.

In conclusion, we should again recall (as, in effect, did Elliott) the dominant influence of the 'display-attention' model described in chapter 2, compared to the models of transfer of meaning or expression. Mass communication is often primarily a business, and show business at that. Its roots are as much in the theatre and the showground as in politics, art or education. Appearance, artifice and surprise may be more important than reality, truth and the obvious. At the core of many media organizations, there are contrary tendencies which are often in tension, if not at open war, with each other.

CHAPTER 7

MEDIA CONTENT: ANALYSIS; REALITY-REFLECTION; GENRES

On speaking about media content

The most visible and accessible evidence of the working of mass media is what they produce and transmit and, as such, it has attracted more attention than any other aspect of the media, from both researchers and commentators. This vast, diverse and changing body of material is conventionally referred to as 'mass media content'. This reference is misleading insofar as it seems to imply that media content has a unity which can be identified and isolated for study in a relatively unambiguous way. We would not pretend to be able to speak of the 'content' of speech communication nor, usually, of books, nor of education (each of them channels, or media of communication), except by specifying more precisely which aspects or parts of the content we are talking about. It is scarcely more justifiable to speak of 'mass media content' in a general way, despite the convention of doing so, especially since its volume and internal variety continually increase and the boundaries around 'mass media' are increasingly hard to discern. At best, we can speak about a particular body of content (a set of messages) clearly delimited by medium, time, place, category or genre.

In this chapter the subject is less the actual messages than ways of finding out and talking about media. Until now, the main contribution of theory has been to help in finding such ways of talking (forms of discourse), although the result has been to offer alternatives for choice rather than any uniquely correct form of analysis and discussion. Diversity of theory and method stems inevitably from the variety of purposes for which analysis is carried out, the diversity of messages transmitted and the ambiguity and multiplicity of meanings of media messages (and of all human communication). This ambiguity of meaning may be introduced by the originator, whether deliberately or not, or it may reside in the forms of language used (especially visual images), or it can be a consequence of the variability of perception and situation of the receiver. The use of mechanical forms of reproduction by mass media does little to reduce the possibilities for ambiguity of meaning from any or all of these three sources.

Despite these cautionary words, it is true that students (and theorists) of mass media have a weakness for generalizing about media content, beyond reasonable limits. They do so mainly on the grounds that messages produced by media tend to have a very stylized, patterned, even 'manufactured' character and that the main features and patterns of meaning can be typified and summarily described in a more or less objective way. The limitations of this assumption can easily be lost sight of, even if one has to adopt it in order to be able to say anything at all even about specific bodies of media content. A second important assumption which is usually made is that the study of content can tell us something over and above what its originators intended to say or transmit. The *primary* interest of content analysis (in contrast, for instance, with the study of literature or education) lies in these secondary aspects. Media content is often taken as evidence of one or more of the following:

— the systematic performance, in terms of quantity or types of output of a media organization;
— the society or culture in which it is produced;
— the producers and their intentions;
— the media organization and its way of working;
— the languages, formats and codes used to record or convey meaning;
— the eventual audiences and their interest;
— the quality of a given body of content measured against external criteria;
— possible effects or effectiveness in reaching some goal.

It is fairly obvious that without being able to adopt the assumptions named and without being able to speak generally about bodies of media content it would be impossible to ask sensible questions about mass communication, of the kind already raised, let alone search for answers. Nevertheless, one has to be clear about the shifting and sometimes shaky foundations of content analysis on which much generalization about mass communication rests.

Purposes of content analysis

Since this chapter is mainly about ways of analysing content and about theories of its relation to society, it makes sense to begin with what is the main source of variation in both — the alternative purposes, briefly summarized above.

Accounting for media as sent and received: quantitative book-keeping and audience research

Here two questions are addressed, but involving essentially the same activity: how much of what sort of content is sent and how much of what sort is received by whom? For the answer, we need descriptions of content which are at the same time descriptions of audiences, since audiences are often defined by what they attend to and by little else (see chapter 8). For the most part, the categories involved for such basic descriptions will be provided by the media institutions themselves and will be recognizable, at a 'commonsense' level. The categories will be mutually exclusive sets of media output, varying only in degree of specification, from whole media (e.g. all television or all newspapers) to content types (e.g. news, advertisements, fiction) to types within types (e.g. 'westerns', personal ads). For book-keeping purposes, no *analysis* of content is required. One undesirable consequence of the practice of describing audiences in terms of content is that open or implicit value judgements about content (e.g. as 'trivial', 'escapist' or 'serious') tend to be transferred to the people concerned, as if such description was more than a very slight and unreliable indicator of 'taste', 'capacity' or 'cultural level'.

There is also a risk of assuming that a pattern of media content choice can be treated as a basic and defining characteristic of a social grouping. More often than not such patterns are either ephemeral or the outcome of more basic determinants, or fail to differentiate one principle of social grouping from other quite different ones (see below, pp. 222–3, for a discussion of audience determination).

Media content as evidence of society and culture

The uses to which content analysis have been put in the study of society and culture are many and varied. Media content happens to be one of the most voluminous and accessible sets of data which may indicate much about a society, and its accessibility extends over time and sometimes across national frontiers. As source material, mass media content has the apparent advantage of being 'non-reactive' to the investigator and not subject to decay. Media content also appears in forms which seem to be much more constant over time than other cultural phenomena. For these reasons it is valued by historians, sociologists and anthropologists. Among the alternative schools, we can single out as most germane in the current context, the 'cultural indicators' approach, well described and exemplified by Rosengren

(1981a), which finds its model in existing 'economic' and 'social' indicator traditions and uses media content as its primary source.

The basic assumption is that both changes and regularities in media content reliably reflect or report some feature of the social reality of the moment. For instance, the degree of preoccupation with news reports of crime or immigration indicates either an increase in these phenomena, or a heightened awareness of these as problematic, or a policy by those with power and influence over the media to call attention to such matters. The theory and method can be applied to all types of content, including entertainment and fiction.

The purpose of cultural indicator analysis is often to test propositions about effects from media on society over time, but it is also a method for the study of social change in its own right and for the comparison of different national societies and cultures. The (media) cultural indicator can be treated either as cause or effect, or neither (see above, p. 95). While newly reformulated (e.g. Rosengren, 1985), it follows a long tradition of work which has fruitfully related historical changes in society to dominant themes and images of content (e.g. Lowenthal, 1961; Johns-Heine and Gerth, 1949). A more recent example is that of Szpocinksi (1987). It will be evident that types of classification for such purposes are likely to be both varied and complex and the current social indicators approach is highly eclectic, in the sense of allowing choice of any indicator which seems relevant to the problem at hand and involving a number of different disciplines (Melischek et al., 1984).

Content as evidence of the communicators and their organization

Insofar as media content is made or chosen by identifiable individuals or groups, it is reasonable to treat it as telling something of their intentions, attitudes and assumptions about the audience. It is also plausible to think that it will reflect something of their social origins and current social class or milieu. In general, the 'mass communicators' are not typical or average as a social category, being generally of middle or lower middle-class position, more educated and cosmopolitan than average, over-representing men as against women and white as against black (where the comparison is relevant). There are few studies which try directly to relate such factors to features of content, but Gans (1979) does indicate a connection between the typical values and outlook of American newsmakers and their social position. He suggests that their relative autonomy is related to the improbability of their threatening the social order.

As suggested in the preceding chapter, typical features of content seem more directly relatable to the nature of media organizations than to the personal characteristics of media personnel. Organizational imperatives tend to over-ride personal preferences, except at the highest level, and media organization 'policy' is more a collective than an individual phenomenon. Many more adapt to it than make it. The 'working theory' of most media communicators is generally that they themselves are neutral carriers who offer what their audiences want. There is obviously some truth in this, but it also obscures the question of responsibility for what is offered and also the extent to which media content does actually reflect or indicate the ideology of its producers, at some level of the organization. There is evidence that self-selection, as well as later socialization does lead to real variation in the composition of the personnel of different media organizations (see above, pp. 150–1). It is also possible to show that different media organizations have consistently different policies or political allegiances. For purposes of shedding light on communicators, the requirements of a suitable language of description of content can range from a simple classification (e.g. advertising versus editorial space of newspapers) to the close dissection of implicit values and ideology.

Content as evidence of effect

Little need be said of an early (but still encountered) tendency to equate evidence of content with evidence of effect, which derives from the commonsense view that so much of any given kind of media content (war stories, romances, 'violence', or whatever) *must* have *some* effect on those who consume it. It should by now be axiomatic that content (whether as sent or as received) does not equal effect because of: the many alternative ways in which messages can be interpreted and applied by their receivers; the fact that societal conditions and contexts encourage some, and discourage other, effects; the sheer inefficiency of the whole media 'delivery' system. There is an almost equally indefensible, and less easily dismissed, tendency to propose evidence of effect without (adequate) study of content.

Good effect research does require a relevant analysis of the content which is supposed to have caused the effects in question — thus something more than simply evidence of 'exposure' to media. Without content analysis, 'effects' which seem related to exposure may simply be the consequence of a third factor which causes both exposure and seeming effects. It is true that content can never be conclusively related to effect, but a characterization of relevant content cannot be dispensed with. Most good content analysis does lead to propositions about possible effects, but the results should be interpreted first of all as themselves *an effect* — whether of media intention, of assumptions about the audience or of working procedures, or all three.

Media content as an object of study in itself

As the study of media has progressed, there has been an increasing amount of work directed towards understanding the languages and forms used by mass media. This may have no further instrumental purposes, but the results are often found useful in other research, for instance into audience response, interpretation, comprehension and on the 'decoding' process generally. To account for how people 'make sense of' media content it helps to know how meanings have been originally 'encoded' and such knowledge is also relevant to studies of media effect (e.g. news comprehension can vary according to aspects of message form, Robinson and Levy, 1986). Much of the work in question draws on older disciplines of linguistics and literary study and reflects a confusing multiplicity of theory and also a lack of reliable methods for revealing just how media texts do 'work'.

The most promising lines of enquiry have been as follows: semiological and structural analysis, which concentrates on the internal relationship (especially contrasts) of elements in texts taken as wholes and also on ties to the wider culture (see below, pp. 185–8); attempts to distinguish and characterize recurrent media formats and genres (e.g. Altheide and Snow, 1979); studies of systematic ideology in content which follow specific hypotheses (e.g. of hegemonic tendency) and also employ the study of connotative and iconic meaning and the methods of semiology (e.g. Glasgow Media Group, 1985); film and television theory which aims to establish distinctive features of film language, grammar and vocabulary of images and to find ways of systematic record and analysis (Monaco, 1981; Metz, 1974). In respect of this last approach, there remain enormous uncertainties and gaps in method but, without advances in this field, it will hardly be possible to claim to be able to describe the content of the most widely received mass media.

Evaluating media performance

A distinction has to be made between content analysis as here broadly intended and the direct assessment of content according to moral or aesthetic criteria, which is beyond the scope or competence of social scientists as such. In social scientific research, the central requirement for content analysis is that there should be objective indicators which can be applied (also objectively) to determine the presence, absence or frequency of qualities of interest to an investigator. The evaluative criteria most commonly involved in what may be termed media *performance analysis* (Krippendorf, 1980) have already been discussed in chapter 5: diversity; objectivity; order; independence; accuracy; various aspects of culture, etc. Such attributes or qualities are rarely, if ever, to be read directly from content, but have to be inferred on the basis of indirect measures or indicators (see pp. 126–33). Usually there is room for debate about the reliability, validity, or appropriateness of the chosen indicator or about the certainty of any conclusions drawn about the level of performance.

The problem can be illustrated from some examples of indicators. The portrayal of 'violence' in media is often measured, but requires attention not only to the presence, absence or degree of any violent act portrayed, but also the context, the degree of realism, the question of implied approval or disapproval, the typical characteristics of perpetrator and victim, the possible types of violence, the legitimacy or not of the act and still further aspects (Gerbner et al., 1976). The measurement of objectivity is bedevilled by the absence of any complete record of reality for comparison, the impossibility, in any case, of any *complete* account of reality, the difficulty of determining what is relevant, the problem of separating fact from value (Hémanus, 1976) and more besides (Hackett, 1984).

Diversity of content has been measured according to the range of, and freedom for, alternative voices or references or social groups portrayed, but any systematic assessment has to take account of the alternative levels of measurement (which body of content), alternative standards of performance (reflection or equal access), the almost unlimited range of topics on which media can be more or less diverse (McQuail and van Cuilenburg, 1983). Until now, content analysis has delivered only very limited answers to the major questions concerning mass media performance, which naturally vary across countries and media systems (See chapter 5).

Conflicts and inconsistencies of purpose

It should be clear that these different purposes, besides leading to different kinds of investigative activity, are based on varied assumptions which cannot all be reconciled. One potential inconsistency has already been explored in discussing the link between media and social change (pp. 95–6): if the media are regarded as a cause of social and cultural phenomena, they cannot equally be regarded as a reflection and indicator, since the media should precede the 'effects'. The sharpest conflict is likely to exist between the common claim of the media that they give the public what it wants and the view that the media determine or shape culture and social life.

A second potential contradiction exists between the view that media content is a social and cultural indicator and the proposition that most salient aspects of media content are attributable to organizational structure and dynamics. The more that media content is thought to 'indicate' culture and society, the less we can expect it to be shaped by the specific features of the production process.

There is also some divergence between a view of content as either the characteristic product of an organizational milieu or a historical time and the view underlying the last mentioned purpose of content study — the elucidation of language, code and structure of meaning. The question at issue is where the meaning of a text is to be found — is it inescapably embedded in the chosen language or form, is it in the purpose claimed by, or attributable to, the media producers, or is it in the varied and unpredictable response and interpretation of the receiver? The choice between these three as to prime location of meaning of content is a crucial one and a central issue for all students of content.

Modes of discussion and methods of analysis

Modern methods for the analysis of mass media content have all been interposed between two pre-existing modes of discourse about content, which might be thought of as forming two poles of a 'dimension': at one end the 'unproblematic' description of content as a set of commonsense types or categories (books, news, plays, etc); at the other end, forms of essentially subjective, moral and aesthetic evaluations of cultural production.

Between these two are several approaches which vary in their degree of complexity, claimed 'objectivity', attention to surface or underlying features of content. They nevertheless share some general characteristics. First, they claim some measure of scientific reliability. They are methods which can, in principle, be replicated by different people and the 'findings' should be open to challenge according to some (not always the same) canons of scientific procedure. Secondly, they are meant to deal with regularity and recurrence in cultural artefacts rather than what is unique and non-reproducible. They are thus less appropriate for application to 'art' than to 'non-art', to the products of the 'cultural elite' than to those of the 'cultural industry'. Thirdly, they all avoid judgements of moral or aesthetic value. Fourthly, despite what has been said of content study for its own sake, all such methods are, in principle, instrumental. They can be used for other purposes, especially for answering questions about the links between content, creators, social context and receivers.

The variety of possibilities within these boundary conditions is wide and best dealt with by describing the two dominant versions of content study, one of which lies closest to the 'commonsense' pole of overt classification and the other nearer the pole of aesthetic and literary judgement. Beyond that, several variants and partial approaches can be distinguished.

Traditional content analysis

The label 'traditional' is given only because this is the earliest, most central and most widely-practised method of analysis. Its use goes back to the early decades of the century (cf. Kingsbury and Hart, 1937), and the most commonly quoted definition was given by Berelson (1952) as 'a research technique for the objective, systematic and quantitative description of the manifest content of communication'.

The basic approach for applying the technique is to: (1) choose a universe or sample of content; (2) establish a category frame of external referents relevant to the purpose of the enquiry (e.g. a set of political parties or countries); (3) choose a 'unit of analysis' from the content (word, sentence, item, story, picture, sequence, etc); (4) match content to category frame by counting the frequency of the references to items in the category frame, per chosen unit of content; (5) express the result as an overall distribution of the total universe or sample in terms of the frequency of occurrence of the sought-for referents.

The procedure is based on two main assumptions: that the link between the external object of reference and the reference to it in the text will be reasonably clear and unambiguous and that frequency of occurrence of chosen references will validly express the predominant 'meaning' of the text in an objective way.

The approach is, in principle, no different from that adopted in surveys of people when one chooses a population (here a media type or subset), samples within it for respondents representative of the whole (here units of analysis — words, items, etc), collects data about individuals according to variables (here the objects in the category system) and assigns values to these variables (here presence or absence, or frequency, of a given reference). As with the survey, such forms of content analysis are held to be reliable (reproducible) and not unique to the investigator. The method produces a statistical summary of a much larger field and it has been used for many purposes, but especially for extracting from content frequency distributions of references to things with a known frequency in 'social reality', for instance, occupations, crimes, strikes, demographic characteristics, political behaviours, opinions and so on. Hence the method lends itself well to purposes of comparing media with reality, the study of social and cultural indicators and certain kinds of effect research.

The approach has many limitations and pitfalls, which are of some theoretical as well as practical interest. The normal practice of constructing a category system before applying it involves the risk of an investigator imposing his or her meaning-system rather than 'taking' it from the content. Even when care is taken to avoid this, any such category system must be highly selective and hence distorting. The result of content analysis is a new text, the meaning of which may, or even must, diverge from the original source material. This result is also based on a form of 'reading' of content which no actual 'reader' would ever, under natural circumstances, undertake. In a certain sense, the new 'meaning' is neither that of the original sender, or of the text itself or of the audience, but a fourth construct, which has to be interpreted with care.

Frequency of occurrence is not the only guide to salience or to meaning and much may depend on aspects of context of a reference, which are hard to capture, or on internal relationships between references in texts which are lost in the process of abstraction. The 'unit of analysis' convenient for sampling and frequency counts may also not be a very meaningful division of content or accord with units of behaviour by audiences.

There are a number of routine problems to do with reliability and with the assumption that overt meaning is really overt. The method tends to assume that training can eliminate from 'coders' of content those large variations of perception which ordinary audience members always exhibit and if no such assumption is made, the range of application of the method may be unduly narrowed.

The boundaries of the kind of content analysis described are, in fact, rather elastic and many variants can be accommodated within the same basic framework. The more one relaxes requirements of reliability, the easier it is to introduce categories and variables that will be useful for interpretation but 'low' in 'objectivity' and somewhat ambiguous. This is especially true of attempts to capture references to values, themes, settings, style and interpretative frameworks. A good many content analyses now display a hierarchy of reliability, extending from the relative 'hardness' of data about the 'topic' of a given unit of analysis to the relative 'softness' of giving values to some classifying variables of style, direction, or general theme. To this extent, the practice of content analysis, although continuing to be systematic, quantitative and descriptive, has tended to depart from Berelson's specification by being less concerned with 'manifest' content and more flexible about objectivity.

Structuralism and semiology

It is impossible in the space available to give a satisfactory account of this subject and one can do little more than apply one of structuralism's own methods and contrast it with 'traditional content analysis' in its pure form. There are several classic statements of the structuralist/semiological approach (e.g. Barthes, 1967; 1977; Eco, 1977) and now several useful introductions and commentaries (e.g. Hawkes, 1977; Fiske, 1982; Burgelin, 1972). A few explanatory words, nevertheless, are needed before making the promised comparison. As to the terms: structuralism is a development of the linguistics of de Saussure (1915) and combines some principles from structural anthropology with the latter. Structuralism differs from linguistics in two main ways: it is concerned not only with conventional verbal languages but also with any sign-system which has language-like properties, and it directs its attention less to the sign-system itself than to chosen texts and the meaning of texts in the light of the 'host' culture. It is thus concerned with the elucidation of cultural as well as linguistic meaning, an activity for which a knowledge of the sign-system is instrumental but insufficient.

Semiology (or semiotics) is the 'general science of signs' (Peirce, 1931–35) and encompasses structuralism and other things besides, thus all things to do with signification, however loosely structured, diverse and fragmentary. The concepts of 'sign-system'

and 'signification' common to linguistics, structuralism and semiology derive mainly from de Saussure. A sign is any 'sound-image'
that acts as a 'signifier' of something 'signified' — an object or concept
in the world of experience, about which we wish to communicate.

Figure 22, based on the work of Peirce on Ogden and Richards
(1923) and on de Saussure illustrates the relationships between these
concepts. According to de Saussure, the process of signification is
accomplished by two elements of the sign, one the *signifier* (e.g. a
letter or sound) and the other the *signified* — which is the mental
concept invoked in a given language code.

Figure 22 Elements of semiology

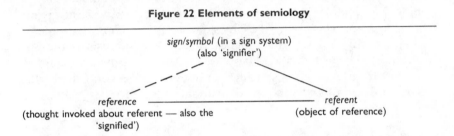

Fundamental here is the *arbitrary* nature of the link between the
sound-image (signifier) and the thing signified (hence the dotted line
in the diagram between 'sign-symbol' and 'reference' — the link is
only imputed). In principle, anything which can make a sense-
impression can act as a sign and this sense-impression has no
necessary correspondence with the sense-impression made by the
thing signified. The importance of this lies in the attention which is
then directed to the whole sign system because it is from this and our
knowledge of it that we derive, or transfer, meaning in communication. The separate signs gain their meaning from the systematic
differences, contrasts and choices which are regulated in the
linguistic or sign-system code and from the values (positive or
negative valence) which are given by the rules of the culture and the
sign-system.

Semiology has sought to explore the nature of sign-systems which
go beyond the rules of grammar and syntax and which regulate
complex, latent and culturally dependent meanings of texts. This has
led to a concern with connotative as well as denotative meaning —
the associations and images invoked and expressed by certain usages
and combinations of signs. In so doing it has been applied to the
recognition of myths, which are pre-existing and value-laden sets of
ideas derived from the culture and transmitted by communication.

In general, denotative meaning has the characteristics of universality (same meaning for all) and of objectivity (references without evaluation), while connotation involves both variable meaning according to the culture of the recipient and elements of evaluation (positive or negative direction).

The relevance of all this for the study of mass communication will be evident. Media content consists of a large number of 'texts', often of a standardized and repetitive kind, which are composed on the basis of certain stylized conventions and codes, often drawing on familiar or latent myths and images present in the culture of the makers and receivers of texts (Barthes, 1972). The application of semiological analysis opens the possibility of revealing more of the underlying meaning of a text, taken as a whole, than would be possible by simply following the grammatical rules of the language or consulting the dictionary meaning of separate words. It has the especial advantage of being applicable to 'texts' which involve more than one sign system and signs (e.g. visual images and sounds) for which there is no established 'grammar' and no available dictionary.

Much media content is of this kind. Such work presupposes a thorough knowledge of the originating culture and of the particular genre. According to Burgelin (1972, p. 317) 'the mass media clearly do not form a complete culture on their own . . . but simply a fraction of such a system which is, of necessity, the culture to which they belong'. Moreover, it follows from the theory summarized above that a text has its own immanent, intrinsic, more or less given, and thus objective, meaning, apart from the overt intention of sender or the selective interpretation of the receiver. As Burgelin also comments (p. 316) 'there is nobody, and nothing, outside the message which can supply us with the meaning of one of its elements'.

This body of theory supplies us with an approach, if not exactly a method, for helping to establish the 'cultural meaning' of media content and thus shedding light on some of the questions underlying the various purposes named above. It certainly offers a way of describing content: it can shed light on those who produce and transmit a set of messages; it is potentially as useful as, perhaps more so than, conventional content analysis in predicting or explaining effects; it has an especial application in certain kinds of evaluative research, especially that which is directed at uncovering the latent ideology and 'bias' of media content.

But it has perhaps contributed most to an understanding of mass communication by revealing essential features of certain media 'genres' in film, television and print which show such a remarkable resilience and persistence over time and a power to 'colonize' mass communication processes. Examples include the dominant 'news' form, certain advertising forms, the western and the detective story or thriller. Not only do such genres comprise a large part of media output, they constrain would-be communicators and they remarkably survive cultural transplantation. It is fundamental to the semiological approach that to understand the meaning of signs we need to take account of the genre in which they appear.

Structural analysis of a genre

An example of a genre analysis is offered by Hall (1973b) in respect of the once traditional 'B movie western' film. This is derived from a general view of a *code* as a meaning system in which signs are organized, with a range of alternative signs and with rules for linking signs in certain sequences (respectively, the paradigmatic and the syntagmic dimensions), and which can draw on some agreement as meaning among 'users' of the code (both encoders and decoders) in a given culture. We can speak of a genre, according to Hall, where coding and decoding are very close and where meaning is thus relatively unambiguous, in the sense of being likely to be received much as it is sent. The classic western movie is then said to derive from a particular myth concerning the original conquest of the west and involving, in brief: displays of masculine prowess and womanly courage; the struggle of good against evil; the working-out of destiny in the open air, etc.

The particular strength of the western genre with an established and agreed basic meaning allows it to generate many variant forms which can easily be understood, though only in relation to the basic original form. Examples of the variant forms are: the psychological western; the parody; the spaghetti western; the comedy western; soap opera western and so on. The genre can be extended to deal with racism, feminism, rural decline and much more, but this range and flexibility derive from a clear understanding of the original myth, even if this is rarely portrayed any longer. The meaning of the variant forms all depends on a reversal of elements in the original code and Hall goes on to suggest from this analysis that the meaning of *violence* in the western cannot be taken literally. He speculates that the basic 'code of the western' gives violent acts the meaning of the demonstration of 'professional cool' — an act of studied efficiency and competence by someone who is a master of contingencies and triumphs over fate. This interpretation would give to the genre a much more universal meaning than it possessed in its original basic form.

Structuralism (or semiology) and content analysis compared

The contrasts with traditional content analysis can now be summarized. Some are already self-evident. First, structuralism is not quantitative, and is even antipathetic to counting as a way of arriving at significance, since meaning derives from relationships, oppositions and context rather than from quantity of references. Secondly, attention is directed to latent rather than to manifest content and latent meaning is regarded as actually more essential. Manifest meaning is much more open to alternative interpretation because it is 'further' from the structure of the text and consists of more random elements. Thirdly, structuralism is systematic in a different way than is content analysis — giving no weight to procedures of sampling and rejecting the notion that all 'units' of content should be treated equally and that the same procedure can be applied in the same way to different texts, as is often the case with content analysis.

Fourthly, structuralism does not allow the assumption that the world of social and cultural 'reality', the message and the receiver, all involve the same basic system of meanings. Social reality consists of numerous more or less discrete universes of meaning, each requiring separate elucidation. The 'audience' also divides up into 'communities' each possessing some unique possibilities or tendencies for attributing meaning. Media content, as we have seen, is also composed on the basis of more than one code, language or sign-system. All this makes it impossible, even absurd, to assume that any category system of references can be constructed in which a given element is likely to mean precisely the same in the 'reality', in the content, to the audience member and to the media analyst. It follows from structuralist theory that it is very difficult to carry out research which relates or even compares findings in one of these 'spheres' with findings in another.

This comparison does not indicate the superiority of one approach over the other, since, despite the claim at the outset that these methods have something in common, there are few criteria which would be appropriate for a joint assessment. Structuralism does not offer a systematic method and is not accountable in its results according to normal standards of reliability. It is not a generalizing method in the same sense as is content analysis because it generalizes about form rather than substance. It offers no way of knowing whether or not its findings are 'representative'. Nor is it in summarizing method, like most descriptive social science methods, including content analysis. Rather it produces a volume of 'findings' that is usually much larger than the text analysed, even if the results may be regarded as broadly true of many other similar examples with the same genre.

Other variants and possibilities

In pursuit of one or more of the objectives stated at the outset, it has often been thought permissible and necessary to depart from the pure form of 'Berelsonian' or 'Barthian' analysis and a number of enquiries use combinations of both approaches, despite their divergent assumptions. A good example of such a hybrid approach is the work on British television news of the Glasgow Media Group (1976; 1980; 1985), which combines rigorous and detailed quantitative analysis of industrial news in relation to the industrial 'reality', together with an attempt to 'unpack' the cultural meaning of specific news stories and elucidate the many methods of signification which comprise the meaning system of television news. The school of 'cultural indicators' as represented by Gerbner and colleagues (see below, pp. 283–4) has also sought to arrive at the 'meaning structure' of dominant forms of television output by way of systematic quantitative analysis of overt elements of television representation.

In principle, any systematic attempt to characterize or typify bodies of content qualifies for inclusion within the range of approaches that has been identified between manifest categorization and critical or moral evaluation. There are also other methods which do not easily belong to either of the main approaches desribed. Three such approaches deserve recognition. One is the psychoanalytic approach favoured at an early stage of content study, which focuses on the motivation of 'characters' and the underlying meaning of dominant themes in the popular (or less so) culture of a given society or period (e.g. Kracauer, 1949; Wolfenstein and Leites, 1947; McGranahan and Wayne, 1948).

A variant (which is not usually psychoanalytic) of the purposeful study of themes and plots and which has developed its own strong tradition concerns the fiction designed especially for women (see Tuchman et al., 1978). An interesting example is offered by Radway (1984) who combines a detailed study of the motives and responses of female readers of mass produced romance stories with an examination of their contents. She describes the basic narrative logic of the romance in a series of stages from an identity disturbance for the heroine, through an antagonistic encounter with an aristocratic male, by way of a separation, to a reconciliation and a sexual union, concluding with a restoration of identity. Radway interprets the dominant tendency of this category of fiction as supportive of patriarchalism:

> the romance also provides a symbolic portrait of the womanly sensibility that is created and required by patriarchal marriage and its sexual division of labour . . . the romance underscores and shores up the very psychological structure that guarantees women's commitment to marriage and motherhood.

The descriptive interpretation offered is not likely to have been reached either by quantitative content analysis or by semiology on its own.

Another longstanding approach has been concerned with form, style and word usage, especially in the service of evaluating media comprehensibility or readability, identifying authorship, or as a form of political intelligence (Lasswell et al., 1952). Thirdly, there is a possibility for a functional content analysis, as yet not widely developed, according to which media, and content within media, can be classified according to the dominant functions served for the audience (see below, pp. 233–7). In this connection mention should also be made of the study of political language (Bell, 1975; Edelman, 1967; Graber, 1976; 1981). Thus Graber (1976) names the following set of functions of political communication which could well serve as a category system for content analysis and, when applied, as a measure of purpose of one main kind of communicator: to arouse attention; to establish linkages and define situations; to make commitments; to create policy-relevant moods; to stimulate action (mobilize); to act directly (words as actions): to use words as symbolic rewards for actual or potential supporters.

Such possibilities are a reminder of the *relative* character of most analysis of content, in that there has invariably to be some outside point of reference or purpose according to which one chooses one form of classification rather than another. While structural analysis seems to avoid this form of relativism and Burgelin claims as much for it, it too can only supply meaning in terms of a much larger system of cultural meanings. The possibilities for speaking about content are thus extensive and without foreseeable limit and no one result will seem to serve all purposes.

One recurrent problem with all methods and approaches is the gap that often exists between the outcome of such work and the perceptions of the creators and producers on the one hand and the audience on the other. The creators tend to think of what is unique and distinctive in what they do, while the latter are inclined to think of content in terms of a mixture of conventional genre or type labels and a set of satisfactions which have been experienced or are expected. The version extracted by the content analyst is thus rarely easily accessible or communicable to the two main sets of participants in the mass communication enterprise (producers and receivers) and often remains a scientific or literary abstraction.

Media content and reality: a unifying theme of research

Because there are many purposes for studying content there are even more numerous and divergent hypotheses about it and no possibility, in consequence, of having any single theory of media content. However, insofar as there is any unity in research involving media content it is provided by the question of the relation between what is represented and some external standard of *reality*. This happens to be the main issue posed by the framework outined in chapter 3 (Figure 9, p. 54), since it concerns the way in which the mediating role of mass communication is carried out. Each of the purposes for content analysis stated at the outset of the chapter can also be framed in terms of this issue. Content is often classified according to expectations concerning its closeness to reality (another use of the scheme suggested by Elliott, p. 153 above) and we conventionally make a key distinction between fact and fiction, past and present, etc. The question of how media relates to society is centrally about the degree to which media content reflects the reality of society. The criteria by which the influence of communicators, their organizations and the production process on the media product is measured and evaluated usually involve some notion of reality reflection.

Hypotheses about media effects also often depend on the same issue. The more there is a gap between media experience and other 'real-life' experience, the more influence is usually attributed to the media. The study of media languages and codes is mainly a study of how references are made to 'reality' and the most common evaluations of media content in informational or moral/cultural terms involve conformity to reality as a main criterion. The typical questions asked are often as follows. Do news reports record events accurately and fully? Whose version of social reality is conveyed? Do the media reflect the full range of views in society? Are social groups and minorities portrayed objectively? Is violence as portrayed in media similar in degree and kind to what occurs in society? Whatever philosophical uncertainties attach to the concept of reality they do not greatly worry media producers, audiences, critics, or even researchers.

There are familiar conventions by which the reality claims of content can be recognized and judged. The highest expectation of 'trueness to reality' is attached to 'news' and to 'information'. Much fiction occupies an intermediate or indeterminate position, but some is clearly marked as reflecting a particular reality of time and place, even if stories and characters are invented. The dominant mode of story-telling at the present time is realistic or naturalistic. There is also a set of contents which are generally regarded as fantasy or abstractions, with correspondingly low reality expectations on the part of their audiences. At the extreme, we find science fiction, supernatural, mythical and horror stories, together with some abstract forms of communication such as music and dance.

Aside from the reasons cited above for such an interest in the reality component of mass communication content, there are political explanations. Wherever there is political control or surveillance of mass media content (thus, everywhere) the attention of controllers is concentrated more on content which might be thought to have some message about current reality. The more severe the control or surveillance, the sharper the attention of controllers to marginal categories, such as historical dramas or possible allegories, and the more these non-realistic forms are used by critical writers to express their views on society. The ban on the novel for centuries in most of Latin America under Spanish state and church control before independence illustrates the acknowledged potential of fiction for subversion and has left a permanent mark on the literature of the region.

Media content and reality: some evidence

Not only does much research have a unifying theme, but there is also a fairly unified answer to the central question. Wherever media content may actually lie on the dimension of reality expectation, it is likely to deviate away from reality as conventionally understood or as open to measurement. Some of the main points of evidence can be summarized and illustrated in advance of possible theoretical explanations.

1. From studies of *news*, the following kinds of systematic deviation from reality have often been identified.

– There is a consistent over-representation of the social 'top' or of elites as *sources* of news. Governments, heads of state, official spokespersons provide views, versions of reality and 'make news' much more than 'lower level' participants in events and 'ordinary people' (e.g. cf. Hackett, 1984; Golding and Elliott, 1979; McQuail, 1977; Beharrell and Philo, 1977).

- The *objects* of news reporting are also more likely to be members of political or social elites. In western media at least, there is no proportional reflection of the society in any statistical sense.
- Events are more likely to figure in the news the more they have a large-scale, dramatic, sudden or violent character. Such events are by definition untypical and in fact the more events are 'true to normal reality', the less newsworthy they are (Hall, 1973a).
- Themes of reporting are likely to show a bias towards dominant (or consensual) social and community values. The 'reverse content analysis' of Breed (1958) suggested this to be true of the typical American newspaper and the 'good of the town' may be more important to local media than simple dissemination of facts.
- Numerous studies have shown a bias in international reporting towards news concerning countries which are culturally, econ-omically and politically 'close', regardless of size or proximity (McQuail, 1977; Gerbner and Marvanyi, 1977; Womack, 1981; Sreberny-Mohammadi, 1984). The nationalistic or ethnocentric bias of news can show up not only in quantitative, but also in qualitative, terms and in the use of language which influences the portrayal of reality. An example of a 'patriotic' bias in language use was provided by the Glasgow Media Group (1985) comparison of British TV news reporting of the sinking of the Argentine ship, the *Belgrano* and a British ship, the *Sheffield*, in the hostilities of 1982. In the former case, there were ninety-six 'casualty statements' in all, of which only twelve used words such as 'death', 'killing' or 'perish', while of 193 casualty statements relating to the British loss, 'death' words numbered eighty-five. The reality of the Belgrano event was presented in a 'softer', more abstract, manner to the British viewer, whatever may have been the explanation.
- In news, women figure less frequently than men and in less varied roles (Baehr, 1980).
- In varying degrees, minorities, deviants and outgroups of many kinds receive differential treatment which bears little relation to their actual numbers or significance (Shoemaker, 1984). The general pattern is of ignoring minority groups which are not troublesome and giving disproportionate attention to those thought to be troublesome for society (Fedler, 1973). The latter are also usually treated negatively, which in itself can involve exagger-ation or misrepresentation of facts (Cohen, 1972). Cohen coined the term 'moral panic' to characterize the collective social response

which the media at times seem to promote in response to deviance.

- Ethnic minorities, especially black minorities in white societies, appear to share some of the disadvantages and distortions of untypical treatment accorded to deviants, although it may be mixed with sympathetic treatment. They are often highlighted as problematic for society even when they are actually reported as victims (Hartman and Husband, 1974).
- Crime reporting tends to far over-represent violent crime against persons (Roshier, 1973; Graber, 1980).

2. In the case of *fiction*, one can make a somewhat similar list of tendencies for the world of the media to diverge from the world as measured in other ways. Some typical findings are as follows.

- Occupational distribution of characters does not follow distributions found in national labour statistics. Generally, there is an over-representation of those in higher status occupations (DeFleur, 1964; Seggar and Wheeler, 1973). Dominant occupations seem to be: medical, legal, law enforcement, show-business, military, at their higher levels.
- Ethnic minorities have been shown frequently to have a disproportionately low status or dubious role in society, even if the situation seems to have 'improved' in the United States, since Berelson's study in 1940 (Berelson and Salter, 1946). Whether the portrayal is favourable or not is less important here than its realism, and policies to 'improve' minority images on television do not always increase conformity to social reality.
- Women, when not, as in the news, relatively invisible, also tend to appear in stereotyped occupational and domestic roles, which do not usually correspond with reality (Tuchman et al., 1978). The pattern of inequality of women in fiction does not correspond with the pattern of inequality in society.
- Violence, as often shown, occurs in amounts and types of media fiction which bears little relation to reality. Gerbner (e.g. with Gross, 1976) has most thoroughly documented this tendency for US television and has formulated a set of 'TV answers' to questions about the reality of American society. These are put to television viewers to see if amount of television viewing is associated with adoption of the 'TV version of the world' rather than the real (statistically) version. For example, the 'TV answer' (based on the incidence of violence in TV fiction) to the question 'what are your chances of being involved in some kind of violence?' in any week is 10 percent, while the 'right answer' (based on crime statistics) is 1 percent.

- Media fiction of all kinds continues systematically to purvey myths about history, present-day society and its institutions, and about human behaviour, especially in matters which involve the nation, crime, sexuality, war.
- Fiction designed for very large (or international) audiences is likely to reflect dominant, 'official' or consensual (non-controversial) viewpoints (e.g. Schlesinger et al., 1983).

As has been emphasized, the expectations about reality representation which are distributed in society and which define different kinds of content and sources are highly variable. It would be foolish to suppose that all those kinds of deviation mentioned are problematic, undesirable or even avoidable. The media are constrained to be both selective and also fairly consistent and the result is inevitably a bias of some kind. In informational matters it is often the departure from normality which is relevant and interesting to have news of, rather than normality (which equals reality by some definitions).

In fiction, expression and communication may best be achieved by way of the portrayal of the unusual, the special case, by providing a contrast with 'normality'. It is also an expectation from fiction, and therefore a purpose, that it should 'take people out of themselves' and distance them from reality. Fiction can use invention and fantasy to comment on reality. Even so the tendencies indicated are not simply to be dismissed on commonsense grounds or as unavoidable. There is little inevitable about the particular forms taken by systematic 'deviation'. Even if the tendencies are not problematic, the implications for effects do not disappear. It is, therefore, important to look at alternative explanations for the evidence which has been summarized.

Theories of reality-deviation

Functional theory

Functional theory offers several possibilities of accounting for the tendencies described, depending on whether we take the point of view of the society or of the individual. From the point of view of the society, media can contribute to continuity, social control, integration and motivation by symbolically rewarding those who conform to the social and economic values and succeed according to them, and by punishing those who do not conform, or who rebel. Hence the positive emphasis on the 'top' and on 'in-groups'. Further, the societal need for 'tension-management' is served by a diversionary emphasis on fantasy, unreality, dreams and 'escape'.

From the individual point of view, the 'undue' emphasis on the elite and on the accepted values may also meet certain needs for models, objects of identification, value reinforcement, while diversion from reality also makes the burdens of reality more bearable. The empirical weakness of the functional explanation lies in the ease with which it can be turned around to suit alternative interpretation. For instance an over-representation of crime or violence may seem to confirm its 'normality' and spread its incidence, while too much fantasy and lack of accurate information unfits a society collectively and individually from coping with its own real environment. There is a limit to the positive function of ignorance.

Conspiracy or hegemony theory

Conspiracy or hegemony theory can, with little exercise of the imagination, be found to account for many of the findings about content as reflecting exercise of societal control by self-interested elites or classes. Their power is likely to be reinforced by public ignorance of social reality, emphasis on the legitimacy of the state and established class institutions, delegitimation of challenges to the social order and diversion of discontent and frustration towards the scapegoat deviants, militants and non-conformists. The weakness, noted already, is the lack of a good explanation of how ruling classes achieve such favourable tendencies in the media, and indeed the difficulty of establishing that they do so at all.

Organizational theory

Several lines of explanation may be subsumed under this heading. The political-economic approach can explain why economic and market forces lead to many of the deviations from reality already noted: the concentration on majority tastes of majority audiences; the lower diversity of media outlets and thus the narrower range of societal access; the value placed on mass production and repetition. In general, what is new, original, informative, diverse, will cost more and be less profitable. Secondly, many of the tendencies described in the preceding chapter would also be predictive of some consistent 'distortions' of reality. Objectivity requirements in news place a high value on higher status sources, as does the need to ensure a supply of news. The somewhat closed or insulated world of the media organization in itself limits the 'reality input' from society. Several pressures in the media environment dictate a need to seek security and safety, although the freedom of media from pressure is greatest in matters of fiction and fantasy (the typology of societal access on p. 153 is relevant here).

Thirdly, much media content is a reworking of themes and images from the past of a culture, often perpetuating elements of a pre-democratic past in which values of race, nation and social hierarchy have been embedded. The available cultural stock on which the media depend is inherently likely to lag behind contemporary reality. In sum, many features of media organization and production process militate against a close engagement with, and reflection of, reality and even against social representatives.

The audience as determinant

One cannot rule out the possibility that many 'deviations from reality' do chiefly reflect the response of the media to the wishes of their audience. Certainly this is the theory which would find most favour with the media themselves (Cantor, 1982). There is a good deal of evidence that audiences do have only a limited interest in reality content (as news, documentary, information) especially where it does not seem very close or relevant to everyday concerns. Audiences do also show a strong preference for fiction, the exciting and unusual, providing it is not too disturbing (which may often mean not very realistic). There is also a demonstrable demand for the more comforting myths, for nostalgia and for social amnesia (Davis, 1981). The dominant definition of media use is probably for relaxation or escape in free time. For many, reality means work and responsibilities which are burdensome and media are valued precisely because they provide an alternative.

There are other explanations for audience tendencies of the kind described but, whatever their plausibility, it is clear that they could not have effects on content directly, but only as filtered through interpretations made by media organizations. An early example of research on media content and social reality (Martel and McCall, 1964) showed that US story magazines tended consistently to over-represent the demographic characteristics of intended readership groups in the universe of characters in stories. This is an example of a tendency on the part of media to offer an ideal rather than a real world for choice and identification. It is consistent with a common self-view of the media that they are an agent of social change, but it is inconsistent with the claim to reflect reality in any direct way. We are left with some uncertainty about how far the actual preferences of the audiences do account for many of the phenomena described.

Comment

Each of these theories has the weakness that it appears to explain everything. They are, consequently, of limited use, since they cannot account for exceptions to general tendencies and they actually explain very little. Since decisions about media content are made in media organizations, it is likely that the best explanations will be found there (Cantor, 1982). However, media organizations are so constrained by pressures of the moment, past traditions and conventions, as well as by their own myths and unthought-out assumptions, that the surface explanations offered by media communicators themselves cannot be accepted at face value.

We are left with organizational factors, outside the realm of individual choice, as the most likely source of explanation for seemingly large-scale reality deviations. We also have some cause for reflection on whether the whole set of propositions about chosen criteria of reality reflection are relevant and adequate. At the very least we need ways of assessing content which are more sensitive to the different ways in which truth about reality may be conveyed. It is time also to abandon assumptions about the unique authority of numbers and to recognize that the 'decoding' skills of experienced audience members are sufficient, when coupled with personal experience of society, to enable them to learn about reality from the most unlikely content.

Media genres and formats

The word 'genre' in common use simply means a kind or type of any object. It was first used in cultural matters to refer to a particular kind of realistic painting in the nineteenth century, but in literary and film theory it has the common usage meaning of any recognizable category or type of cultural product. In film theory, it has been especially controversial, because of its links with structuralism and because of the tension between individual creative authorship and location in a genre. An emphasis on the genre tends to stress the extent to which the value of a work comes from the culture rather than from the individual artist, who simply follows the rules laid down by the particular school of production. For use in relation to most mass media content, however, the concept of genre can be useful and is not especially controversial, since the question of artistic authorship does not usually arise and a somewhat 'materialist' usage of the word is in order (Andrew, 1984).

For our purpose, genre can refer to any category of content which has the following characteristics:

- It has an identity recognized more or less equally by its producers (the media) and its consumers (media audiences);
- This identity (or definition) relates to its purposes (e.g. information, entertainment, or subvariants); its form (length, pace, structure, language, etc); and its meaning (reality reference).
- It has been established over time and observes familiar conventions. It tends to preserve cultural forms, although these can also change and develop within the framework of the original genre (see the discussion of the western movie above, p. 188);
- A particular genre, as already implied, will follow an expected structure of narrative or sequence of action, draw on a predictable stock of images and have a repertoire of variants of basic themes.

The genre may be considered as a practical device for helping any mass medium to produce consistently and efficiently and to relate its production to the expectations of its customers. Since it is also a practical device for enabling individual media users to plan their choices, it can be considered as a mechanism for ordering the relations between the two main parties to mass communication. According to Andrew (1984, p. 110) genres (of film):

> are specific networks of formulas which deliver a certified product to a waiting customer. They ensure the production of meaning by regulating the viewers' relation to the image and narrative construction for him or her. In fact, genres construct the proper spectators for their own consumption. They build the desires and then represent the satisfaction of what they have triggered.

This view implies a high degree of media determinism which needs to be qualified, but it is at least consistent with the aspirations of media organizations to control the environments in which they operate.

While the genre is a useful general concept for finding one's way in the luxuriant abundance of media output and for finding some organizing principles to help describe and categorize content, it is not a very powerful tool of analysis, since there are simply too many possibilities for applying it. The distinction between one genre and another is also not to be ascertained objectively and the coincidence of recognition and understanding by producers and audience, named above as a characteristic of a genre, is not easy to demonstrate. It is more likely to hold good for the case of films and books where individual acts of choice are made and paid for, guided by publicity, than for television where, arguably, one genre blurs into another for the typical unselective viewer.

Despite these comments, the genre concept has been found helpful and it has been used particularly by Altheide and Snow (1979) to develop a mode of analysis of media content, employing the additional terms 'media logic' and 'media format'. The first refers essentially to a set of implicit rules and norms which govern how content should be processed to take most advantage of the characteristics of a given medium and fit the needs of the media organization (including their view of the needs of the audience).

The operation of a media logic, according to Altheide (1985) implies the existence of a media 'grammar' which governs how time should be used, how items of content should be sequenced and what devices of verbal and non-verbal communication (codes) should be used. Altheide sees content as tailored to fit media formats and formats as tailored to fit listener/viewer preferences and capacities. The formats are essentially sub-routines for dealing with specific themes within a genre. For instance, Altheide describes a 'format for crisis' in television news, which transcends the particularities of events and gives a common shape to the handling of quite different news stories. The main conditions necessary for handling a crisis in the news on a continuing basis are: *accessibility* (to information or to the site of the crisis); *visual quality* (of film or tape); *drama and action*; *relevance* to the audience; *thematic unity*.

Following the same line of thought, Mazzoleni (1987) has suggested that, in the field of political communication, a 'media logic' has tended to encroach on a 'political logic' in the selection and presentation of politics, during campaigns especially, showing itself in more attention to personalities and details of campaign events rather than to abstract political ideas. He has applied the hypothesis to the case of a traditionally very politicized television system, that of Italy (see also Hallin and Mancini, 1984). Without the same terminology, a very similar hypothesis had already been applied to the study of election campaigns in the United States (Graber, 1976) and in Denmark (Siune, 1981).

Graber (e.g. 1981) has made notable contributions to the study of political languages in general and its television versions in particular. She confirms the points made by Altheide in her comment that 'television journalists have developed repertoires — another possible term for frames, logics or sub-genre formats of highly stereotyped cues for many specific situations in politics'. She argues convincingly that the encoding and decoding of audiovisual languages is essentially *different* from that of verbal languages in being: more associational, connotative, unstructured; and less logical, clearly defined, delimited.

The systematic analysis of audiovisual languages is still at an early stage, despite much attention from theorists of film and print. An exploration of this fertile terrain lies outside the scope of this book, but a few more remarks are in order on the distinctive features of audiovisual 'languages', if the term is allowable. A comparison between print media and film/television media suggests the following contrasts which derive from language rather than social factors. Television (and film) is, in general: less regulated by agreed codes; more ambiguous in meaning; lacking in clear authorship (or indication of source); more open; more concrete; more universal; more information-rich.

It does not appear that the distinctive features of television have yet been harnessed to achieve more communicative effectiveness. Both print and audiovisual media have their own in-built inefficiencies and both are severely limited by human information-processing capacity. It may be the case that the full potential of audiovisual languages (and the same applies to alpha-numeric-pictorial forms) has simply not yet been realized in a period of rapid change of technology and experimentation with new forms and purposes of communication media.

Before leaving the subject of genres and formats and related concepts, it is worth emphasizing that they can, in principle, cut across the conventional content categories of media output, including the divide between fiction and non-fiction. This is not too surprising, given the long tradition which allows fiction to draw on real-life situations or historical events for its subject matter, although it may undermine the reality claims of media news and information. Schlesinger et al. (1983) provide a valuable demonstration by analysing the portrayal of terrorism on British television in news, documentary, current affairs and dramatic fiction.

They make an additional contribution to an understanding of the constraints on fictional portrayal of reality referred to above and its potential effect, by introducing two conceptual dimensions into their analysis. These are: 'open' versus 'closed' portrayal and 'tight' versus 'loose' story treatment. An open portrayal is one which allows room for more than one perspective on a topic (in their case, terrorism), including alternative or oppositional viewpoints. A closed portrayal gives an official, dominant or consensual view only. The 'tighter' the storyline, the more a viewer is led to the conclusion chosen by the author, editor or presenter. The two are correlated, but can operate independently and both can apply equally to 'reality' and to fiction. Their own conclusion is that TV news tends to be both 'closed' and 'tight', while documentary and fiction are more variable. However, the larger the audience for fictional portrayals of terrorism the more 'closed' and 'tight' it seemed to be, thus converging on the 'official' picture of reality as portrayed in the news.

In this chapter, for reasons of economy only one genre — that of news — is dealt with in any detail, partly also because it has received so much research attention. In the light of what has been said about genres it may be worth adding a cautionary word or two in advance. First, there is a large range of styles and sub-types within such a broad category as 'news', varying according to medium, intended audience, national culture, etc. This variety may call into question the existence of *a* news genre. Secondly, in a given medium, one type of media logic associated with one medium, often extends into another, bringing inter-genre boundaries into question. For instance, there is reason to think that TV entertainment (and advertising) has a strong influence on the manner of TV news-giving and on the construction of the news bulletin.

The news genre

The centrality of news

It is arguable that the newspaper is the archetype as well as the prototype of all modern mass media (Tunstall, 1977, p. 23) and certain, in any case, that the central ingredient of the newspaper and of those media modelled on it, radio and television, is what we call news. It merits special attention in a discussion of media content just because it is one of the few original contributions of mass media to the range of forms of human expression. It is also the core activity according to which a large part of the journalistic (and thus media) profession defines itself. According to Tuchman (1973–74). 'It would appear that news judgement is the sacred knowledge, the secret ability of the newsman, which differentiates him from other people'.

Further, news provides the component which elevates or distinguishes something called a newspaper from other kinds of media, earns it the protection of free press theory or the sanctions of authoritarian theory, and by convention allows it to express opinion in the name of the public. Media institutions could barely exist without news and news could not exist without media institutions since, unlike almost all other forms of authorship or cultural creation, newsmaking is not something that can be done privately or even individually. The institution provides the machinery for distribution and the guarantee of credibility and authority.

What is news?

While the question is one which journalists themselves find distinctly metaphysical and difficult to answer except in terms of their intuition, 'feel' and innate judgement, attempts to answer it by analysis of media have been revealing. It happens that the two 'founding fathers' of the sociology of news were both former or practising journalists and drew on their own experience in answering the question of the nature of the news. Walter Lippman (1922) focused on the process of news-gathering, which he saw as a search for the 'objective clear signal which signifies an event'. Hence, 'news is not a mirror of social conditions, but the report of an aspect that has obtruded itself'. Our attention is thus directed to what is noticeable (and worthy of notice) in a form suitable for planned and routine inclusion as a news report.

It is for this reason that newspapers survey such places as police stations, law courts, hospitals, legislatures, where events are likely to be first signalled. The second early commentator on news, Robert Park (1940), paid much more attention to the essential properties of news. His starting point was to compare it with another 'form of knowledge', history, which is also a record of past events, and to place news on a continuum that ranges from 'acquaintance with' to 'knowledge about'. News has its own location on such a continuum, being more than the first and less than the second. The result of Park's comparison of news with history can be distilled into a few main points:

- News is timely — about very recent or recurrent events.
- News is unsystematic — it deals with discrete events and happenings and the world seen through news alone consists of unrelated happenings, which it is not the primary task of news itself to interpret.
- News is perishable — it lives only when the events themselves are current and for purposes of record and later reference other forms of knowledge will replace news.

- Events reported as news should be unusual or at least unexpected, qualities which are more important than their 'real significance'.
- Apart from unexpectedness, news events are characterized by other 'news values' which are relative and involve judgements about likely audience interest.
- News is mainly for orientation and attention-direction and not a substitute for knowledge.
- News is predictable. This paradoxical and provocative point is explained by Park (p. 45) as follows:

> if it is the unexpected that happens it is not the wholly unexpected which gets into the news. The events that have made news in the past, as in the present, are actually the expected things . . . it is on the whole the accidents and incidents that the public is prepared for . . . the things that one fears and that one hopes for that make news.

The same point has subsequently been put more succinctly by Galtung and Ruge (1965) in the remark 'news' are actually 'olds'. This assertion makes sense in the light of what has been said about strategies of news-gathering and news production and we can add that readers will have from past experience an expectation about the kind of events they will find reported in the news and that newspapers will try to meet these expectations.

There have been other contributors to the general characterization of news, amongst them Warren Breed (1956) who listed the following terms descriptive of news: 'saleable', 'superficial', 'simple', 'objective', 'action-centred', 'interesting' (as distinct from significant), 'stylized', 'prudent'. He also suggested several dimensions along which an item of news might be placed: news versus truth; difficult versus routine (in terms of news-gathering); information versus human interest. Further sources of variation in news have to do with its significance for future events, its relationship to editorial control, its function for the reader, its visibility to the public, its visibility to newsmen.

According to Hall (1973a), there are three basic 'rules of news visibility': (1) its link to an event or occurrence (the component of action); (2) its recency; and (3) its newsworthiness or link to some important thing or person. Noteworthy, in Hall's view, is that news is itself responsible for creating over time the 'consensus' knowledge, by which newsworthiness is recognized by newspeople and accepted as such by the public. He writes: 'the ideological concepts embodied in photos and texts in a newspaper do not produce new knowledge about the world. They produce recognition of the world as we have already learnt to appropriate it'.

News and human interest

In Breed's characterization, news is at one point contrasted with 'human interest', implying that the former has to do with serious information, the latter with something else — perhaps entertaining, personalized, sensational. In practice it seems hard to separate the two and both have been elements in the newspaper since its earliest appearances.

A classic study by a pupil of Park, Helen McGill Hughes (1940), examined the relationship between the two forms of content and argued that the (American) newspaper had been 'transformed from a more or less sober record into a form of popular literature'. In her view, a human interest story is not intrinsically different from other news stories, but takes its character from the particular attitude which the writer adopts to the reader — it is a story which is intended to divert, but also one which is told, as it were, from the reader's point of view. It can, in consequence, be told only by a reporter who is 'able to see the world as his readers do'. Hence it is more akin to gossip or the folk tale.

The characteristics of news are derived to a larger extent than is sometimes recognized from much older traditions of story telling and it has been suggested by Darnton (1975) that our conceptions of news result from 'ancient ways of telling stories'. The tendency for news reports to be cast in the form of a narrative, with principal and minor actors, connected sequence, heroes and villains, beginning, middle and end, signalling of dramatic turns, a reliance on familiar plots, has often been noted.

In general the tendency for media to replace and incorporate earlier story-telling and moralizing forms has been termed the 'bardic function' by Fiske and Hartley (1978), a function which cuts across the line dividing 'reality' from 'fictional' content. While it may seem diversionary to pay much attention to elements of news which are subsidiary to informational purposes, it remains the case that much newspaper content is more akin to 'human interest' than 'news' about politics, economics and society (Curran et al., 1981). Human interest is vital to the economics of news and it helps us to understand the nature of 'news values'.

News values and the structure of news

One general conclusion from the many studies of news content is that news exhibits a rather stable and predictable overall pattern when measured as to quality and conventional categories of subject matter. There are variations from one country to another and one medium type to another and the pattern is naturally responsive to major events, such as war and world crisis. Nevertheless, the stability of news content is often quite remarkable to those who argue that the content of news is very much determined by a variety of external political, ideological and cultural constraints and by internal organizational and technical requirements. Some of these matters have already been discussed and here we shall attend mainly to internal tendencies connected with the nature of news as it has been characterized above.

The single most valuable source in the quest for explanation has been the work of Galtung and Ruge (1965) who identified and inter-related the main factors influencing the selection of (foreign) news. In essence there are three types of factors: organizational; genre-related; socio-cultural. The organizational factors are the most universal and least escapable and they have some 'ideological' consequences. Thus news media prefer: 'big' (large-scale or 'major') events; events which are clear and unambiguous; events which occur in a time-scale which fits the normal production schedule (usually within 24 hours); events which are easiest to pick up and report and which are easily recognizable and of accepted relevance (cultural proximity).

Among genre-related factors are: a preference for events which fit advance audience expectations (consonance with past news); a bias towards what is unexpected and novel within the limits of what is familiar; a wish to continue with events already established as newsworthy; a wish for balance among types of news events. Galtung and Ruge distinguish only socio-cultural influences that derive from 'north European' culture and especially news values favouring events which are about elite persons, elite nations and negative happenings. Events with all these values are believed to produce most audience interest and these values are consistent with several of the organizational and genre-related selection requirements. Thus 'bigness' goes with eliteness; personal actions fit the short time-scale and are least ambiguous and most 'bounded'; negative events often fit the time schedule, are unambiguous and can be personalized (e.g. disasters, killings, crimes, etc).

This framework has been found to apply fairly widely beyond the case from which it was first derived and beyond foreign news alone. It tells a certain amount about the kind of event that will tend to be reported and, by implication, about what will be neglected. Thus it is predictive of a pattern of one general kind of news 'bias'. News will not tend to deal with: distant and politically unimportant nations;

non-elites; ideas; institutions and structures; long-term undramatic processes (e.g. social change itself); many kinds of 'good news'. The theory does not offer a complete explanation of all regularities of news composition and an alternative, less psychological and more structural, approach to explanation has been recommended by Rosengren (1974) who argues that several features of news flows can be accounted for by political and economic factors. He demonstrates that flows of trade between countries are good predictors of mutual news attention and one might expect that within countries the giving or withholding of attention might have as much to do with political and economic factors as with the news values of individual news selectors.

The question of news structure has sometimes tended to be argued in terms of 'bias', yet it need not be so, especially as the term has the connotation of a deliberate tendency to mislead (McQuail, 1986b). It is noteworthy that the characterization of news offered above does not place great emphasis on objectivity and its correlates, such as truth and accuracy. Indeed, since judgements of news value are agreed to be relative and based on a 'feel for the news' at the particular moment of time, there must be strong elements of subjectivity. Objectivity is no more than a mode of procedure, as noted above (pp. 130–1), little different in journalism than in history or social science (Benet, 1970). Journalists do not usually claim to tell in the news what is *objectively* most important, significant or relevant for their audiences since, in the dominant western liberal tradition, there are no criteria for objectivity in this sense, although Nordenstreng (1974) provides an interesting step in this direction. In the light of all the evidence about regularities of news content it is hard to resist Gerbner's (1964) conclusion that 'there is no fundamentally non-ideologically, apolitically, non-partisan, news-gathering and reporting system'.

Two versions of the news sequence

Despite the progress of media research and theory there remains a gap between two different conceptions of the newsmaking process in which the ideas discussed play a part and the gap tends to separate the 'commonsense' journalistic view from the position which derives from content and media organizational analysis. Four elements are related in a different sequence in the two views: events; criteria of news selection (news values); news interests of the public; news report. The 'view from the media' emphasizes the reality-responsive quality of news and the analytical viewpoint the structured and autistic nature of the news selection process. According to the former view, the sequence is as follows:

events ⟶ news criteria ⟶ news report ⟶ news interest

This sequence begins with the world of unpredictable happenings which 'obtrude' and break the normality and to which news media respond by applying criteria concerning relative significance for their public. They compile objective news reports of the chosen events and the public responds with attention and interest or not, a datum which feeds into subsequent selection behaviour. The alternative model of the sequence is:

news interest ⟶ news criteria ⟶ events ⟶ news report

Here the starting point is experience of what gains the attention of the public, which contributes to a rather stable and enduring set of news criteria, including the organizational and genre requirements. News events are only recognized as newsworthy if they conform to these selection criteria. News reports are then written in conformity to news criteria, guided more by the news organization's own requirements and routine practices than by reference to the 'real world' of events or what audiences 'really' want or need. It is not necessary to make an absolute choice between the models, but they cannot both be true to what happens. The second version is a further illustration of the deployment of the 'attention-display' model described in chapter 2.

The form of the news report

A good deal of attention has recently been paid not only to the nature of news as a concept, and to the influences which shape its production, but also to the form in which it appears. Part of the claim that news is a particular cultural genre or type, in the same sense as the novel, feature film or opera, rests on observations about the constancy, predictability and universality of the news form. While much recent attention has been paid to television news (e.g. Glasgow Media Group, 1976; 1980; 1985; Frank, 1973; Altheide, 1974; 1985; Altheide and Snow, 1979; Schlesinger, 1978; Gans, 1979; Hetherington, 1985), there is a good deal of overlap between the main features of news in the newspapers and on television. This is not surprising, given the origin of television news, but the seemingly small difference that has been made by developments in visual reporting is rather remarkable. The elements of form shared by press and radio or television fall into three main categories: those to do with recurrence; and those relating to neutrality and facticity.

It should be borne in mind that two levels of formation are involved — one on the level of the separate news item and the other the whole news 'packet' (newspaper page or news bulletin or radio or television). While the media are comparable in this respect, the newspaper or page has to be structured spatially and the television news temporally, giving rise to some obvious differences of device.

Several researchers have been struck by the great regularity of structure of the news vehicle (newspaper or bulletin) which seems only partly accountable in terms of the needs of the production process (Van Dijk, 1983). Newspapers and bulletins are regular in appearance, but also length or duration and in the balance of types of content, when divided into 'topic categories', such as 'foreign', 'political', 'sport', 'economic', 'human intrest', etc (McQuail, 1977). In television news the average duration of items shows a high degree of constancy, so that the number of items does not vary much from one 'bulletin' to another and there is even a relationship between type of content and average duration (Glasgow Media Group, 1976). Some of these features of regularity are found to be much the same in different countries (Rositi, 1976). What is striking is the extent to which a presumably unpredictable universe of events seems open to incorporation, day after day, into much the same temporal or spatial frame. It is true that deviations occur, at times of crisis or exceptional event, but the news form is posited on the notion of normality and routine and might be thought to reinforce the notion of normality through its regularity.

The second main aspect of news form has to do with indications of order and devices for structuring the whole. Analyses of news content show two main devices for indicating the relative significance of events reported. One is relative primacy of items in the newspaper space or the time of the bulletin. According to what the Glasgow Media Group (1980) calls 'viewers' maxims' it will be understood that first appearing items are most 'important', and that, generally, items receiving more time are also more important. It is common knowledge that newspages, newspapers and news bulletins are put together with a view to their overall appearance or possible effect and are not a random set of items, even after allowance has been made for the principle of order of importance.

However, it has not been easy to turn daily observation into systematic theory or general statement. Television news bulletins are generally constructed with a view to arousing initial interest, by highlighting some event, maintaining it by diversity and human interest and holding back some vital information to the end (sports results and weather forecast), sending the viewer away with a light touch at the close. The suspicion persists that there is more to the overall balance of items than the mechanics of keeping attention and the Glasgow Media Group argue that it has to do with an underlying 'primary framework' or view of the world which is essentially ideological.

Rositi's (1976) search for the latent organization in the television news of four European countries led to rather modest, but interesting, results: 'perhaps the only latent organization to be found at the level of the entire news program is that described as the movement from a fragmented image of society in its recomposition through the homogeneity of interests and political representation'. The regularities described characterize the dominant 'western' news form and it is likely that media operating under different 'press theories' will exert different kinds of regularity.

There are almost certainly significant and systematic differences between television news-giving in different societies. A comparison of US and Italian television news, for instance, led to the conclusion that each system's news gives a quite different conception of what politics is about (Hallin and Mancini, 1984). The main differences were attributed to the much larger space occupied by a public sphere, other than the state, in the case of Italy, with the result that US journalists have a much larger role as representatives of the public than they adopt, or are attributed, in Italian circumstances.

Much news form is clearly devoted to pursuit of objectivity in the sense of facticity or factualness. The language of news is 'linear', elaborating an event report along a single dimension with added information, illustration, quotation, discussion. According to the Glasgow Media Group (1980, p. 160) 'the language of news seems to be in a form which would allow of a fairly simple test of its truth or falsity. It has the appearance of being entirely constative (propositional and capable of being shown to be true or false) and not performative'. Both terms are taken from Austin and have been used by Morin (1976) in an attempt to describe the basic ambiguity of the news discourse. According to her (structuralist) analysis of the news form, an event has to be rendered into a 'story about an event' and the process of doing so involves a negotiation between two opposed modes — that of the 'performative', which is also the interpretative and the 'fabulative' (story-telling) mode, and that of the 'constative' which is also the 'demonstrative' and factual mode. Thus pure facts have no meaning and pure performance stands far from the irreversible, rationally-known, fact of history. In her view, different kinds of story involve different combinations of both and can be plotted against the two 'axes' of the television discourse.

There is little doubt of the vital nature of facticity to the news genre. As Smith writes 'The whole idea of news is that it is beyond a plurality of viewpoints' (1973, p. 174). In his view, without an attribution of credibility by the audience news could not be distinguished from entertainment or propaganda. This may point to one reason why Gans' (1979) seemingly reasonable plea for 'multi-perspectival news' is unlikely to receive universal acclaim and why the secular trend in news development has been away from ideology and towards neutrality. Much of what remains unsaid here about the nature of the news form has to do with devices for maintaining the claim to credibility, which involve, in television news, the inclusion of film and tape containing direct evidence, illustration, interview and discussion, part of which is directed towards establishing a 'balanced presentation', which in the news culture is strongly related to credibility.

CHAPTER 8
THE MEDIA AUDIENCE

Duality of the audience

The term 'media audience' has a wide currency and a rather simple surface meaning as the aggregate of persons forming the readers, listeners, viewers for different media or their component items of content. As such, there would seem little scope for alternative theories of the audience. Yet this apparently straightforward phenomenon conceals different ways of looking at such aggregates and wide variations in the reality and conception of the audience.

The most important source of variation, and thus the source of alternative theories about the audience, is its fundamentally dual character. It is a collectivity which is formed either in response to media (channels and content) or out of independently existing social forces (when it corresponds to an existing social group or category or the result of activities by a social group to provide itself with its own channels of communication (media). Often it is inextricably both at the same time.

Thus fans of a particular writer, musical group or television series are its audience, but an audience which cannot easily be localized in time or place and may have no other existence as a social group. At the other extreme, the residents in a small community may have their own local newspaper which serves their needs but which has played no part in bringing the community into being or defining its boundaries or determining its continuity. There are many empirical variants of the relationship between media as source and people as receivers which produce different kinds of audience and many questions in the study of audiences which have arisen from this diversity.

The issues to be dealt with in this chapter are all in one way or another connected with the fact that audiences are both a cause of, and a response to, a supply of messages. These issues have to do with the extent to which an audience is a social group, the degree and kinds of activity which audiences can and do engage in, the forces which contribute to the formation of audiences and the extent to which media 'manipulate' their audiences or are, in turn, responsive to them. We look first at the audience concept itself, since it can appear under different names or with different meanings for the same name. These alternative versions of the audience sometimes stand for different ways of perceiving the same thing and sometimes for different realities.

The rise of the audience

The historical roots of the audience phenomenon have contributed much to the shaping of current meanings of the audience concept. The original 'audience' was the set of spectators for drama, games, spectacles, for performances of all kinds which have taken different forms in different civilizations and stages of history. Despite variations, some central features of the pre-media audience have persisted and still shape our understanding and expectation.

- The audience was planned for in advance and thus organized.
- It was localized in place and time, often with special provisions to maximize the quality of 'reception'.
- It belonged to the *allocutory* (direct address) mode of communication (see p. 41).
- The settings for the audience (theatres, halls, churches, arenas, etc) were designed with indications of rank and status of spectators.
- It was a *public* and open gathering.
- It was the result of *individual* and *voluntary* acts of choice.
- These acts were motivated by expectations of *enjoyment* or related experiences of admiration, amusement, pity, relief, terror, etc.
- It was subject to potential or actual *control* by authority of city or state.
- In sum, it was an *institutionalized* form of collective social behaviour with the features listed above.

All these features remain, although they are no longer adequate on their own to account for the audiences of present-day mass communication. The changes in the nature of the audience are the result of changes in communication technology and changes in society. The former have made new kinds of formation possible, the latter have changed the nature and scale of demand for public communication provision. Both kinds of change continue, so that both the concepts and the realities of audiences are continually changing.

The first major historical addition to the audience idea follows the invention of printing (but is also associated with social change) and is the development of a *reading public* — consisting of those who engage in private reading and provide the following for particular authors, publications and genres (including the newspaper). This development tended to *delocalize* the audience, make it *less time-bound* and diversify its basis. Identifiable reading publics could exist without a unique location in time and space. It also introduced a clearer social-economic division of audiences and also a differentiation according to interest, taste, education, politics, religion, as societies began to experience more rapid social and political fragmentation in the print era.

The second main development was the growing commercialization of most forms of public performance and communication, but especially of the print media, leading to larger-scale operation and the separation out of advertising and other media industries. This development strengthened the tendency for media to recruit and shape audiences according to their own plans and interests. It reinforced the concept of audience as an aggregate defined by a set of interests rather than as a social group able to act autonomously.

Thirdly, electronic media have helped further to delocalize and socially 'decompose' the audience, detaching its members from each other and from the senders. The ties of space and time have been loosened and patterns of communication and associated types of relationship have been diversified accordingly. In terms of the alternative patterns of communication described earlier (Figure 7, p. 41) there is now more possibility and likelihood for interactive *exchange*, for *search* and for the registration by sources of audience choices and uses. It is also much easier to record and re-use content at the convenience of the receiver, rather than as determined by the sender. The audience is thus less predictable or open to planning and management than in the ideal-typical case of the original audience as characterized above. While the audience is, in one sense, decomposed and less manageable, from the point of view of the sender, the changes can be interpreted as increasing receiver, and therefore audience, autonomy and diversity.

If one summarizes the consequences of changes for that version of the 'original' audience described above, it would be in the following terms. Audiences in the elementary sense of aggregates giving attention to media sources are less open to planning and prediction by sources: the allocutory (direct address) mode is no longer dominant; reception does not involve participation in a *public* in any sense (either of being a public or of being open); control by authority over reception is much lower; and, in general, the degree of institutionalization is much lower. With these points in mind, we can turn to a review of the main variant concepts of audience which are to be found in common usage and in the research literature about mass media.

Alternative concepts of the audience

The audience as aggregate of spectators, readers, listeners, viewers

This is the audience in its most recognizable form and the version employed in most research for the media themselves. Its focus is number — the total number of persons reached by a given 'unit' of media content and the number of persons within this total of given demographic characteristics of interest to the sender. In practice, the application of the concept is not so simple and leads eventually to considerations beyond the purely quantitative.

Clausse (1968) has indicated some of the complexities of distinguishing varying degrees of participation and involvement by audiences. The first and largest audience is the population which is *available* to receive a given 'offer' of communication. Thus all with television sets are in some sense the television audience. Secondly, there is the audience which actually *receives*, in varying degrees, what is offered — the regular television viewers, newspaper buyers, etc. Thirdly, there is that part of the actual audience which *registers* reception of content and finally there is a still smaller part which *'internalizes'* what is offered and received. Clausse puts this another way by pointing to a series of reductions, from the whole population of society, to the 'potential public' for a message, to the 'effective public' which actually attends, to the 'particular message public' within that and finally to the public actually 'affected' by the communication.

In general, this concept of audience goes no further than the point of reception, or giving of attention, which can be recorded in various ways or estimated after the event, since the commercial or professional interest of the media senders is usually satisfied by such information. Elliott (1972) has made some critical remarks about the limiting effects of this concept of the audience as a body of spectators. The more the maximization of the number of spectators is taken as an end in itself, the less likely is there to be any concern with real communication in the sense of an 'ordered transfer of meaning' (see above, p. 44).

The audience as mass

The meaning of the mass has already been discussed (pp. 30–1) as a key element in the ideal type of mass communication and as originally defined by Blumer (1939) and other sociologists (e.g. Mills, 1956). We can recapitulate by saying that this view of the audience emphasizes its large size, heterogeneity, dispersion, anonymity, lack of social organization and fleeting and inconsistent composition. The mass has no continuous existence except in the minds of those who want to gain the attention of and manipulate as many people as possible. According to Raymond Williams (1961, p. 289) there are no masses, 'only ways of seeing people as masses'. It has, even so, tended to become a standard by which media are judged — the larger and more instantaneous the audience, the more socially significant. It has also become a standard for judging the audience — the more it approaches a mass, the lower must be its culture and taste. The verbal accident which has equated mass with the audience for mass media should not mislead us to favour this conception.

The audience as a public or social group

The key element in this version of the audience is the pre-existence of an active, interactive and largely autonomous social group which is served by particular media, but does not depend on the media for its existence. The idea of a public has already been discussed as it appears in sociology and liberal-democratic theory (see above, p. 31). It was, for example, defined by Dewey (1927) as a 'political grouping of individuals brought into being as a social unit through mutual recognition of common problems for which common solutions should be sought'. Such a grouping needs various means of communication for its development and continuity but, according to Mills (1956), the mass media had developed in such a way as to hinder the formation of publics.

We can, nevertheless, see evidence of the continuing existence of various audience formations with the characteristics of a public. Although rarely identified as such, most societies have an 'informed public' — that section of the audience which is most active in political and social life and draws on many sources of information, especially the elite, opinion-forming and specialist press. Secondly, many countries retain some element of the party press or a press which does have political connections with readership groups (Seymour-Ure, 1974). Here the membership or supporters of a particular party form a public which is also an audience. Thirdly, there are local or community audiences for a local publication, of the kind described by Janowitz (1952). In such cases the audience tends to coincide with the membership, especially the most active members, of a pre-existing community, hence social group (Stamm, 1985). Finally, there are numerous particular audiences formed on the basis of an issue, an interest, or an occupation which may have their own forms of social interaction and are not simply the creation of a media supply.

Instances of such publics are mainly to be found in relation to print media, since film and television have tended in their most commonly instituted forms to avoid links either with more elite 'informed publics', or with party political groups, or with localities. This is less true of radio, but still partly so. There are also exceptions in relation to television, for instance where channels are deliberately profiled by social-economic or taste differences (as in Britain) or by politics (as, to some degree, in France and Italy) or by language and culture (as in Belgium and Switzerland) or by politics and/or religion (as in the Netherlands) or by local community (as in the United States). In general, greater channel capacity and/or societal diversity are associated with the persistence or emergence of audiences for television which have more of the characteristics of social groups or publics. These characteristics include: a degree of self-consciousness and identity, possibilities for internal organization and interaction and for having some autonomous influence on what is offered.

The audience as market

While social-cultural developments led to the original audience and political developments to the concept of the public, it was economic developments in the last century that gave rise to the 'audience as market' concept. A media product is a commodity or service offered for sale to a given body of potential consumers, in competition with other media products. These potential or actual consumers can be referred to as a market and in the United States, where media are almost entirely commercial, it is customary, even in academic contexts, to refer to potential audiences as 'markets', sometimes indicating specific population areas, sometimes indicating aggregates of population characterized in some other way (e.g. young women, farmers or left-handed golfers).

The audience so designated has a dual significance for media, first as set of potential customers for the product, and secondly as an audience for advertising of a certain kind, which is the other main source of media revenue. Thus a market for a media product is also likely to be a market for other products, for which the media will be an advertising vehicle and thus a way of 'recruiting' potential customers for other products (Smythe, 1977). While it is necessary for commercially financed media to regard their audiences as markets in both senses and convenient, sometimes, to characterize given audiences in terms of lifestyle and consumption pattern, there are a number of consequences of this approach for ways of perceiving the audience, which can be expressed as follows.

- It specifies the link between media and their audiences as a consumer-product relationship, hence 'calculative' from the point of view of the consumer and manipulative from the point of view of the sender — in any case it is not a moral or social relationship, as in the case of the audience as public.
- It gives little emphasis to the internal social relationships of the audience: they are a set of individual and equal consumers sharing certain demographic or cultural attributes. This feature of audience markets has been modified by the development of a social relations approach to audience study and a recognition of personal influence, but it still largely holds.
- The audience characteristics most relevant to this way of thinking are social-economic and the stratification of the audience by income and consumption patterns claims special attention.
- From a market perspective, the key fact about audiences is their attention-giving behaviour, expressed mainly in acts of purchase (sales, box office) or viewing, listening and reading choices (ratings). Such data provide the criteria for the success or failure of media content, rather than measures of effective communication or intrinsic quality. The salience of the display-attention model (see p. 45, above) is accentuated by treating audiences as markets.
- The market view is inevitably the view 'from the media'. We never conceive of ourselves as belonging to markets, rather we are placed in market categories or identified as part of a target group by others.

To summarize, we can define the audience as market as an 'aggregate of potential consumers with a known social-economic profile at which a medium or message is directed'. There are similarities with the mass concept (p. 30), since the very largest market (whole population) will have the features of a mass, but market thinking pays much more attention to differentiation within the total available audiences and is concerned with matching media product to believed needs and interests of receivers. In market thinking, there is also attention to cultural tastes and preferences as well as to number or to purely social-economic criteria. Among the audience concepts named, the widest gap lies between market and public, since they diverge sharply in the way they attend to audience origin, to the degree and kind of audience identity and activity, and to the purpose and function of communication.

A typology of audience formation

The diversity of concepts of audience can be made sense of in relation to the initial proposition about its duality, according to the scheme presented in Figure 23. There are two fundamental types of origin of various audiences, but each has at least two sub-types. In reality, of course, sources and actual audiences cannot be so neatly separated out and identified.

Figure 23 The sources of audience formation: a typology

Society as source		Media as source	
I Existing public or social group membership (Group or Public)	II Individual need or purpose arising in social experience (Gratification Set)	III Content (Fan Group or Taste Culture)	IV Channel or medium (Medium Audience)

What is proposed essentially in this scheme is that an audience will belong primarily to one of these sub-categories, which can be further characterized as follows:

I *Group or public.*
– Concomitant with an existing social grouping (e.g. community, membership of political, religious or ethnic minority) and with shared social characteristics of place, social class, politics, culture, etc.
II *Gratification set.*
– Formed on the basis of some individual purpose or need existing independently of the media, relating, for instance, to a political or social issue, a general need for information or for some emotional, affectual satisfaction.
III *Fan group or taste culture.*
– Formed on the basis of an interest in a particular type of content (or genre) or attraction to a particular personality or a particular cultural/intellectual taste.
IV *Audience of a medium.*
– Recruited to and held by habit or loyalty to a particular media source — e.g. a newspaper, magazine, radio or television channel.

These categories are not, of course, mutually exclusive and the primary character of a given audience is not easy to determine empirically. The assessment has to be made on the basis of wider knowledge of a media system and a society. The following remarks explain more fully why and how the four types are to be differentiated.

The first type (group or public) corresponds largely with the concept of audience as public which has already been described. There are more likely to be some normative ties between audience and source and, within the audience, there is likely to be some interaction and sense of identity and purpose. Such audiences are likely to be more stable over time than others, with continuity of membership and to respond to, and have some participation in, what is offered.

The second kind of audience (gratification set), based on a particular need or purpose, is also likely to be fairly homogeneous in terms of its composition, active in expressing demands which shape supply, and also selective. Such audiences are, however, not social groups, but aggregates of individuals engaged in consumer behaviour. They belong to the category of market or aggregate described above. The activity and rational selectivity to be observed is expressed in individual behaviour and the members will not usually see themselves as a particular group or as a market.

The audience defined by content (fan group or taste culture) consists of sets of fans or followers of authors, personalities, genres, but otherwise lacking any clear social definition or categorization. Its composition will change over time, although some such audiences may also be stable. Its existence is owed entirely to the content offered and when this changes (as, for instance, at the end of a long-running show or the death or decline of a star), the audience has to disperse or reform in other ways. Occasionally such kinds of audience are encouraged by the media to form into social groups (as with fan clubs) or they spontaneously transform themselves into social groups. There is, consequently, an element of normative attachment, especially where a high degree of identification or involvement occurs. Nevertheless manipulation of this kind of audience attachment is common and often actively associated with merchandising of products linked to media images, characters, themes etc.

There are many examples of the channel or medium audience and loyalty to channels is also encouraged by the media for commercial reasons. Whether formed spontaneously or by manipulation, such loyalty can give to this kind of audience some of the characteristics of the public or social group-stability over time, boundaries, awareness of identity. For most commercial media, however, audiences of this kind are more like aggregates or markets, and relationships between audience and source are rarely likely to be other than non-moral and calculative. Its members are typically consumers of the media product in question and for other products to be advertised or merchandised.

There is a degree of tension as well of simple differentiation involved in the contrast between society-origination and media-origination, which underlies the typology described. The former goes with strong social and normative ties and mutuality of benefit, while the latter is mainly characterized by (would-be) manipulation from above and (individual) self-interested calculation from 'below'. One is a view 'from society', the other a view 'from the media'. It might also be argued, however, that the former is associated with stronger social control and the latter with more individual choice in a free market for information and culture. It would not be appropriate to make a simple value judgement, even if much of the normative social theory which is applied to media seems to favour the values associated with 'society-origination'. These values can be rationally argued for, but are sometimes based on nostalgia for a lost community and solidarity.

The contrast also has implications for research into audiences, since society-originated audiences are likely to require more qualitative and intensive methods and more study of social and political contexts. The research needs in respect of the media-originated audience are more easy to satisfy by extensive quantitative survey research, in which precise behavioural measures of attention-giving play an important part. The audiences of fans drawn to particular genres have, however, also increasingly attracted their share of intensive research as the motives for such interests seem to call for interpretation (e.g. Radway, 1984; Liebes and Katz, 1986; Levy, 1977, Ang, 1985). An obvious connection exists between the differentiation of audiences and the distinctions made earlier in the book between models of communication (p. 45), since the 'audience as public' (Type I) concept is appropriate to a communication/sharing model, while the media-originated audience types go better with either a 'performance-gratification' or a 'display-attention' model.

Sources of change

Each of the types and concepts of audience described is dependent in some way on a given set of media-technological possibilities and social-historical circumstances and is subject to change. The most significant sources of change at present are:

- The multiplication of media channels and expansion of offer.
- The increasing individualization of reception and use and the

detachment from fixed and accountable systems of distribution (especially as a result of VCRs, cables and satellite).
- The development of interactive media based on computers and cable links, allowing for more search, choice and exchange (see above, pp. 16–17).
- The increased tendency for content to flow across national frontiers.

One consequence of the first two is that it becomes increasingly difficult to predict who will comprise the audience for a given 'item' or to know after the event who was in the audience. It is simply more difficult than in the early days of the media to 'account' for the audience experience and to answer the question 'who receives what?'. The growth of 'interactive' media, although still at a very early stage, is likely further to promote the fragmentation and specialization of media use, but also to give the audience member a potentially more active role. Under pressure of current media changes, the whole concept of the audience as a group or set receiving much the same content at the same time and place is increasingly anachronistic.

The 'de-nationalization' of media reception and content works in the same direction, reducing the social and cultural homogeneity of audiences and accelerating a conception of mass communication as another branch of international marketing. However, this is not the only direction of change, since electronic media also make local and specialist media more viable and the outcome is more likely to be a move towards international and unified form and content on the one hand and, on the other, towards more local and differentiated content. The loser is quite likely to be the media which have operated at the level of the nation state — itself somewhat in decline in various parts of the world.

Under conditions of great diversity of supply and flexibility of use by individuals, the early concept of audience as mass seems less appropriate. There are fewer opportunities for an audience to form as a heterogeneous mass, although when it does happen, it is on a scale greater than ever before — as with world audiences for sporting events. The challenge to the audience as public has other sources and arises from two main tendencies: one within media themselves which, as they professionalize, have tended to weaken their direct links with political and social movements; the other, the trend to 'secularization' (decline in ideology) and growth in consumer-mindedness in many western societies in the last decade or two.

Nevertheless, it is likely that the 'public' is only changing its manifestation, becoming more localized, issue- and interest-specific, less identified with either a 'single' informed elite public or the following of a major political party. If anything, the market concept is likely to become even more widely current under the conditions briefly described, since the application of yet more media innovations, the greater production of media content of all kinds and the increase of available time and money to spend on media, require yet more detailed specifications of target groups and the cultivation of more and more specialized 'markets'.

One conceptual development which is related to these changes is the appearance of the notion of a 'taste culture', which recognizes the importance of non-demographic factors and also the fleeting and overlapping nature of audiences. One definition of taste culture has been attributed by Lewis (1980) to Herbert Gans as an 'aggregate of similar content chosen by the same people'. The concept makes it easier to detach choice making from social background and to regroup acts of choice according to similarity of content rather than to channel or medium location or to demographic variations. (This corresponds to type III in Figure 23.) The concept is compatible with market thinking and challenges older conceptions of a socially and culturally stratified audience system. Thus taste cultures may be difficult to place in any hierarchical scheme and are a consequence in part of the genuine classlessness of some uses of leisure time and of media interests and in part of the success of the cultural industry in establishing a 'one-dimensional society' (Marcuse, 1964).

The social character of audience experience

Group properties of audiences

In order to deal with the main questions about the audience raised at the start of this chapter, a somewhat arbitrary separation is made between the issue of whether audience experience is 'social' and that of audience 'activity'. In discussing alternative conceptions of the audience it has become clear that the solution to the first issue depends partly on how one chooses to regard the audience — whether as aggregate or social group — and partly on the facts of the case: some audiences do have a group character and some, strictly speaking, are no more than aggregates.

In practice, there is a continuum, with 'mass' at one end and 'small close-knit group' at the other, along which actual audiences can be located. There is, however, more to be said before audiences can be identified in such a way and the purpose of the following discussion is to look at some of the theory and evidence that would be helpful in locating audiences according to the degree to which they exhibit group-like properties.

Much sociological effort has been devoted to studying the properties of groups, and Ennis (1961) has provided a useful starting point for the study of audience as group by naming the main criteria which should be applied (drawing on Merton, 1957). He distinguished 'boundary' properties from those of 'internal structure'. It is the latter which are of most concern here, since the question of audience boundaries can usually be settled empirically and the main issues have already been discussed.

If an audience corresponds more or less to an existing group — a public, a party membership, a minority, an association, a community, etc — it inherits the characteristics of the group-like collectivity in question as to membership 'qualification', size, degree of engagement, stability over time, location in space, etc. This also reminds us that media audiences can acquire the boundary properties that groups have and may perhaps give rise to group formation. Audiences do sometimes correspond to the boundaries of a demographic group (e.g. age group) and may exhibit other group properties, such as feelings of identity with an age or peer culture.

It is sometimes argued that, since local media use is correlated with attachment to a community, the introduction of new local media may help to strengthen the solidarity of the neighbourhood and give it some enduring identity. It is also the case that media often give rise to subsets of 'fans' who may become organized sufficiently to recognize and interact with each other. This leads us to consider the second set of properties, those to do with internal structure, and here Ennis names three in particular: the degree of social differentiation; the extent of interaction; the existence of systems of normative controls. With some 'stretching', these can still provide the headings for a discussion of the social character of the audience.

Social differentiation

Since we are dealing with the 'internal structure' of audiences at this point, it is not strictly relevant to discuss the question of the social stratification of different audiences and more is said below about audience composition. However, it is worth recalling that, within a given audience, there are almost always differences of interest, attention, perception and effect associated with social differentiation.

Thus the behaviour of a given audience group is almost always patterned by the factors that more generally shape social behaviour. To that extent, audience behaviour is almost inevitably 'social'.

More pertinent to the discussion, perhaps, is the evidence that has accumulated through studies of personal influence (Merton, 1949; Katz and Lazarsfeld, 1955) which shows that given audience groups can have an internal structure related to media use and type of content. Thus, there is a recognized informal hierarchy separating those more expert on a certain content or subject from those less expert. This kind of social differentiation often reflects features of the rest of social life and is not directly caused by the media, though media use offers the occasion for its expression and perhaps reinforcement. While the social differentiation of audiences may correspond to the stratification pattern of society, it need not do so. Thus Katz and Lazarsfeld found such associations in the identification of opinion leaders for certain kinds of subject matter (e.g. public affairs) but not others (e.g. fashion). The development of 'taste-cultures', relatively free from class determination, may also tend to promote a dissociation between social stratification and audience composition.

Social interaction

Sociability

Of the several aspects to be considered, the most obvious is that of the sociability of the behaviour itself, which varies according to the nature of the medium (see chapter 1). It is some time since the concept of media use as solitary, atomized and alienated behaviour was tested against the evidence and found wanting. As Friedson (1953) remarked: 'mass communications have been absorbed into the social life of the local groups' and even the seemingly most private and individual act of media choice, going to a cinema, has been repeatedly shown to be, first, a social act with someone else and usually, secondarily, a communication act (Jowett and Linton, 1980).

The primary medium for most people, television, is frequently watched in family group settings and is closely integrated into patterns of family interaction, just as music listening is often an integral part of youth peer group behaviour. It is true that some media, especially books and radio, provide opportunities for solitary enjoyment and are chosen for this reason at certain times (Brown,

1976), but it is rare for media use to be an obstacle to sociability. There is quite a lot of research to support the view that media use is either a means towards better social relations (e.g. Riley and Riley, 1951; Noble, 1975; Hedinsson, 1981) or, where loneliness is enforced, a possible compensation or substitute for companions.

Social uses

There is a good deal of evidence to support the view that media use is more social than otherwise and some recent research by James Lull (1982), based on participant observation of family media use, has confirmed, or added to, what had already been established. His work provides a useful framework and presents a 'social uses' typology with five main types: structural; relational; affiliation or avoidance; social learning; competence/dominance. The first of these, 'structural', refers to uses of media as background, providing companionship, regulating patterns of activity and talk. Mendelsohn (1964) had earlier described radio as 'bracketing' the day and creating 'moods'. The relational heading is similar to what had earlier been called the 'coin of exchange' function. The media provide common ground for talk, topics, illustrations — pegs on which to hang opinions. The 'affiliation' dimension refers to media as an aid to gaining or avoiding physical and verbal contact and also to the function of the media in increasing 'family solidarity', maintaining relationships and decreasing tension. 'Social learning' has mainly to do with various aspects of socialization. 'Competence/dominance' has to do with such things as role enactment and reinforcement, with validation of arguments, with being an 'opinion leader' or 'first with the news'.

Social isolation

A good deal of attention, especially in relation to children and young people, has been given to the potentially isolating effects of media use, a concern which has mainly expressed itself in anxiety over 'excessive' or 'addictive' use of media, especially television, although the same fears were once expressed about films. Very heavy attention to media, especially if one is alone, has often been interpreted as a form of self-isolation, even alienation, a withdrawal from reality.

We shall return shortly to the subject of 'normative regulation', but here it should at least be noted that very high usage of media competes for time with normal social interaction. There are two relevant bodies of evidence: one suggesting that high use is correlated with poor social adjustment and other indications of problems (e.g. Maccoby, 1954; Horton and Wohl, 1956; Pearlin, 1959; Halloran et al., 1970; McLeod et al., 1965); another associating high media use (especially television) with other kinds of social marginality, such as sickness, old age, unemployment, poverty.

Two main theses suggest either that media work against 'good' social adjustment and relationships, or that poor social circumstances are reflected in media use, either because the media offer some compensation or simply because they are a time-filler (Rosengren and Windahl, 1972). In the event, research has confirmed neither proposition in any general way. It is clear that high media use can go with and even promote good social contact (e.g. Hedinsson, 1981) and also that poor social circumstances may even deprive people of the small motivation needed to make extensive use of media (Meyersohn, 1968).

Audience-sender relationships

In speaking of social interaction within the audience, the obvious reference is to personal contacts between people, but the question of a certain kind of social relation between audience and sender can also belong here. At several points, reference has been made to the possibility for a relationship to be established or maintained between a sender and a public by way of the mass media. This can occur either when a sender is genuinely trying to communicate or when both sender and receiver are trying to achieve the same ends. It has, however, often been noted that individuals in audiences establish (mainly vicarious) relationships with mass communication, especially with characters, stars or personalities in fiction and entertainment. This has aptly been called 'para-social interaction' (Horton and Wohl, 1956) and its various forms have been described in different ways. Although difficult to study scientifically, the phenomenon is very familiar — programme fans are strongly affected by what happens to fictional characters and talk about them as if they were real. Realistic and long-running 'soap operas' with fixed characters seem to lend themselves most to dissolving the line between fiction and reality.

Noble (1975) has suggested two concepts for dealing with this kind of involvement: 'identification' and 'recognition'. He attributes the first to Schramm et al. (1961) who defined it as 'the experience of being able to put oneself so deeply into a TV character and feel oneself to be so like the character that one can feel the same emotions and experience the same events as the character is supposed to be feeling'. This concept implies some 'identity-loss', while 'recognition' does not, and even contributes to identity forming.

Thus recognition is being able to interact with well-known television characters as if they were similar to known people in real life. Noble writes (pp. 63–4)

> these characters serve as something akin to screen community with whom the viewer regularly talks and interacts . . . this regularly appearing screen community serves for many as an extended kin grouping, whereby the viewer comes into contact with the wider society beyond his immediate family.

The emphasis is on the positive aspect of vicarious social interaction, rather than on its common association with social withdrawal and inadequacy.

Normative controls

The existence of systems of normative control in relation to mass media use seems at first counter to the view that uses of media are voluntary, free-time, 'out-of-role' activities, more or less unrelated to social obligation. While media use is relatively uncontrolled compared to other types of institutional involvement, it follows from the fact of normative regulation of the institution by society that there should be discriminations and valuations made in relation to audience use. In practice, audience research continually uncovers the existence of value systems which regulate 'media behaviour' in several ways.

First, there are values governing content and often involving fine distinctions, depending on context, between one type of content and another. Secondly, there are valuations of different media and time given to media as against other uses of time. Thirdly, there are expectations held by the audience about the obligations of media producers and distributors to provide certain services and meet certain obligations. Much the same set of values governs each of these aspects, although they are applied in different ways by different groups.

The values about content are rather familiar and stem from traditional judgements embedded in the culture and handed on mainly by the institutions of education, family and religion. They apply first to certain kinds of content, favouring what is informational, educational or moral over entertainment, the immoral and the 'low-cultural'. As Bourdieu (1986) has extensively shown, aesthetic judgements are also related in predictable and very structured ways to occupational (therefore class) position. One consequence is a carry-over to judgements about media channels, so that the media with stronger entertainment associations, such as television and film, carry a lower value than newspapers and books. Thus parents are more inclined to limit the use of television than newspaper or book reading, even though the last-named appears to have stronger connotations of 'escape' than do other media (Brown, 1976).

It is mainly in the imposition of norms for media use in family contexts that we are aware of normative control of media (Geiger and Sokol, 1959; Hedinsson, 1981; Brown and Linné, 1976), but similar normative prescriptions have a much wider distribution. For instance, Steiner (1963) found a tendency for respondents to show a certain amount of guilt over high levels of television use and some kinds of content preference. In general, he attributed this to a legacy from the protestant ethic, which frowns on 'unproductive' uses of time. Among middle-class audiences, especially, a sensitivity to this value persists. Steiner and others have found a tendency for this to show more in words than in behaviour and although it may be in decline, it seems likely that the broad value system remains and exerts some influence on actual behaviour as well as on self-reports of behaviour (Neumann, 1982).

The question of audience attitudes to the media has been a rather frequent matter of investigation, usually in the context of inter-media comparisons (cf. Comstock et al., 1978, pp. 128–40). People voice complaints about media and they also appreciate them. Positive appreciation usually outweighs criticism, but the point here is that audiences regard it as a matter on which they should have views — the performance of the media is a matter for public opinion. Audiences expect to be informed and entertained and expect conformity to some norms of good taste and morality and perhaps also patriotism and other values. This takes us some way from the question of the audience as a group, but it is a reminder that the mass media are not protected from the application of normative judgements at whatever is the appropriate level of operation — be it that of the local community, the nation or even the international community.

One last aspect of the normative status of media should be raised and that has to do with the absolute level of attachment to media. Some writers have made very strong claims for the dependence of people on their media and Steiner (1963) reports that many would feel quite lost without television. Although there is little doubt that people often exhibit strong feelings of deprivation when denied television or newspapers (Berelson, 1949), there is some uncertainty about the strength of attachment at normal times. Himmelweit and Swift (1976), for instance, on the basis of a longitudinal study of media use and preferences, conclude that 'the media form part of the background rather than the foreground of the leisure life and interests of adolescents and young men: they are used far more than they are valued'. The truth is probably that dependence, and hence valuation, varies a good deal according to circumstances and that under some conditions, especially of confinement to home and low income, the strength of attachment and level of appreciation is indeed very high, whether for television, books or radio.

Audience activity, satisfactions and uses

The kinds of question indicated by this heading extend over a broad range and can only be answered by saying something more about progress in the field of research labelled 'the uses and gratifications' approach, which has been centrally concerned with the choice, reception and manner of response of the media audience. The extent to which an audience can be considered active is related, first of all, to the degree to which a clearly and consistently motivated selection takes place, but extends to matters of conscious reflection on the media experience and of the application of benefits derived from media to other purposes in life. Each of these topics has been dealt with by way of the research approach named. That there is *some* measure of selectivity by audiences among channels and types of content is a basic presupposition of the whole media industry which can hardly be doubted (e.g. Zillman and Bryant, 1985), but there is a surprising amount of dispute about how much selectivity there actually is and a good deal of evidence to show that a lot of media use is habitual and unselective (e.g. Goodhart et al., 1975; Barwise et al., 1982).

The best evidence of selectivity derives from the consistent profiling of media behaviour and types of content chosen according to such familiar demographic variables as income, education, age or gender (Blumler, 1979; Espé and Seiwert, 1986) and evidence of the varying appeal of different kinds of content or genres. The development of 'taste cultures' mentioned earlier and the documented phenomenon of loyal groups of fans (and of positive avoiders) for major international soap operas also lends pragmatic support for the existence of real selectivity, even if both are consistent with a good deal of passive acceptance of what the media choose to offer. The investigation of selectivity has often been hampered by the social value attached to certain kinds of media and content, which leads to subjective misreporting of actual media use (Steiner, 1963).

The relevance of the 'uses and gratifications' research tradition rests on the fact that its practitioners have set themselves against the notion of a passive audience and it involves a number of assumptions, of which a key item is that the audience makes a conscious and motivated choice among channels and content on offer. There are several varieties of theory (see McQuail and Gurevitch, 1974; McQuail, 1985a), although the earliest and dominant version tended to be functionalist in formulation. One much quoted statement of a functionalist version of the theory reads as follows. The approach is concerned with

> (1) the social and psychological origins of (2) needs, which generate (3) expectations of (4) the mass media or other sources which lead to (5) differential patterns of media exposure (or engagement in other activities), resulting in (6) need gratifications and (7) other consequences, perhaps mostly unintended ones (Katz et al., 1974, p. 20).

Thus, the causes of media use are held to lie in social or psychological circumstances which are experienced as problems and the media are used for problem resolution (the meeting of needs), in matters such as information seeking, social contact, diversion, social learning and development. If media use were unselective, then it could not be accounted in any significant degree as an instrument for problem solving, or even carry much meaning attributed by the user. Much work done over a period of forty years seems to show that audience members can and do describe their media experience in functional (i.e. problem-solving and need-meeting) terms. There is a recurrent pattern to the ideas which people produce about the utility of their media behaviour, the main elements having to do with: learning and information; self-insight and personal identity; social contact; diversion, entertainment and time-filling (see above, pp. 72–4). The responses also vary a good deal according to the type of media content involved.

In the decade since the statement by Katz et al. was written, a good deal of research has been carried out, which has further specified the nature of motives, expected media gratifications and uses and led to theoretical revision. The further progress in naming specific gratifications has not greatly altered the picture we already possessed, but the basic proposition stated above does now call for reformulation (see Rosengren et al., 1985). Some of the preoccupations of early research and theory have proved to be dead ends or seem less relevant to understanding audience formation and behaviour. In particular, the emphasis on *needs* has been much reduced, since the concept has proved theoretically and methodologically slippery and, to a certain extent, redundant. Secondly, the expectation that differentiation by use and gratification would help in explaining effects has been reduced, in the face of difficulties of verification.

A reformulated version of the basic proposition would put more emphasis on certain key linkages: between social background and experience and expectations from media; between prior expectations and use of media; between expected satisfactions and those obtained from media, with consequences for continued use. A new statement might now read: (1) Personal social circumstances and psychological dispositions together influence both (2) general habits of media use and also (3) beliefs and expectations about the benefits offered by media, which shape (4) specific acts of media choice and consumption, followed by (5) assessments of the value of the experience (with consequences for further media use) and, possibly, (6) applications of benefits acquired in other areas of experience and social activity. There is still an implied logical sequence which looks conscious and rational, expressed in this way, but it is much less mechanistic or dependent on functionalist assumptions than the earlier version.

It is also more open to investigation, helped by certain theoretical and conceptual developments. Firstly, the concept of expectation has been clarified in terms of an 'expectancy-value approach' (Palmgreen and Rayburn, 1985). The essence is a view of media use behaviour as a function of a belief that a particular kind of media content will have attributes which carry a negative or positive valuation for the audience member. This simple proposition opens the way to a clearer formulation of the research task: relevant attributes can be identified, respondents can be asked how they value each attribute and whether or not they apply to specific content (or media). The same researchers (e.g. in Rayburn and Palmgreen, 1984) have also contributed to the handling of the linkage between expectation, media use and assessment after the event, by proposing a clear distinction between the first and the third of these — in the terms 'gratifications sought' versus 'gratifications obtained'. The relation (of association or disassociation) between the two empirical measures can help considerably to account for media use patterns and, possibly, some part of message effect or effectiveness.

A further advance has been on the question of measuring media activity. This concept has been clarified by Levy and Windahl (1985) by distinguishing two underlying dimensions: one of time (the communication sequence) and the other of audience orientation. According to the first, we can locate relevant activities in time as before, during, or after the media 'exposure'. According to the second dimension, we can separate different kinds of activity, especially selection, involvement and use (or application). The two dimensions can be cross-classified to identify sub-categories of media activity which are open to investigation.

Some advance has been made on the question of relating social background to media choice and response, although it remains one of the most intractable problem areas. For instance, Blumler (1985) has made a distinction, based on extensive evidence, between 'social origins' and (ongoing) social experiences. The former seem, in general, to be more likely to go with predictable constraints on the range of choice and with compensatory, adjustment-oriented media expectations and uses. The second are much less predictable and variable in their sequence and direction of effect and often go with 'facilitation' of media use — with positive choice of, and application of, media use for personally chosen ends. Media use can thus be seen to be both limited and motivated by complex and interacting forces in society and in the personal biography of the individual. This is a sobering thought for those who hope to explain as well as describe patterns of audience behaviour.

It is worth drawing attention, in the context of theoretical advance, to one of the most intractable tasks which has faced research into audience motivation — that of explaining the often extraordinary appeal of certain kinds of entertainment (Tannenbaum, 1981). Reference has already been made to a research effort designed to explain the appeal of the soap opera, but other kinds of entertainment may take precedence or equal rank in popular appeal, especially those involving excitement and violence. One investigator, Zillman (1980; Zillman and Bryant, 1985) has shown, using mainly experimental methods, that people form mood-specific preferences for media content, such that boredom leads to a choice of exciting content and stress a choice for relaxing content. Avoidance, escape and diversion can be demonstrated as operative factors, as can a general factor of 'arousal' or excitement which is attributed to certain media content.

More specifically, according to Zillman, the attraction of drama to spectators depends on three main elements: conflict between protagonists; valuation of the latter (as good or bad) by spectators;

experience of feelings of enjoyment or anger according to the success or failure of chosen protagonists. This process is clearly the object of manipulation by the creator. These various contributions to understanding the appeal of cultural content, however summarily described here, have, when inter-related, a considerable potential for explaining choice and involvement of audiences (thus media activity). They can go some way to account for one of the familiar paradoxes indicated by Zillman, that of the great appeal of 'bad news' as well as of fictional disaster and horror.

It can be argued (as in McQuail, 1984) that theory and investigation of media motivation and use should pay more attention to the particular subject matter and also observe a clearer distinction between 'cognitive' and 'cultural' types of content and media use, following the fundamental distinction made by Carey (1975) between a 'transmission' model and a 'consummatory' (end in itself) view of communication. The first deals in rational uses, especially of information, for chosen ends, and is consistent with a functional view and a sequential logic. The second view tends to undermine the notion of the audience as engaging in rational, accountable behaviour. The key difference is that symbolic cultural experience is characterized by an element of liberation from temporal and spatial constraint and subject to shaping by highly variable and unpredictable patterns of taste and content preferences, leading to emotional and/or aesthetic satisfactions. The cognitive model of use is based on a mixture of individual interests (also very variable) and purposes of a more rational-accountable sort.

Advances in theory have been too recent to yield a great deal in the way of definitive answers to any of the questions about linkages named above, but there seems more chance than in the past, not only of describing and accounting for media use patterns, but also of integrating research into the audience with 'reception' research, described below, and with studies of media effect and effectiveness. There is also some reason to think that the cogent criticisms made by Chaney (1972) and Elliott (1974) of uses and gratifications research are less applicable than when originally made.

Theories of audience composition

The description of audiences has been a perennial task of audience and market research and a by-product of almost all studies of media use and effect. There are many more data about the media audience than data of any other kind, yet they have been of little value in understanding the process of mass communication. Most such sets of data are time- and place-bound, although they do reveal the working of a small number of basic factors which seem to influence the size and composition of media audiences.

The two most commonly recurring factors have to do with age and social class (or income and education), because both tend to determine the availability of free time and money for media use. Age influences availablility and content choice. Thus, as young children, we are confined more or less to the range of family chosen media and watch more television. As we acquire freedom, we make more independent choices and go outside the home, leading to a pattern of radio listening and cinema-going. With acquisition of our own family and work responsibilities, we return to a domestic context, but with different interests, giving more time to newspaper reading and information generally.

With more spare income after the growing up of our own children, media consumption diversifies and then contracts again with old age, leading to a return to more domestic media (television and books) and more 'serious' content choices. Social class position, as represented by income, governs the pattern of media use and, within this pattern, higher income tends to diminish the place of television because of wider non-media leisure choices. High education and professional work responsibility may also lead to different content choices — more informational content or content favoured by dominant educational and cultural values.

Such findings and others which relate, with less consistency, to differences of gender and locality help to describe and predict the overall shape of audiences and the underlying factors at work are not hard to recognize. However, there are differing explanations of the formation of audiences and the specific or typical patterns which are found and it is relevant to the purposes of this chapter to look at the various theories or part-theories that have been advanced. Those that follow are not all mutually exclusive and vary in their completeness and specificity. They tend to divide into three main groups, reflecting an emphasis on: 'media supply' as a determinant; on the conditions of distribution and possible reception; or on audience 'demand'.

Media institutional history

The reference is to two main factors which account for a given overall audience structure. One factor is media history, since the media have grown on the basis of successive appeals to limited social groups and have gradually extended their reach, without bridging some social 'gaps', and they have even institutionalized some of them, especially those between social strata or classes. Thus the daily newspaper was developed primarily for a male, urban middle-class readership, with functions in political and business life, and it still tends to have a greater appeal for the social groups for which it was originally intended. Television, on the other hand, borrowed from film and radio and established itself as a domestic and entertainment medium appealing most to those most often at home, thus women and children and those with fewer resources.

The second factor is the success of particular media, especially print media, in establishing and maintaining an identity or 'persona' to which a certain kind of audience has been drawn. This theory is likely to appeal to media themselves and is a distinctly 'supply-side' explanation. History plays a part here, in that at any given time the range of media will contain a number of titles or content forms which are retaining, or gradually losing, audiences composed according to some original specifications. Varying loyalty of audiences and varying economic fortunes both enter into the total, rather complex, explanation of audience pattern.

Market management

This is also a 'supply-side' theory, referring to the influence of advertising on media institutions. Commercial media have to match their product to a given market of consumers for the media product itself and for other goods for which it is an advertising vehicle. The readership 'profile' as well as size is thus of great importance to success or failure and market management aims to optimize the audience composition from this point of view. The extent to which this has affected the structure of the British national press is well described by Hirsch and Gordon (1975) and Curran (1986) and we can often interpret many features of audience composition as the outcome of attempts at media market management.

Response to audience demand: giving the public what it wants

This might be termed an 'individual differences' theory and is one which also appeals to the media themselves. In essence it says only that observed patterns of audience composition are the result of large numbers of individual acts of choice, each guided by differences of taste, interest, intellectual capacity and opportunity. Under competitive conditions, laws of supply and demand should ensure that the public as a whole gets what it wants. This pragmatic and common-sense theory holds that different kinds of content, provided on the basis of research and experience, will tend to appeal to audiences of predictable size and composition.

Differential leisure resources and media availability

The stress here is less on content and active choice of content than on differential 'availability' for media reception of social groups. The opportunity to receive (under conditions of equal distribution) depends mainly on three individual variables: amount of free time, educational level and money. The general pattern of media use, as between social categories, can be seen as the complex outcome of each of these factors. Thus women and children and the old tend to have more time and less money available and consequently attend relatively more to media which are cheapest and most time demanding. Such simple associations are cut across by differences of income and education, both of which widen the range of content which is effectively accessible and also the number of alternatives to mass media for informational or diversionary purposes.

Functional theory

The essentials of this theory have already been outlined in discussing the motivations of audience members and the 'uses and gratifications' of media. The consequences for audience composition are clear enough, since we should expect that audiences will tend to seek, if not get, what they 'need' to solve problems or maximize their satisfactions. Insofar as 'problems' and 'needs' are rooted in social conditions or personality and life-circumstances, audience composition will reflect the connection between certain kinds of content and the recurring or typical needs of particular social groups.

This is clearly a 'demand-side' theory and, of all those named here, the most open to operationalization and testing and with most potential for explanation. It is weakened, however, by the discovery that there is no 'one-to-one' relationship between content type and function, so that the same content can meet varied 'needs'. An extension of functional theory would be that the general shape of audience composition will reflect the overall distribution of needs and functions in the society and will be a 'natural' or 'best' solution to the 'communication needs' of society. There is a risk here of assuming that what the audience gets is what it wants and also what it needs.

A social–cultural explanation

If we regard attention to mass media as part of a wider process of attention-giving, we should explain patterns of media use according to the same principles governing other communication (here attention-giving) behaviour. Individuals (and eventually groups or categories) have a more or less given social location and surrounding 'life space' (Kurt Lewin's term). They pay attention to things they encounter within this life space and develop a structure of attention-giving which is appropriate to their social location. In general, we can expect attention to what is close, familiar, positive, unthreatening, equal or subordinate in social power and we can expect avoidance of objects with reverse characteristics.

Such an explanation would, for example, predict working-class avoidance of content which is unfamiliar, socially or physically remote, or likely to recall powerlessness in work contexts or intellectual inadequacy. There are other situations of varying dependency and powerlessness which might produce similar patterns of selection and avoidance. Examples include the development of youth sub-cultures in opposition to the official culture of the school (Murdock and Phelps, 1973) or generally in resistance to society (Hall et al., 1978). Music is often the main focus. In general, this explanation emphasizes the location of media artefacts within a universe of socially defined objects. One acquires an orientation to such artefacts through experiences which are likely to be shared with others. The orientation thus becomes a collective phenomenon.

Concluding note

Underlying these different approaches lies an implicit division of factors into those that facilitate choice and those that constrain and suppress. Between media supply on the one hand and demand on the other are a set of 'filter conditions', some of which relate to individual differences, others to culture and social structure. While changes of media supply can have some effect on the pattern of demand and demand can also affect supply, many of the conditions are slow to change, hence the stability over time of patterns of media consumption.

The audience as decoder: reception theory and research

It has already been pointed out that one source of meaning of media texts is to be found in the 'reading' made by the ordinary receiver, that is, the audience member. An attention to the decoding of media messages by audiences dates back to the earliest days of research into persuasive mass communication, even if the terminology has changed. Then the topic was dealt with under the heading of selective attention, perception, interpretation and retention. In sum, what receivers got from messages was the key dependent variable in effect research. This way of conceiving the audience role in the communication process has not disappeared for certain purposes, but it has been supplemented by other theoretical frameworks which share a concern for exploring or predicting the variable interpretation of information or of cultural content. This may now be regarded as a very active field for research and theory, even if the results are still somewhat elusive.

It has three or four newer theoretical sources. One is the 'uses and gratifications' approach already described, which is mainly concerned with expectations or derived satisfactions from media, but which, insofar as it is concerned with motivation and response, also has to pay close attention to the ways in which content is interpreted or anticipated. The motivations associated with media choice and the functions assigned to content by audience members are located within specific frames of meaning constructed by audiences. A second source derives from critical theory of 'hegemonic' influence from ideological content. Much weight attaches to the notion that dominant or 'preferred' meanings (Hall, 1973b) are embedded by producers into content and constrain the audience to extract a certain pre-chosen meaning. Theorists such as Hall accept the possibility of alternative decodings, some of which may involve 'seeing through' the ideological bias and turning the message around to allow 'oppositional' readings. Other readings allow various degrees of distance from the preferred meaning to be taken up by the receiver. Most such theory deals with informational content, but it can apply to cultural production more widely.

A third source of interest in audience decoding (not unrelated to that described) is concerned with the analysis of cultural products from the 'reader's' point of view and has a connection with the growing school of 'reception analysis' in literary critical studies. Radway (1984) provides an example of a study which combines the study of a particular popular genre (pulp romance novels, with their patriarchal ideology) with a study of how and why women readers are attracted. This approach, which does have conceptual links to both critical and functionalist theory (Schroeder, 1987) is also represented by attempts to account for the cross-cultural appeal of very popular television serials like Dallas, despite the seemingly restricted cultural setting of the original versions (e.g. Ang, 1985; Liebes and Katz, 1986).

Yet a further contribution to the study of audience reception comes from another growth point in media research — that dealing with news comprehension, where it has seemed necessary, in order to make progress, to have some view of the frames of interpretation brought to (television) news by audiences (Gurevitch and Levy, 1986). These frames are also described as 'metamessages' by these authors: 'latent meanings that are embedded in *audience decodings* of mass media messages and that link the aggregated structure of individually created meanings to macrosocial phenomena' (p. 162). Their assumption is that audiences, much like journalists, have 'tacit theories' to frame their understanding of events in the world and to help in 'processing' incoming information.

The theory and research described covers a wide terrain and is not yet very far advanced, but it is bound to leave its mark on future audience research. The theoretical propositions being tested are still very general, but come down to four main points:

- audience members bring, from their own experience, pre-formed frames of interpretation to their media experience;
- these frames have a stable structure, thus some collective existence over and above their individual variation;
- frames can be taken over from the media or shaped by the audience itself out of its own needs and experiences;
- the same content can be given different meaning (compared with deduction from text or sender intention) and can have different meanings in different cultural settings.

There is a good deal of fragmentary evidence from past research for active and selective audience interpretation, but no clear answer. Research generally confirms that audiences do deploy frameworks of meaning of some kinds and that media probably play a part in forming them (thus, there is some hegemonic tendency). There is still too little evidence for a clear assessment on this point and there are many conceptual and methodological problems to overcome

(Dahlgren, 1985; Gurevitch and Levy, 1985b; Sigman and Fry, 1985; Richardson and Corner, 1986).

The influence of the audience on content

A central issue in this chapter has been the varying dependency or activeness of the audience and there remains for consideration the matter of audience response or 'feedback'. While it is already evident that the competence and power of the audience to influence the producer/distributor depends very much on the character and setting of the audience in question, there are a number of general mechanisms by which senders and receivers are brought into a mutual relationship. These are described in the following paragraphs.

Critics and fans

The traditional concept of the audience or readership group assumed two important elements of institutionalized response. One was the critical apparatus, operating on behalf of, mainly, middle-class publics and in relation to more elite kinds of content. The range of institutionalized critical attention has widened considerably to cover much television, popular music, films and reading, partly as an extension of the media's own requirements as an industry. At the same time, the gap between critics and fans, the other important element, has tended to narrow. Thus many different kinds of media and content have their more or less discriminating, enthusiastic and knowledgeable followers, whose role is not so different from that of the critic. This is a development which has also been encouraged by the media and plays a part in its self-publicity. While critics and fans certainly evaluate, it is less clear that they play much part in modifying performance or in shaping supply, except in helping to identify, amplify and prolong what is currently popular or in vogue.

Institutionalized accountability

There are now numerous forms in which the claim of the audience, as an interest group in society to influence media content, has been recognized. The rise of public broadcasting has stimulated many such developments, since radio and television were often established as services with an assumption of accountability to the public as a whole. The range of instruments of control is large and varied and the main forms can only be named. These include: control through parliament; committees and commissions of enquiry; legal instruments of control; councils of readers, viewers or listeners; authorities which set and apply codes of standards in the public interest; press councils; systems of subsidy and support. Most such instruments and forms tend, in liberal democracies, to have a limiting rather than a positive role — they are more likely to restrict than prescribe.

The working of the market

According to many proponents of media freedom, the main (and best) means of control and influence is the exercise of free choice under conditions of a free market.

Direct 'feedback'

The traditional form of response for the audience has been institutionalized by the media themselves in the form of 'letters to the editor' and phone calls to radio and television stations. Although these have come to form an important component of media there is some doubt about their real value as feedback (Singer, 1973) and they are very open to manipulation by the media themselves, with few widely-held conventions about how letters should be treated and selected. For very large-scale media, it is doubtful whether such direct response can either express the wishes of the audience or inform the media.

The use of 'audience images'

The problem for the media of addressing themselves effectively to chosen audiences, or any audiences, has already been raised (chapter 6) and it arises again in the present context. There is a very indirect and inadequate form of influence on content through the practice by media sources of constructing 'images' of the audiences or anticipated audiences for which they shape their messages (Bauer, 1958; Pool and Shulman, 1959). According to Gans (1957, p. 318) 'The audience participates in the making of a movie through the audience image held by the creator'. This construct may be based on personal experience, imagination or a stereotype, but it helps the creator to 'test' the product in the course of its formation. The existence of this tendency has been widely attested to and it has several times been concluded that such audience images are either shaped by professional self-interest or a very narrow range of social experience (Burns, 1977; Gans, 1979). Gans suggests, for instance, that newsmakers adopt an audience image that conforms largely to their own middle-class social milieu. He notes also that four basic kinds of image are invoked: the interested (like themselves); the uninterested; the rejected (e.g. intellectual critics); the invented (any image which satisfies their own wishes).

Audience research

The various possibilities for research to influence the supply of media will have been illustrated at many points in this book and there is no need to review them here. Most relevant are those kinds of research which the media undertake to guide their own operations. Abraham Moles (1973) has given a useful guide to research as feedback and pointed out that possibilities for influence from research depend especially on the potential for quantification and on the time-scale of application. Thus, numerical findings which can be quickly applied are most likely to have some influence. However, we also have considerable evidence that media communicators tend to resist or reject the findings of research, either because these are not understood or because they are perceived as threatening. Thus any influence they have is likely to be with management. In the case of research carried out outside media organizations there is unlikely to be any direct influence on mass communicators or on management, unless it is sponsored by powerful interests, clients or governments.

It is obviously possible for research to play a creative role in matching the purposes of communicators to the needs, interests and capacities of the public (cf. Belson, 1967; Katz, 1977) and clearly a number of audience research departments attached to public service broadcasting in several countries pursue this objective actively. Yet it is also likely that, on balance, such research is used more for the media than 'on behalf of' the public, let alone 'by' the public as a means of influence. The last claim could not perhaps be made for very much academic research, although this is more inclined to take the 'side' of the public than of the media senders.

In concluding this section and the chapter, it is worth recording the existence of an ambiguity about desirability of audience influence. While one norm supports responsiveness to and interaction with the audience, another safeguards the autonomy of the communicator on grounds of creativity, personal freedom and possibilities for change.

Conclusion: a shift of balance of audience types

Changes are occurring in many countries in the amount and range of what is offered by way of old and new media channels to potential audiences. For the most part, these changes are not the direct result of any initiative or deeply-felt need or unmet demand on the part of audiences. They are more the result of changes within the media industry (more concentration of ownership and control over existing media and many new entrants), changes in the ground-rules of nation states, pressures to take up and exploit new technology for commercial and economic reasons (McQuail and Siune, 1986). Such change is not likely to invalidate the broad lines of theory drawn in this chapter, which, with all their variation, point to audience behaviour as having a stable basis on social experience, in various kinds of self-perceived need and in different forms of normative regulation.

Media abundance creates problems for audience research, but also for the audience (individually experienced). As long as the new abundance consists mainly of 'more of the same', which still seems to be largely the case, the likelihood is that pre-existing patterns of choice will survive or re-establish themselves, sometimes in changed forms. This view is consistent, however, with a broad shift in the distribution of audience types towards that indicated as type III (fan group or taste set) in Figure 23. These are audiences based on the appeal of certain kinds of content, stars, presenters, authors, etc. At the same time, this also implies a reduction in the degree and strength of connection between audiences and organized sources. Ties are less likely to be normative and the control of media over their audiences is also lower.

There are several inter-related reasons for this trend, but the following are primary. First, 'the audience' is becoming more fragmented in social and spatial composition, although its members still need some guidelines for their choice of media content. Secondly, distribution of media content is becoming more separated from production (especially true of audiovisual media). Thirdly, the distributors still need to gain and keep the attention of audiences of known and stable characteristics (for purposes of gaining revenue), although not, as in the past, of stable composition (the *same* members). The best available device for doing so is to profile and package the offer in terms of styles, tastes, genres, special interests and stars or personalities.

CHAPTER 9

PROCESSES OF MEDIA EFFECTS

The premise of media effect

The entire study of mass communication is based on the premise that there are effects from the media, yet it seems to be the issue on which there is least certainty and least agreement. This apparent uncertainty is the more surprising since everyday experience provides countless examples of small effects. We dress for the weather under the influence of a weather forecast, buy something because of an advertisement, go to a film mentioned in a newspaper, react in countless ways to television, radio or music. We live in a world where political and governmental processes are based on the assumption that we know what is going on from press and television and radio. There are few people who can trace no piece of information or opinion to a source in the media, and much money and effort is spent in directing media to achieve such effects.

And yet it is true that much doubt exists about the degree, incidence and kind of effects and our knowledge is insufficient to make any but the most simple prediction about the occurrence of an effect in a given case. Even where we can make a prediction, it is usually based on experience and rule of thumb rather than on a precise knowledge of how a given effect has occurred or might occur. It is the availability of such pragmatic knowledge, based on experience, that enables the media and their clients to continue without too much self-questioning.

There are many good reasons for scientific uncertainty and even common sense and 'practical knowledge' waver when faced with some of the possibilities of media effect in the contested areas of morals, opinion and deviant behaviour which attract most public notice. On many such matters there can be no question of the media being a primary cause and we have no real 'explanation' of patterns of thought, culture and behaviour with deep social and historical roots. Furthermore, it makes little sense to speak of 'the media' as if they were one thing, rather than an enormously diverse set of messages, images and ideas, most of which do not originate with the media themselves but come from society and are sent 'back' to society.

It is thus not at all easy to name a case where the media can plausibly be regarded as the sole or indispensable cause of a given social effect. Despite the difficulties and the inevitable inconclusiveness, the question of media effects has proved as fascinating and unavoidable for social scientists as it has for the media themselves and the general public. If we did not fundamentally believe the media to have important long-term consequences, we could not devote so much time to their study.

The natural history of media effect research and theory

The development of thinking about media effects may be said to have a 'natural history', since it has been strongly shaped by the circumstances of time and place and influenced by several 'environmental' factors: the interests of governments and lawmakers; the needs of industry; the activities of pressure groups; the purposes of political and commercial propagandists; the current concerns of public opinion; the fashions of social science. It is not surprising that no straight path of cumulative development of knowledge can easily be discerned. Even so, we can distinguish a number of stages in the history of the field which indicate some measure of ordered progression and of cumulation.

Phase i: all-powerful media

In the first phase, which extends from the turn of the century until the late 1930s, the media, where they were well developed, were credited with considerable power to shape opinion and belief, change habits of life, to mould behaviour actively more or less according to the will of those who could control the media and their contents (Bauer and Bauer, 1960). Such views were based not on scientific investigation, but on observation of the enormous popularity of the press and the new media of film and radio and their intrusion into many aspects of everyday life as well as public affairs. These beliefs were shared and reinforced by advertisers and by propagandists during the First World War. In Europe, the use of media by dictatorial states in the interwar years and by the new revolutionary regime in Russia appeared to confirm what people were inclined to believe — that the media could be immensely powerful. It was in the context of such beliefs, and with an inclination to accept them, that research of a scientific kind using the survey and experiment, and drawing largely on social psychology, was begun.

Phase ii: theory of powerful media put to the test

The second phase, the opening of which is marked best in the literature by the series of Payne Fund Studies in the United States in the early 1930s (Blumer, 1933; Blumer and Hauser, 1933; Peterson and Thurstone, 1933), continued until the early 1960s. Many separate studies of the effects of different types of content and media, of particular films or programmes, of entire campaigns, were carried out. Attention was mainly concentrated on the possibilities of using film and other media for planned persuasion or information (e.g. Hovland et al., 1949; Lazarsfeld et al., 1944; Star and Hughes, 1950) or for assessing (with a view to control measures) the harmful effects of media in respect of delinquency, prejudice, aggression, sexual stimulation. Over the course of the period the nature of research changed, as methods developed and evidence and theory suggested new kinds of variable which should be taken into account. Initially, researchers began to differentiate possible effects according to social and psychological characteristics; subsequently they introduced variables relating to intervening effects from personal contacts and social environment, and latterly according to types of motive for attending to media.

What now seems like the end of an era was marked by some expression of disillusion with the outcome of this kind of media effect research (e.g. Berelson, 1959) and by a new statement of conventional wisdom which assigned a much more modest role to media in causing any of their planned or unintended effects. The still influential and useful summary of early research by Joseph Klapper, published in 1960 (though dating from 1949), set the seal on this research phase by concluding that 'mass communication does not ordinarily serve as a necessary or sufficient cause of audience effects, but rather functions through a nexus of mediating factors' (p. 8).

It was not that the media had been found, under all conditions, to be without effects, but they were shown to operate within a pre-existing structure of social relationships and a particular social and cultural context. These social and cultural factors tended to have primacy in shaping the opinions, attitudes and behaviour under study and also in shaping choice, attention and response to media on the part of audiences (e.g. Blumler and McQuail, 1968). It was also clear that learning of information could occur without related attitude change and attitude change without changes in behaviour (e.g. Trenaman and McQuail, 1961). This new sobriety of assessment was slow to modify opinion outside the social-scientific community. It was particularly hard to accept for those who made a living out of advertising and propaganda and for those in the media who valued the myth of their great potency. Those with political motives for using or controlling the media did not feel they could risk accepting the conclusions of researchers.

Phase iii: powerful media rediscovered

Hardly had the 'no (or minimal) effect' been written into the textbooks when it was being challenged by those who doubted that the whole story had been written and were reluctant to dismiss the possibility that media might indeed have important social effects and be an instrument for exercising social and political power (Lang and Lang, 1959; Key, 1961; Blumler, 1964; Halloran, 1965). One reason for reluctance to accept a 'minimal effect' conclusion was the arrival of television in the 1950s and 1960s as a new medium, with even more power of attraction than its predecessors and with seemingly major implications for social life. The third phase of theory and research, which is still with us, is one in which effects and potential effects are still being sought, but according to revised conceptions of the social and media processes likely to be involved.

Early investigation had relied very heavily on a model (borrowed from psychology) in which correlations were sought between degree of 'exposure' to media stimuli and measured changes of, or variations in, attitude, opinion, information or behaviour. The renewal of effect research was marked by a shift of attention towards: long-term change; cognitions rather than attitude and affect; the part played by intervening variables of context, disposition and motivation; collective phenomena such as climates of opinion, structures of belief, ideologies, cultural patterns and institutional forms of media provision. Much of the chapter which follows is taken up with a review of these newer theories of effect and of modifications of early direct effect models. While there are many contributors to, and causes of, the revival of interest in effects, it was Noelle-Neumann (1973) who coined the slogan 'return to the concept of powerful mass media' which serves to identify this research phase. The revival of (new) left thinking in the 1960s also made an important contribution by crediting the media with powerful legitimating and controlling effects in the interests of capitalist or bureaucratic states.

This version of the history of media effect research is not universally shared. For instance, in an assessment of research on mass communication and public opinion, Lang and Lang (1981) argue that such a picture (especially concerning the 'minimal effect' conclusion) is more the result of one particular interpretation gaining undue currency than an outcome which can be substantiated from the research itself conducted during the 'second phase'. They write 'The evidence available by the end of the 1950s, even when balanced against some of the negative findings gives no justification for an overall verdict of "media impotence"' (p. 659). In their view, the 'no effect' myth was due to a combination of factors: undue concentration on a limited range of effects — especially short-term effects on individuals (for instance during elections) instead of on broader social and institutional effects; and undue weight given to two publications — Katz and Lazarsfeld's *Personal Influence* (1955) and Klapper's *The Effects of Mass Communication* (1960). Nevertheless, they concede that the myth was influential enough to close off, temporarily, certain avenues of research.

Before leaving the historical aspect of research into media effects, it is worth reflecting on a suggestion by Carey (1978) that variations in belief in the power of mass communications may be accounted for by history itself:

> it can be argued that the basic reason behind the shift in the argument about the effects from a powerful to a limited to a more powerful model is that the social world was being transformed over this period. . . . Powerful effects of communication were sensed in the 'thirties because the Depression and the political currents surrounding the war created a fertile seed for the production of certain kinds of effects. Similarly, the normalcy of the 'fifties and 'sixties led to a limited effects model. In the late 'sixties a period of war, political discord and inflation combined to expose the social structure in fundamental ways and to make it permeable by the media of communication.

We can only speculate about the reasons for this association in time, which indeed may be only coincidence. Even so, it is true that people often know about crises through the media and may associate the message with the medium; in times of change and uncertainty it is also highly probable that people are more dependent on media as source of information and guidance (Ball-Rokeach and DeFleur, 1976; Ball-Rokeach, 1985); media are more likely to be effective on matters outside immediate personal experience and the components of the current, as of past, world crises are of that kind; finally, under conditions of tension and uncertainty, government and business or other elites and interests are likely to try to use media for influence and control. All these are arguments for the view that the effect and power (potential effect) of media may indeed be greater under certain historical conditions.

Levels and kinds of effect

In speaking of 'media effects' we are necessarily referring to what has already occurred as a direct consequence of mass communication, whether intended or not. The expression 'media power', on the other hand, refers to a potential for the future or a statement of probability about effects, under given conditions. 'Media effectiveness' is a statement about the efficiency of media in achieving a given aim and can apply to past, present or future, but always implying intention. Such distinctions can often be important for precision of speaking about the media, although it is hard to keep to a consistent usage. Even more essential for research and theory is to observe the distinction between 'level' of occurrence, distinguishing at least the levels of: individual; group or organization; social institution; whole society; and culture. Each or all can be affected by mass communication and effects at any one level always imply effects at other levels. It happens that most research has been carried out at the individual level, with consequent difficulties for drawing conclusions about effects at collective or higher levels, as recommended in the current research phase.

Perhaps the most confusing aspect of research on effects is the multiplicity and complexity of the phenomena involved. Broad distinctions are normally made between: effects which are cognitive (to do with knowledge and opinion); those which are affectual (relating to attitude and feelings); effects on behaviour. These distinctions have been treated in early research as distinct and following a logical order, from the first to the third (see below). In fact it is no longer found easy to sustain the distinction between the three concepts or to believe the unique logic of that particular order of occurrence. To add to the complexity, much of our evidence comes from replies to questionnaires which are themselves individual acts of verbal behaviour from which we hope to reconstruct collective phenomena, often with an inextricable mixture of cognitive and affectual elements.

A final word should be said at this point about another kind of differentiation — that of type and direction of effect. In his summary, Klapper (1960) distinguished between 'conversion', 'minor change' and 'reinforcement' — respectively: change according to the intention of the communicator; change in form or intensity; confirmation by the receiver of his or her own existing beliefs and opinions. This three-fold distinction needs to be widened to include other possibilities, especially at the supra-individual level, leading to the following:

media may
: cause intended change (conversion)
: cause unintended change
: cause minor change (form or intensity)
: facilitate change (intended or not)
: reinforce what exists (no change)
: prevent change.

The categories are mainly self-explanatory, but the facilitation of change refers to the mediating role of media in wider processes of change in society, as discussed in chapter 4. Both of the last two named imply no effect, but involve different conceptions of media working. Reinforcement is an observable consequence of selective attention by the receiver to content which is congruent with existing views, aided perhaps by a generous supply of such content.

The second, 'preventing change', implies deliberate supply of one-sided or ideologically-shaped content in order to inhibit change in a conforming public. The 'no change' effect from the media, of which we have so much evidence, requires very close attention because of its long-term consequences. It is indeed a somewhat misleading expression, since anything that alters the probability of opinion or belief distribution in the future is an intervention into social process and thus an effect.

Processes of media effects: a typology

In order to provide an outline of developments in theory and research we begin by inter-relating two of the distinctions which have already been mentioned: between the intended and the unintended and between short-term and long-term. This device was suggested by Golding (1981) to help distinguish different concepts of news and its effects; thus deliberate short-term effects may be considered as 'bias'; short-term non-deliberate effects fall under the heading of 'unwitting bias'; deliberate and long-term effects indicate 'policy'; while long-term and non-deliberate effects of news are 'ideology'. Something of the same way of thinking helps us to map out, in terms of these two co-ordinates, the main kinds of effect process which have been dealt with in the literature. The result is given in Figure 24.

The main entries can be briefly described although their meaning will be made more explicit in the discussion of theory which follows:

Individual response: the process by which individuals change, or resist change, in response to messages designed to influence attitude, knowledge or behaviour.

Media campaign: the situation in which a number of media are used to achieve a persuasive or informational purpose with a chosen population, the most common examples being found in politics, advertising, fund-raising, public information for health and safety. Campaigns tend to have the following characteristics: they have specific and overt aims and a limited time-span and are thus open to assessment as to effectiveness; they have authoritative (legitimate) sponsorship and their purposes tend to be in line with consensual values and the aims of established institutions.

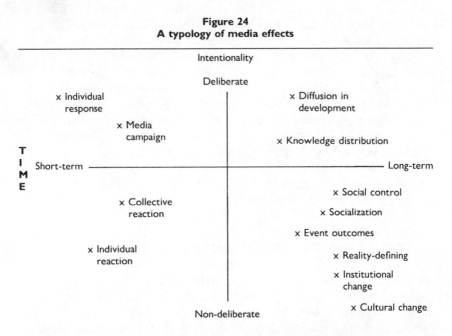

Figure 24
A typology of media effects

Individual reaction: unplanned or unpredictable consequences of exposure by a person to a media stimulus. These have mainly been noticed as imitation and learning, especially of aggressive or deviant acts (including suicide) but also of 'prosocial' ideas and behaviour. Other types of effect include: the displacement of other activities: the imitation of styles and fashions; the identification with heroes or stars; sexual arousal; reactions of fear or anxiety.

Collective reaction: here some of the same individual effects are experienced simultaneously by many people, leading to joint action, usually of an unregulated and non-institutional kind. Effects from fear, anxiety and anger are the most potent, leading to panic or civil disturbance.

Diffusion in development: the planned diffusion of innovations for purposes of long-term development, using a series of campaigns and other means of influence, especially the interpersonal network and authority structure of the community or society.

Knowledge distribution: the consequences of media activity in the sphere of news and information for the distribution of knowledge between social groups, the variable awareness of events (diffusion), the priorities assigned to aspects of 'reality'.

Socialization: the informal contribution of media to the learning and adoption of established norms, values and expectations of behaviour in given social roles and situations.

Social control: refers here to systematic tendencies to promote conformity to the established order and reaffirm the legitimacy of existing authority, by way of ideology and the 'consciousness industry'. Depending on one's social theory, this can be placed either as a deliberate, or as an unintended extension of socialization. Because of this ambiguity, it is 'located' near the midpoint of the vertical co-ordinate.

Reality-defining: a similar process, but differing in its having more to do with cognitions (knowledge and opinion) than values and arising not from deliberate attempts to manipulate but from the systematic tendencies in media to present an incomplete version of reality, shaped by their own operating needs and procedures.

Institutional change: the result of unplanned adaptations by existing institutions to developments in the media, especially affecting their communication functions.

Event outcomes: referring to the part played by media in conjunction with institutional forces in the course and resolution of major 'critical' events of significance to the whole society (see Lang and Lang, 1981). Examples could include revolution, major domestic political up-heavals, matters of war and peace.

Cultural change: shifts in the overall pattern of values, behaviours and symbolic forms characterizing a sector of society (e.g. youth), a whole society or a set of societies.

These entries in Figure 24 are intended to stand for processes of effect differentiated according to level, time-span, complexity and several other conditions which have been briefly indicated. In some cases, the same basic model is sufficient to deal with more than one of the processes since the difference of specification is not fundamental. The discussion which follows deals with these effect processes in terms of a number of basic models, summarizing the current state of theory in relation to each.

Individual response and individual reaction

The S-R model

These two entries in Figure 24 can be dealt with together since they share the same underlying model, that of stimulus response or conditioning. Its main features can be simply represented as follows:

single message ⟶ individual receiver ⟶ reaction

It applies more or less equally to intended and to unintended effects although it does not show the difference between a response (implying some interaction with the receiver) and a reaction (which implies no choice or interaction on the part of the receiver). A more elaborated version of the basic process as it occurs in persuasion is indicated by McGuire (1973) in the form of six stages in sequence: presentation — attention — comprehension — yielding — retention — overt behaviour. This elaboration is sufficient to show why stimulus-response theory has had to be modified to take account of selective attention, interpretation, response and recall. The model, in whatever form, is highly pragmatic, predicting, ceteris paribus, the occurrence of a response (verbal or behavioural act) according to the presence or absence of an appropriate stimulus (message). It presumes a more or less direct effect in line with the intention of the initiator or an unambiguous element built into the message.

In discussions of media effect, this has sometimes been referred to as the 'bullet' or 'hypodermic' theory, terms which far exaggerate the probability of effect and the vulnerability of the receiver to influence. Much has been written of the inadequacy of such a theory and DeFleur (1970) has shown how this model has had to be modified in the light of growing experience and research. First, account has had to be taken of individual differences since, even where expected reactions have been observed, their incidence varies according to difference of personality, attitude, intelligence, interest, etc. As DeFleur writes, 'media messages contain particular stimulus attributes that have differential interaction with personality characteristics of audience members' (1970, p.122). This is especially relevant, given the complexity of most media messages compared with the kind of stimulus used in most psychological experiments. Secondly, it became clear that response varies systematically according to social categories within which the receiver can be placed, thus according to age, occupation, lifestyle, gender, religion, etc. DeFleur notes, with some overstatement, that 'members of a particular category will select more or less the same communication content and will respond to it in roughly equal ways' (p.123).

Mediating conditions

The revision of the S-R model involved the identification of the conditions which mediated effects. McGuire (1973) indicated the main kinds of variable as having to do with source, content, channel, receivers, destination. There is reason to believe that messages stemming from an authoritative and credible source will be relatively more effective, as will those from sources that are attractive or close (similar) to the receiver. As to content, effectiveness is associated with repetition, consistency and lack of alternatives (monopoly situation). It is also more likely where the subject matter is unambiguous and concrete (Trenaman, 1967).

In general, effect as intended is also likely to be greater on topics which are distant from, or less important for, the receiver. Variables of style, types of appeal (e.g. emotional or rational) and order and balance of argument have been found to play a part, but too variably to sustain any generalization. Channel factors offer least scope for generalization, but as between mass media, print and television have been shown to differ in certain effects, sometimes for self-evident reasons, sometimes because of the difference in type of audience attachment.

Generally, research has failed clearly to establish the relative value of different modes (e.g. audio, visual, etc) in any consistent way, although the written or spoken verbal message seems to take primacy over pictorial images, according to measures of recall or comprehension (McQuail, 1985b). As we have seen, a number of obvious receiver variables can be relevant to effect, but especial notice should perhaps be given to variables of motivation, interest and level of prior knowledge.

The degree of motivation or involvement has been singled out as of particular importance in the influence process and in determining the sequence in which different kinds of effect occur (Krugman, 1965). According to Ray (1973) the normal 'effect hierarchy', as found, for instance, in the work of Hovland et al., (1949), is a process leading from cognition (the most common effect) to affective response (like or dislike, opinion, attitude) to 'conative' effect (behaviour or action). Ray argues, with some supporting evidence, that this model is only normal under conditions of high involvement (high interest and attention). With low involvement (common in many television viewing situations and especially with advertising) the sequence may be from cognition directly to behaviour, with affective adjustment occurring later to bring attitude into line with behaviour (reduction of dissonance, Festinger, 1957). In itself, this formulation casts doubt on the logic and design of many studies of persuasive communication which assume attitude to be an unambiguous correlate and indicator of behaviour.

In any non-laboratory situation of mass communication, individual receivers will choose which stimulus to attend to or to avoid, will interpret its meaning variably and will react or not behaviourally, according to choice (Bauer, 1964). This seriously undermines the validity of the conditioning model since the factors influencing selectivity are bound to be strongly related to the nature of the stimulus, working for or against the occurrence of an effect. Our attention should consequently be drawn away from the fact of experience of a stimulus towards the mediating conditions described above, especially in their totality and mutual interaction. This approach to the effect problem is more or less what Klapper (1960, p.5) recommends and describes as a 'phenomenistic' approach — one which sees 'media as influences working amid other influences in a total situation'.

Source-receiver relationships

There have been several attempts to develop theories which would account for different kinds of relationships at the individual level between sender (or message sent) and receiver, in addition to the thought already expressed that trust in — and respect for — the source can be conducive to effect. One framework is suggested by French and Raven (1953), indicating five alternative forms of communication relationship in which social power may be exercised by a sender and influence accepted by a receiver. The underlying proposition is that influence through communication is a form of exercise of power which depends on certain assets or properties of the agent of influence (communicator). The first two types of power asset are classified as 'reward' and 'coercion' respectively. The former depends on there being a gratification for the recipient from a message (enjoyment, for instance, or useful advice), the latter depends on some negative consequence of non-compliance (uncommon in mass communication). A third is described as 'referent' and describes the attraction or prestige of the sender, such that the receiver identifies with the person and is willingly influenced, for affective reasons.

Fourthly, there is 'legitimate' power, according to which influence is accepted on the assumption that a sender has a strong claim to expect to be followed or obeyed. This is not very common in mass communication, but may occur where authoritative messages are transmitted from political sources or other relevant institutional leaders. Finally, there is 'expert power', which operates where superior knowledge is attributed to the source or sender and accepted by the receiver. This situation is not uncommon in the sphere of media information-giving and may apply to the influence of 'news' and the effects of experts used for comment or advice.

It appears to be a further specification of the condition that messages from authoritative and respected sources are more effective than others, but these types of communicative power refer not just to a message or a source, but to a relationship between receiver and sender in which the former plays an active part and which gives rise to the necessary definitions of the situation. Such relationships are only established on a relatively long-term basis and thus pre-date and survive any given instance of communication. One might add that more than one of these power sources is likely to be operative on any one given occasion.

Another rather similar attempt to account for the incidence of effects (especially on opinion) has been made by Kelman (1961). He names three processes of influence. One of these, 'compliance', refers to the acceptance of influence in expectation of some reward or to avoid punishment. Another, 'identification', occurs when an individual wishes to be more like the source and imitates or adopts behaviour accordingly (similar to 'referent' power). A third, 'internalization', is intended to describe influence which is guided by the receiver's own pre-existing needs and values. This last named process may also be described as a 'functional' explanation of influence (or effect), since change is mainly explicable in terms of the receiver's own motives, needs and wishes.

Katz (1960) has recommended this approach to explaining the influence of mass communication in preference to what he considers to have been the dominant modes of explanation in the past. One of these he describes as based on an 'irrational model of man', which represents people as a prey to any form of powerful suggestion. An alternative view depends on a 'rational model', according to which people use their critical and reasoning faculty to arrive at opinions and acquire information. The latter would be consistent with a view of the individual as sovereign against propaganda and deception. Katz finds both views mistaken and less likely than a 'functional' approach to account for communicative effect, thus giving most weight to the needs of receivers and to their motives for attending to communication. He suggests five main functions which attitude formation (and thus communication use) is likely to fulfil: instrumental; adjustive (maintaining cognitive balance) or utilitarian; ego-defensive; value-expressive; knowledge (giving meaning and experience).

A model of behavioural effect

These developments of theory take one a good way from the simple conditioning model and help to account for some of the complexities encountered in research into media effect. It is obvious that in situations of unintended effect, some individuals will be more prone than others to react or respond to stimuli, 'more at risk' when harmful effects are involved. An elaboration of the basic stimulus-response for the case of television viewing has been developed by Comstock et al., (1978) to help organize the results of research in this field. It rests on the presupposition that media experience is no different in essence from any other experience, act or observation which might have consequences for learning or behaviour.

The process depicted by the model, and shown in Figure 25, takes the form of a sequence following the initial act of 'exposure' to a form of behaviour on television (TV act). This is the first and main 'input' to learning or imitating the behaviour concerned. Other relevant inputs are the degree of excitement and arousal (TV arousal) and the degree to which alternative behaviours (TV alternatives) are depicted: the more arousal and the fewer behaviours (or more repetition), the more likely is learning to take place. Two other conditions (inputs) have to do with the portrayal of consequences (TV perceived consequences) and the degree of reality (TV perceived reality): the more that positive consequences seem to exceed negative ones and the more true to life the television behaviour, the more likely is learning (P TV act) to take place. All these inputs affect the probability of learning the action (the effect), but ultimately any resulting behaviour is conditional on there being an opportunity to put the act into practice. Apart from opportunity, the most important condition is 'arousal', since without arousal (connoting also interest and

Figure 25
**A simplified version of Comstock et al.'s (1978) model of television effects on
individual behaviour (from McQuail and Windahl, 1982)**

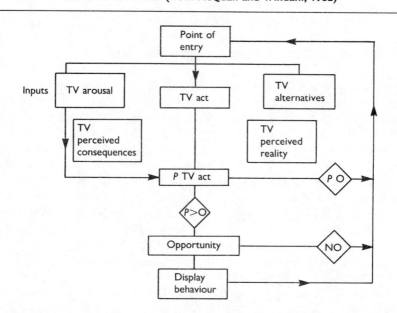

attention) there will be no learning. While full confirmation of this model from research is not yet available, it is quite an advance on the simple conditioning model and useful for directing attention to key aspects of any given case.

This model was intended to help organize research results, including those concerning the possible effects of the representation of violence in media. There is no space or need to summarize this field of study since it is periodically well reviewed (e.g. Howitt and Cumberbatch, 1975) and since the underlying process of effect is much the same as for 'prosocial' effects. It is sufficient to note the following at this point: the balance of evidence supports the view that media can lead to violent behaviour and probably have done so (cf. Surgeon General, 1972); these effects occur mainly as a result of 'triggering' of aggressive acts, imitation, identification with aggressive heroes, 'desensitization', leading to a higher tolerance for real violence.

There are also substantial areas of dispute: about the extent to which media provide release from aggressive feelings rather than provoke aggressive acts (Baker and Ball, 1969); about the applicability of laboratory findings to natural settings; about the relative importance of fictional versus 'real-life' portrayal of violence; about the independence of media as an influence; about the overall significance of whatever contribution media actually make to the level of violence in society.

Collective reaction — panic and disorder

Two main kinds of effect are here in question: widespread panic in response to alarming, incomplete or misleading information and the amplification or spreading of mob activity. The 'contagion effect' describes one important aspect of both. The first kind of effect is instanced by the much-cited reaction to the Orson Welles radio broadcast of the *War of the Worlds* in 1938 when simulated news bulletins reported a Martian invasion (Cantril et al., 1940). The second is demonstrated by the hypothesized effect of the media in stimulating civil disorder in some American cities in the late 1960s. In the first case there remains uncertainty about the real scale and character of the 'panic', but there is little doubt that the conditions for panic reaction to news could well arise, given the increase of civil terrorism and the risk of nuclear attack or, more likely, of nuclear accident. Rosengren (1976) reports an instance of alarm spread by media about the latter.

We are dealing here with a special case of rumour (see Shibutani, 1966), but the media contribute the element of reaching large numbers of separate people at the same moment with the same item of news. The other related conditions for panic response are anxiety, fear and uncertainty. Beyond this, precipitating features of panic seem to be incompleteness or inaccuracy of information leading to the urgent search for information, usually through personal channels, thus giving further currency to the original message.

Because of the threat to the established order, non-institutionalized and violent collective behaviour have been extensively studied and the media have been implicated in the search for causes of such behaviour. It has been suggested that the media, variously, can provoke a riot, create a culture of rioting, provide lessons on 'how to riot', spread a disturbance from place to place. The evidence for or against these propositions is very fragmentary although it seems to be acknowledged that personal contact plays a larger part than media in any ongoing riot situation. There is some evidence, even so, that the media can contribute by simply signalling the occurrence and location of a riot event (Singer, 1970), by publicizing incidents which are themselves causes of riot behaviour, or by giving advance publicity to the likely occurrence of rioting.

While the media have not been shown to be a primary or main cause of rioting (Kerner et al., 1968), they may influence the timing or form of riot behaviour. Spilerman (1976) lends some support to this and other hypotheses, on the basis of rather negative evidence. After failing, through extensive research, to find a satisfactory structural explanation of many urban riots in the United States (i.e. explanations in terms of community conditions), he concluded that television and its network news structure was primarily responsible, especially by creating a 'black solidarity that would transcend the boundaries of community'. In treating together the topic of panic and rioting, it is worth noting that the most canvassed solution to the dangers just signalled, the control or silencing of news (Paletz and Dunn, 1969) might entail a local panic through lack of interpretation of observable neighbourhood disturbances.

An interesting variant of this theme of media effect arises in the case of media reporting (or not) of terrorism. Much violence or disorder is either planned or threatened for political objectives, by persons seeking, however indirectly, to use the media, giving rise to a complex interaction between the two. In an analysis of this problem, Schmid and de Graaf (1982) argue that violence is often a means of access to mass communication and even a message in itself. The media are inevitably implicated in this process because of the weight they attach to reporting violence.

An interesting example of possible effect is the sequence of aircraft hijacking crimes in 1971–2, which showed clear signs of being modelled on news reports. Holden (1986) reported correlational evidence of a similar kind which seems to point to an influence from media publicity. Schmid and de Graaf also show the existence of strong beliefs by police and a moderate belief by media personnel that live coverage of terrorist acts does encourage terrorism. More difficult to assess are the consequences of refusing such coverage. There has been other empirical support for the theory that press reports can 'trigger' individual but widespread actions of a pathological kind. Phillips (1980) has reported empirical data showing that suicides, motor vehicle fatalities, commercial and non-commercial plane fatalities have a tendency to increase following press publicity for suicides or murder-suicides. He has also (1982) reported similar evidence linking the portrayal of suicide in television fiction to the real-life occurrence of suicide, although the findings have been challenged on methodological grounds (Hessler and Stipp, 1985). There seems, at least, enough evidence to make a plausible case for an imitation or 'contagion' effect of some aggregate significance.

The campaign

General features of the campaign: a model

The defining characteristics of a campaign have already been indicated, but we should pay special attention to the fact that campaigns have typically dealt with well-institutionalized behaviour that is likely to be in line with established norms and values. They are often concerned with directing, reinforcing and activating existing tendencies towards socially-approved objectives like voting, buying goods, raising money for good causes, achieving better health and safety, etc. The scope for novelty of effect or major change is thus often intrinsically limited and the media are employed to assist other institutional forces. Certainly most of the research and theory available to us about campaigns has been carried out in such circumstances and we know relatively little about campaigns, insofar as they exist, to promote objectives that are unusual or new.

A second point to bear in mind is that campaigns have to work ultimately through the individuals who receive and respond to messages and thus many of the conditions of effect which have been described also apply to campaigns. However, the organized and large-scale character of campaigns makes it desirable to sketch a revised model of campaign influence, as in Figure 26.

Figure 26 Model of campaign influence process

COLLECTIVE SOURCE	SEVERAL CHANNELS	MANY MESSAGES	FILTER CONDITIONS	VARIABLE PUBLIC REACH	EFFECTS
			Attention		Cognitive
			Perception		Affective
			Group situation		Behavioural
			Motivation		

The model draws attention to key features of the process. First, the originator of the campaign is almost always a collectivity and not an individual — a political party, government, church, charity, pressure group, business firm, etc. The known position in society of the source will strongly affect its chances of success in a campaign. Secondly, the campaign usually consists of many messages distributed through several media and the chances of reach and effect will vary according to the established nature of the channels and the message content. Thirdly, there is a set of 'filter conditions' or potential barriers which facilitate or hinder the flow of messages to the whole or chosen public. Several of these have already been discussed and they are to some extent predictable in their operation, although only in very broad terms.

Attention is named because without it there can be no effect — it will depend on the interest and relevance of content for the receivers, on their motives and predispositions and on channel-related factors. Perception is named, since messages are open to alternative interpretations and the success of a campaign depends to some extent on its message being interpreted in the same way as intended. Research has indicated the occurrence of 'boomerang' effects, for instance in attempts to modify prejudice (e.g. Cooper and Jahoda, 1947; Vidmar and Rokeach, 1974), and it is a constant preoccupation of commercial and political campaigners to try to avoid counter-effects which will aid the 'opposition'.

Much has been written of the part played by the group in mediating the effects of campaigns (e.g. Katz and Lazarsfeld, 1955) and more is said below about 'personal influence'. Here we should only note that campaigns usually come from 'outside' the many groups to which people belong, according to age, life circumstances, work, neighbourhood, interest, religion, etc. Thus much of the history of media campaign research has been a struggle to come to terms with the fact that societies are not so conveniently 'atomized' and individuated as the first media campaigners had expected. Group allegiance, or its absence, has strong consequences for whether messages are noticed and then accepted or rejected. Motivation refers to the variable of type and degree of expected satisfaction on the part of the audience member which can influence either learning or attitude change (Blumler and McQuail, 1968). The revival of an interest in audience motives and in the needs and gratification approach more generally (see pp. 233–7) was influenced by the search for better prediction and explanation of effect processes.

These 'filter conditions' together determine the structure of the public reached and the success of a campaign is ultimately dependent on a reasonable 'fit' between composition of the planned 'target' public and the actual public reached. Finally, the entry in the model for 'effects' reminds us of the enormous diversity of possible effects, some of which will be intended and others not, some short-term and some long-term. Again, a successful or 'effective' campaign will depend on some match between planned effects and those achieved. The criteria for effectiveness have thus to be set by the sender, but evaluation should also take account of side-effects which have to be weighed in the overall balance.

The model is a reminder of the complexity of campaigns and the ease with which they can go wrong. There is a very large literature on political campaigns (well reviewed in Kraus and Davis, 1976) and on other kinds of campaign (Rice and Paisley, 1981) but no way of summarizing the results except to remark that some do seem to succeed (Mendelsohn, 1973) and some to fail (Hyman and Sheatsley, 1947), with partial failures and partial successes accounting for most cases in the research literature and probably in the reality. While success or failure can usually be accounted for in terms of the various conditions which have been named, it is worth adding a few extra remarks.

First, in many areas of social life, especially in politics and commerce, the campaign has become deeply institutionalized and has acquired something of a ritual character. The question then arises, not whether campaigns produce this or that marginal advantage, but whether it would be possible not to campaign (or to advertise) without disastrous results. Secondly, campaigners do not usually control the reality of a situation or reports about it and circumstances may intervene to destroy or invalidate the message of a campaign. However, the more power to manipulate the reality (e.g. government by policy making or information giving), the more control over the outcome of a campaign. Thirdly, most campaigns that have been studied take place under conditions of competition (counter-campaigning or with alternative courses argued).

Rather too much of the theory that we have has been influenced by these circumstances and we know relatively little about campaigning for objectives that are not contested, under conditions which make it difficult to avoid otherwise trusted media sources. These are not very widely occurring circumstances, but they can occur, especially outside the 'western, industrialized' context, and evidence about them could modify existing theory.

Finally, it is worth emphasizing that campaigns do ultimately depend rather heavily on the relationship between sender and receiver and there are several ways in which relations favourable to successful campaigning are forged. Several aspects have been discussed in the context of individual level effects, but attention should be paid to the attractiveness, authority and credibility of media and sources. Especially important are moral or affective ties between audiences and media and audience belief in the objectivity and disinterest of sources. There is, however, some inherent conflict between objectivity and what is, by definition, a partisan activity. This has two consequences: the fact that other media may work against campaigns; and that an aim of many campaigners is to ensure either publicity or favourable coverage in the 'objective' media, especially in news. The capacity to do this is not unrelated to general power position in the society.

Personal influence in campaign situations

In the study of mass media effects the concept of 'personal influence' has acquired such a high status that it has, in a recent critical discussion (Gitlin, 1978), been referred to as the 'dominant paradigm'. While, in principle, the concept is relevant to any effect regardless of intention or time-span, it is appropriate to deal with it in relation to the campaign, partly because it originated in the study of campaigns and partly because the circumstances of medium-term and deliberate attempts at persuasion and information are most conducive to the intervention of personal contacts as relevant and accountable sources of influence. The underlying idea of personal influence is a simple one expressed, in the words of its originators (Lazarsfeld et al., 1944, p. 151) as follows: 'ideas often flow from radio and print to the opinion leaders and from them to the less active sections of the population'.

Thus two elements are involved: the notion of a population stratified according to interest and activity in relation to media and the topics dealt with by mass media (in brief 'opinion leaders' and 'others'); the notion of a 'two-step flow' of influence rather than a direct contact between 'stimulus' and 'respondent'. The original evidence for these ideas was presented in a study of the 1940 US presidential election campaign and by Katz and Lazarsfeld (1955). Since that time many students of campaigns have tried to incorporate the role of personal influence as a 'variable' in their research and more sophisticated campaign managers have tried to apply the ideas for the more successful management of the commercial, political or social campaign purpose.

Not only has the 'personal influence' hypothesis had a strong effect on research and campaigning, it has also played an important part in mass communication theory, and even media ideology. It has been invoked to explain the paucity of evidence of direct media effect and to counter the view, advanced first by mass society theorists and later by proponents of ideological determinism, that the media are powerful and rather inescapable shapers of knowledge, opinion and belief in modern societies. The 'ideological component' of personal influence theory lies in the supposition that individuals are 'protected' by the strength of personal ties and by the group structure within which they acquire knowledge and form judgements. Much research and thought devoted to the question have gradually led to a lower degree of emphasis on the simple proposition as expressed above (Robinson, 1976).

First, subsequent research, while confirming the importance of conversation and personal contact as accompaniment and perhaps modifier of media influence, has not clearly demonstrated that personal influence always acts as a strong independent or 'counter-active' source of influence on the matters normally affected by mass media. Some of the evidence originally advanced by the proponents of the concept has also been re-examined, with differing conclusions (Gitlin, 1978). Secondly, it has become clear that the division between 'leaders' and 'followers' is variable from topic to topic, that the roles are interchangeable and there are many who cannot be classified as either one or the other. Thirdly, it seems probable that the flow is as likely to be multi-step as two-step.

Finally, it seems clear that direct effects from the media can occur without 'intervention' from opinion leaders and highly probable that personal influence is as likely to reinforce the effects of media as to counteract them. Despite these qualifications and comments on the personal influence thesis, there are circumstances where inter-personal influence can be stronger than the media: the overthrow of the Shah of Iran seems to provide a well-documented case in point (Teheranian, 1979).

Diffusion in a development context

It is not easy to find documented cases of media applied consciously to promote long-term change. Most evidence relates to the many attempts since the Second World War to harness media to campaigns for technical advance or for health and educational purposes in the Third World, though often following models developed in the United States (Katz et al., 1963). Although early theory of media and development (e.g. Lerner, 1958) portrayed the influence of media as 'modernizing' simply by virtue of bringing western ideas and appetites (see above, p. 97) the mainstream view of media effect has been as a mass educator in alliance with officials, experts and local leaders, applied to specific objectives of change.

A principal chronicler of, and worker in, this tradition has been Everett Rogers (1962; Rogers and Shoemaker, 1973) whose model of information diffusion envisaged four stages: information; persuasion; decision or adoption; confirmation. This sequence is close to McGuire's stages of persuasion (see above, p. 260). However, the role of the media is concentrated on the first (information and awareness) stage, after which personal contacts, organized expertise and advice, and actual experience take over in the adoption process. The diffusionist school of thought tends to emphasize organization and planning, linearity of effect, hierarchy (of status and expertise), social structure (thus personal experience), reinforcement and feedback. Rogers (1976) has himself signalled the 'passing' of this 'dominant paradigm', its weakness lying in these same characteristics and its over-reliance on 'manipulation' from above. The alternative theories of development allot to mass media a rather small role, with benefits depending on their remaining close to the basis of the society and to its native culture.

It is worth noting that mass communication is itself an innovation which has to be diffused before it can play a part in diffusion processes of the kind familiar in modern or developed societies (DeFleur, 1970). It may also be that for media to be effective, other conditions of modernity have also to be present — e.g. individuation, trust in bureaucracies, understanding of media authority, legitimacy and objectivity, etc.

Distribution of knowledge

As we enter a new 'area' of our media effect typology (Figure 24) we have to deal with a set of topics and concepts which are difficult to locate in terms of the two main variables of time and purposiveness. They are, however, united by a concern with cognition: each has to do with information or knowledge in the conventional sense. One has to do with a major media activity, news provision. Another deals with differential attention to issues and objects in the world: 'agenda-setting'. A third covers the general distribution of opinion and information in society, potentially leading to the 'knowledge gap' as an effect.

These different kinds of media effect are included under the rather neutral label, 'distribution of knowledge', since the media do actually distribute and the result can be expressed as a distribution in the statistical sense. Alternative terms such as 'control' or 'management' of information would imply a consciously directed effort. This would accord with some general theories of media but not with others and the evidence for 'manipulation' in this field is not conclusive (Weaver, 1981). The kinds of effect dealt with here cannot be accommodated within any of the models so far presented, but they can be considered as falling within the scope of the model which follows (Figure 27).

News learning and diffusion

The diffusion of news in the sense of its take-up and incorporation into what people 'know' is mainly a short- or medium-term matter, but with long-term and often systematic consequences. It is also open to alternative formulations as to purpose: the media do intend in general that their audiences will learn about events but they do not normally try to *teach* people what is in the news. The question of how much people understand and remember from the news has only recently begun to receive much serious attention (e.g. Findahl and Höijer, 1981; Robinson and Levy, 1986) and most research has so far concentrated on 'diffusion' — the spread of news as measured by the capacity to recall certain named events. Four main variables have been at the centre of interest here: the extent to which people know about a given event; the relative importance or salience of the event concerned; the volume of information about it which is transmitted; the extent to which knowledge of an event comes first from news or from personal contact. The possible interactions between these four are complex, but one model of the interaction is expressed by the J-curved relationship between the proportion who are aware of an event and the proportion who heard of the same event from an interpersonal source (Greenberg, 1964).

The J-shape expresses the following findings: when an event is known about by virtually everyone (such as the assassination of Kennedy in 1963), a very high proportion (over 50 percent) will have been told by a personal contact (associated conditions here being high event salience and rapid diffusion). When events are known by decreasing proportions of the population, the percentage of personal contact origination falls and that of media source rises (associated conditions are lower salience and slower diffusion rates). However, there is a category of events which is known about ultimately by rather small proportions of a whole population. These comprise minorities for whom the event or topic is highly salient and the proportion of knowledge from personal contact rises again in relation to media sources, because personal contact networks are activated.

Theory about news diffusion is still held back by the bias of research towards a certain class of events, especially 'hard news', with a high measure of unexpectedness (Rosengren, 1973 and 1987). In order to have a fuller picture of processes of news diffusion we would need more evidence about 'soft news' and more about routine or anticipated events. We are also limited by the difficulty of estimating event importance independently of amount of attention by the media, bearing in mind the differing interests of different sectors of the society.

News learning research (reviewed by Robinson and Levy, 1986) has been increasing, especially in respect of television and with particular reference to possible lessons for the improvement of the information capacity of news. The results so far have tended to confirm the outcome of much basic communication research of decades past (Trenaman, 1967), that story interest, relevance and concreteness aid comprehension and that both prior knowledge and the habit of discussion of news topics with others are still important, in addition to favourable educational background. Robinson and Levy consider television to be over-rated as a source of knowledge of public affairs and also that several common news production and presentation practices often work against adequate comprehension of news by audiences.

Agenda-setting

This term was coined by McCombs and Shaw (1972) to describe in more general terms a phenomenon that had long been noticed and studied in the context of election campaigns. Lazarsfeld et al. (1944) referred to it as the power to 'structure issues'. An example would be a situation in which politicians seek to convince voters as to what, from their party standpoint, are the most important issues. This is an essential part of advocacy and attempts at opinion shaping. As a hypothesis, it seems to have escaped the general conclusion that persuasive campaigns have small or no effects. As Trenaman and McQuail (1961) pointed out: 'The evidence strongly suggests that people think about what they are told . . . but at no level do they think what they are told'. The evidence at that time and since collected consists of data showing a correspondence between the order of importance given in the media to 'issues' and the order of significance attached to the same issues by the public and the politicians.

This is the essence of the agenda-setting hypothesis, but such evidence is insufficient to show a causal connection between the various issue 'agendas'. For that we need a combination of: content analysis of party programmes; evidence of opinion change over time in a given section of the public (preferably with panel data); a content analysis showing media attention to different issues in the relevant period; and some indication of relevant media use by the public concerned. Such data have rarely, if ever, been produced at the same time in support of the hypothesis of agenda-setting and the further one moves from the general notion that media direct attention and shape cognitions and towards precise cases, the more uncertain it becomes whether such an effect actually occurs. Davis and Robinson (1986) have also criticized past agenda-setting research for neglecting possible effects on what people think about: *who* is important; *where* important things happen; and *why* things are important.

Most evidence (e.g. Behr and Iyengar, 1985) is inconclusive and assessments (e.g. Kraus and Davis, 1976; Becker, 1982) tend to leave agenda-setting with the status of a plausible but unproven idea. The doubts stem not only from the strict methodological demands, but also from theoretical ambiguities. The hypothesis presupposes a process of influence from the priorities of political or other interest groups, to the news priorities of media, in which news values and audience interests play a strong part, and from there to the opinions of the public. There are certainly alternative models of this relationship, of which the main one would reverse the flow and state that underlying concerns of the public will shape both issue definition by political elites and those of the media, a process which is fundamental to political theory and to the logic of free media. It is likely that the media do contribute to a convergence of the three 'agendas' but that is a different matter from setting any particular one of them.

Knowledge gaps

It has been a long-standing assumption that the press, and later broadcasting, have added so greatly to the flow of public information that they will have helped to modify differences of knowledge resulting from inequalities of education and social position (Gaziano, 1983). There is some evidence from political campaign studies to show that 'gap-closing' between social groups can occur in the short term (e.g. Blumler and McQuail, 1968). However, there has long been evidence of the reverse effect, showing that an attentive minority gains much more information than the rest, thus widening the gap between certain sectors of the public. Tichenor et al. (1970) wrote of the 'knowledge gap hypothesis' that it 'does not hold that lower status population segments remain completely uninformed (or that the poorer in knowledge get poorer in an absolute sense). Instead the proposition is that growth of knowledge is relatively greater among the higher status segments'. There is certainly a class bias in attention to 'information-rich' sources and strong correlations are persistently found between social class, attention to these sources and being able to answer information questions on political, social, or economic matters.

There are two aspects to the knowledge gap hypothesis, one concerning the general distribution of aggregate information in society between social classes, the other relating to specific subjects or topics on which some are better informed than others. As to the first 'gap', it is likely to have roots in fundamental social inequalities which the media alone cannot modify. As to the second, there are many possibilities for opening and closing gaps and it is likely that the media do close some and open others. A number of factors can be named as relevant to the direction of media effect. Donohue et al. (1975) put special emphasis on the fact that media do operate to close gaps on issues which are of wide concern to small communities, especially under conditions of conflict, which promote attention and learning.

Novak (1977) has given particular attention to the broad issue of the incidence and consequences of information gaps associated with divisions of social and economic power. At the same time, he directs attention to practical solutions which would be helpful to specific groups with identifiable 'information needs' and known 'communication potential', the latter referring to the various resources which help people to achieve goals through communication activity. Useful in Novak's contribution is the emphasis not only on form, presentation and manner of distribution in the 'gap-closing' enterprise but also on the kind of information involved, since not all information is equally useful to all groups. In general, motivation and perceived utility of information influence information seeking and learning, and these factors come more from the social context than from the media.

It has, however, been argued that different media may work in different ways and that print media are more likely to lead to a widening of gaps than is television (Robinson, 1972) because these are the favoured sources for the favoured classes. The suggestion that television can have a reverse effect (benefiting the less privileged) is based on the fact that it tends to reach a higher proportion of a given population with much the same news and information and is widely regarded as trustworthy. However, much depends on the institutional forms adopted in a given society.

In Europe, public broadcasting arrangements and, in the US, to a lesser extent, network television, ensured that television became a very widely attended and fairly homogeneous source of common information on national and international concerns. Under current conditions of change this national homogeneous audience for information is threatening to fragment, with television becoming a more differentiated source of information more akin to print media. Knowledge gap theory would indicate a widening of the gaps as a result, since the already information-rich, with higher information skills and more resources, would move even further ahead of informationally 'lower' strata. Robinson and Levy's (1986) evidence does not increase confidence in the capacity of television to close knowledge gaps.

Long-term change, planned and unplanned: a model

We enter an area where there is much theory and speculation but little firm evidence of confirmed relationships between the mass media and the phenomena under discussion: systems of values, beliefs, opinions, social attitudes. The reasons for this uncertainty are familiar: the matters are too large and complex to investigate reliably or fully; they involve broad historical and ideological judgements; the direction of influence between media and social phenomena can nearly always be two-way and is often unclear. Where evidence exists, it does little more than illustrate and add to the plausibility of a theory and it may be difficult ever to expect more. Nevertheless, we are dealing with one of the most interesting and important aspects of the working of mass communication and can at least try to develop an intelligent way of talking about what might happen.

Each of the effect processes to be discussed can occur in western liberal societies without intention being present in any significant, visible, or well-organized manner. Yet we should also recognize that these same processes are central to normative and ideological control, to the composition and maintenance of public belief systems, climates of opinion, value patterns and forms of collective awareness posited by many social theorists. It is hard to conceive of a society without such phenomena, however difficult they are to specify and quantify. Thus something of the sort is happening and the media are implicated. More important than determining the precise degree of intention is the question of direction. Do the processes favour conservation or change, and in either eventuality, in whose interest? Without some attention to this question, however provisional and beyond the scope of 'media theory' alone to answer, the discussion of these matters is rather pointless.

The model given in Figure 27 indicates some features common to various kinds of (variably) unplanned and long-term effects which

Figure 27
Process model of social control and consciousness-forming

SOURCE	CONTENT	FIRST EFFECT	SECOND EFFECT	THIRD EFFECT
Unspecified multiple sources: media in general	Messages with stable and systematic structure	Available stock of knowledge, values, opinions culture	Differential selection and response	Socialization Reality definition Distribution of knowledge Social control

have been attributed to mass media, irrespective of purpose or direction.

First, the outcomes of the various processes all posit some pattern and consistency over time in media output. Secondly they presuppose an initial cognitive effect, of the kind partly discussed. Thus the media provide materials for recognizing and interpreting reality beyond what is available from personal experience. What is termed in the model the 'second effect' refers to the encounter between what is made available and people in audiences. Here the set of 'filter conditions' signalled in the case of the campaign operate in much the same way, but especially those which have to do with social group and cultural environment. Beyond this, the processes listed as 'third effects' need to be discussed separately, having already paid attention to 'knowledge distribution'.

Socialization

That the media play a part in the early socialization of children and the long-term socialization of adults is widely accepted, although in the nature of the case it is almost impossible to prove. This is partly because it is such a long-term process and partly because any effect from media interacts with other social background influences and variable modes of socialization within families (Hedinsson, 1981). Nevertheless, certain basic assumptions about the potential socialization effects from media are present in policies for control of the media, decisions by media themselves and the norms and expectations which parents apply or hold in relation to the media use of their own children. An anomalous, but not contradictory, strand in the assumption of media as a socialization agent is the high attention given to media as potentially desocializing — challenging and disturbing the setting of values by parents, educators and other agents of social control.

The logic underlying the proposition that media do socialize or desocialize involves a view of socialization as the teaching of established norms and values by way of symbolic reward and punishment for different kinds of behaviour. An alternative view is that it is a learning process whereby we all learn how to behave in certain situations and learn the expectations which go with a given role or status in society. Thus the media are continually offering pictures of life and models of behaviour in advance of actual experience. Studies of children's use of media (e.g. Wolfe and Fiske, 1949; Himmelweit et al., 1958; Brown, 1976; Noble, 1975) confirm a tendency for children to find lessons about life and to connect these with their own experience. Studies of content also draw attention to the systematic presentation of images of social life which could strongly shape children's expectations and aspirations (e.g. DeFleur, 1964; Tuchman et al., 1978). These studies focus especially on occupation and sex roles, but there is also an extensive literature on political socialization (e.g. Dawson and Prewitt, 1969; Dennis, 1973).

McCron (1976) points to a basic divergence of theory, one strand emphasizing the consensual nature of social norms and values and another viewing media along with other agencies of social control as tending to impose on subordinate groups the values of dominant classes. The latter perspective emphasizes the central conflicts of society and the possibility of change through resistance and renegotiation of meanings. In this view, the media are neither 'prosocial' nor 'antisocial' but tending to favour the values of an established order and probably of a dominant class. In whichever formulation, the general theory that media have a socialization effect is hard to doubt, but only indirectly founded on empirical evidence, mainly concerning content and use.

Reality defining

That media offer many representations of the reality of society has already been argued and some aspects of the nature of this 'reality' have been discussed. One possible effect has been discussed under the heading of 'agenda-setting'. If the media can convey an impression about priorities and direct attention selectively among issues and problems they can do much more. The step from such a ranking process to wider opinion-forming is not a large one, and the theory of media socialization contains such an element. The basic process at work may be described by the general term 'defining the situation' and its importance rests on the familiar sociological dictum of W.I. Thomas that 'if men define situations as real they are real in their consequences'. Another general term for the same process is 'creation of a symbolic environment' (Lang and Lang, 1981).

The spiral of silence: opinion formation

In the sphere of opinion-forming one interesting theory has been developed by Noelle-Neumann (1974), starting from the basic assumption that most people have a natural fear of isolation and in their expression of opinion try to identify and then follow majority opinion or the 'consensus'. The main source of information about the consensus will be the media and, in effect, journalists, who may have considerable power to define just what is the prevailing 'climate of opinion' at a given time on a given issue, or more widely. The general term 'spiral of silence' has been given by Noelle-Neumann to this phenomenon because the underlying logic holds that the more a dominant version of the opinion consensus is disseminated by mass media in society, the more will contrary individual voices remain silent, thus accelerating the media effect — hence a 'spiralling' process. Her evidence suggests that such a process occurred in Germany in the 1960s and 1970s, to the benefit of the ruling Social Democratic Party, because of a generally left tendency among journalists of the major media.

A somewhat similar view of opinion-shaping by the American media in the 1970s, although with a politically different tendency, is given by Paletz and Entman (1981), who reported the propagation of a 'conservative myth' — the conventional journalistic wisdom that America had turned sharply away from the radicalism of the 1960s. As they show, however, there was no support for this interpretation from opinion polls taken over the period in question, thus failing to uphold the 'spiral of silence' thesis.

Among the scarce empirical enquiries, we can mention two Swedish studies reported in Rosengren (1981b) comparing trends both in newspaper editorial opinion and in public opinion. One of these, by Rikardsson, showed a very close relationship between Swedish public opinion on the Middle East issue and that of the Swedish press, both of them deviating from 'world opinion' as measured by opinion polls in several other nations. There was no time-lag on which to base a conclusion about the direction of effect. Another study, by Carlsson, on the relationship over time between party support, economic conditions and editorial direction of the press, concluded that political opinions are probably moulded first by economic conditions and second by media content. However, they found their data tending to support the standpoint of Noelle-Neumann and other proponents of 'powerful mass media'. The spiral of silence theory is a close neighbour to mass society theory and involves a similar, somewhat pessimistic, view of the quality of social relations (Taylor, 1982). According to Katz (1983), its validity will depend on the extent to which alternative reference groups are still alive and well in social life.

Structuring reality — unwitting bias

Common to much theory in this area is the view that media effects occur unwittingly, as a result of organizational tendencies, occupational practices and technical limitations. Thus Paletz and Entman (1981) attributed the propagation of a conservative myth mainly to 'pack journalism', the tendency of journalists to work together, arrive at a consensus, cover the same stories and use the same news sources. A good deal has been said in earlier chapters about the consequences of organizational and 'media culture' factors on content, and thus, potentially, for effect. The notion that media 'structure reality' in a way directed by their own needs and interests has provided the theme for some research with strong implications for effect.

An early example was the study by Lang and Lang (1953) of the television coverage of the return of McArthur from Korea after his recall, which showed how a relatively small scale and muted occasion was turned into something approaching a mass demonstration of welcome and support by the selective attention of cameras to points of most activity and interest. The reportage was seeking to reproduce from rather unsatisfactory materials a suitable version of what had been predicted as a major occasion. The reporting of a large demonstration in London against the Vietnam war in 1968 appeared to follow much the same pattern (Halloran et al., 1970). The coverage was planned for an event pre-defined (largely by the media themselves) as potentially violent and dramatic and the actual coverage strained to match this pre-definition, despite the lack of suitable reality material.

The evidence of an actual effect on how people define reality is not always easy to find. However, in their study of how children came to define the 'problem' of race and immigration Hartman and Husband (1974) do seem to show that in this respect dominant media definitions are picked up, especially where personal experience is lacking. Another, different, kind of effect is documented by Gitlin (1981) in relation to media coverage of the American student radical movement in the late 1960s. Here the media played a major part in shaping the image of this movement for the American public, partly according to their own needs (e.g. for action, stars, conflict), and caused the student movement itself to respond to this image and adapt and develop accordingly.

Most of the effects referred to here derive from 'unwitting bias' in the media, but the potential to define reality has been exploited quite knowingly. The term 'pseudo-events' has been used to refer to a category of event more or less manufactured to gain attention or create a particular impression (Boorstin, 1961). The staging of pseudo-events is now a familiar device in many campaigns (McGinnis, 1969), but more significant is the possibility that a high percentage of media coverage of 'actuality' really consists of planned events which are intended to shape impressions in favour of one interest or another. Those most able to manipulate actuality coverage are those with most power, so the bias, if it exists, may be unwitting on the part of the media, but is certainly not so for those trying to shape their own 'image'.

Cultivation theory

Among theories of long-term media effect, some prominence should be given to the cultivation hypothesis of Gerbner (1973) which holds that television, among modern media, has acquired such a central place in daily life that it dominates our 'symbolic environment', substituting its message about reality for personal experience and other means of knowing about the world. The message of television is, in Gerbner's view, distinctive and deviant from 'reality' on several key points, yet persistent exposure to it leads to its adoption as a consensual view of (American) society. The main evidence for the 'cultivation' theory comes from systematic content analysis of American television, carried out over several years and showing consistent distortions of reality in respect of family, work and roles, ageing, death and dying, education, violence and crime. This content is said to provide lessons about what to expect from life and it is not a very encouraging message, especially for the poor, women and racial minorities.

The propagation and take-up of this 'television view' is essentially the 'cultivation' process referred to (Hawkins and Pingree, 1980). The second main source of evidence in support of the theory comes from surveys of opinion and attitude which seem to support the view that higher exposure to television goes with the sort of world view found in the message of television. It is not easy to assess this part of the evidence and several authors have raised doubts about the interpretation of the television message (e.g. Newcomb, 1978) and about the causal relationship posited between television use data and survey data concerning values and opinions (Hughes, 1980; Hirsch, 1980; 1981).

There is also some reason to doubt whether the 'cultivation' effect would occur elsewhere than in the United States, partly because television content and use are often different and partly because the limited evidence from other countries is not yet very confirmatory. In relation to images of a violent society, Wobor (1978) finds no support from British data and Doob and McDonald (1979) report similarly from Canada. A longitudinal study of Swedish children (Hedinsson, 1981, p. 188) concluded, however, that evidence amounted to, 'if not a direct support, at least a non-refutation of Gerbner's theory'. However plausible the theory, it is almost impossible to deal convincingly with the complexity of posited relationships between symbolic structures, audience behaviour and audience views, given the many intervening and powerful social background factors.

A remaining point of uncertainty about the cultivation hypothesis has to do with the origin and direction of the effect. According to its authors, 'television is a cultural arm of the established industrial order and as such serves primarily to maintain, stabilize and reinforce rather than to alter, threaten or weaken conventional beliefs and behaviours' (Gross, 1977, p. 180). The statement brings the cultivation effect very close to that posited by the critical theorists of the Frankfurt School and not far from later Marxist analysis. While Gerbner has paid some attention to the institutional origins of content (e.g. Gerbner, 1969) and recognized the importance of 'institutional process analysis' (Gerbner, 1977), this work has remained largely undone and the two bodies of theory remain some distance apart. One seems over-'positivistic' and the other over-theoretical and one-sided. Perhaps cultivation theory really belongs towards the end of the section that follows.

Social control and consciousness-forming

A number of media effects have already been discussed which might belong under this heading, since the idea of socialization includes an element of social control and some, at least, of the reality-defining tendencies that have been discussed seem to work in favour of an established social order. The effects still to be considered are thus not so different in kind, nor are they always easy to assess in terms of their purposefulness: to know, that is, who is doing what to whom with what objective.

There are varying positions to be taken up. One is the view that the media act generally, but non-purposively, to support the values dominant in a community or nation, through a mixture of personal and institutional choice, external pressure and anticipation of what a large and heterogeneous audience expects and wants. Another view is that the media are essentially conservative because of a combination of market forces, operational requirements and established work practices. A third view holds that the media are actively engaged on behalf of a ruling (and often media-owning) class or bourgeois state in suppressing or diverting opposition and constraining political and social deviance. This is essentially the Marxist view of media as an instrument for the legitimation of capitalism (Miliband, 1969; Westergaard, 1977),

These alternative theories vary in their precision, in their specification of the mechanisms by which control is exercised and in the attribution of conscious power. However, they tend to draw on much the same evidence, most of it relating to systematic tendencies in content with very little directly about effects. A good deal of the evidence concerning content has already been discussed. Most relevant here are those many assertions, based on systematic content analysis, to the effect that the content of media with the largest audiences, both in news or actuality and in fiction, is supportive of social norms and conventions (an aspect of socialization and of 'cultivation'). It has also been shown to be distinctly lacking in offering fundamental challenges to the national state or its established institutions and likely to treat such challenges offered by others in a discouraging way.

The argument that mass media tend towards the confirmation of what exists is thus based on evidence both about what is present and about what is missing. The former includes the rewarding (in fiction) of 'conformist' or patriotic behaviour, the high attention and privileged (often direct) access given to established elites and points of view, the observably negative or unequal treatment of non-institutional or deviant behaviour, the devotion of media to a national or community consensus, the tendency to show problems as soluble within the established 'rules' of society and culture. One outcome of the 'cultivation' research of Gerbner et al. (1984) is evidence of a link between dependence on television and the adoption of consensual or middle of the road political views.

The evidence of media omission is, in the nature of things, harder to assemble but the search for it was begun by Warren Breed (1958) who, on the basis of what he called a 'reverse content analysis' (comparing press content with sociological community studies), concluded that American newspapers consistently omitted news which would offend the values of religion, family, community, business and patriotism. He concluded that ' "power" and "class" are protected by media performance'. Comparative content analyses of news in one or several countries have added evidence of systematic omission in the attention given to certain issues and parts of the world. Detailed studies of news content such as those by the Glasgow Media Group (1976; 1980) or by Golding and Elliott (1979) have documented some significant patterns of omission. More importantly, perhaps, they have shown a pattern of selection which is so consistent and predictable that a corresponding pattern of rejection can be inferred.

Golding (1981) wrote of the 'missing dimensions' of power and social process in the television news of more than one country. The absence of power is attributed to: the imbalance of media attention over the world; the concentration on individuals rather than corporate entities; the separation of policy options from the underlying relations of political and economic power. Social process is lost by concentration on short-term, fleeting events rather than deeper, long-term changes. In Golding's view, the outcome is a kind of ideology showing the world as unchanging and unchangeable and one likely to preclude 'the development of views which might question the prevailing distribution of power and control' (p. 80). The explanation also lies in the complex demands of news production and its place within the media industry. Herbert Gans (1979) reached not dissimilar conclusions about the generally conservative tendencies of the main American news media and is inclined to attribute this to organizational and occupational demands rather than conspiracy. He also lays stress on the reflection in news of the characteristic outlook and social milieu of those who make the news and tend, in the absence of better information, to assume an audience much the same as themselves.

The view that media are systematically used for purposes of

legitimation of the state in capitalist society has often to rely heavily on evidence of what is missing in the media. Stuart Hall (1977, p. 366), drawing on the work of both Poulantzas and Althusser, names those ideological processes in the media as: 'masking and displacing'; 'fragmentation'; 'imposition of imaginary unity or coherence'. The first is the failure to admit or report the facts of class exploitation and conflict. The second refers to the tendency to deny or ignore common working-class interests and to emphasize the plurality, disconnection and individuality of social life. The third refers to the 'taking for granted' of a national consensus, common to all classes and people of goodwill and common sense.

There is some evidence for the latter two of these processes and it would probably not be difficult to argue that the main mass media of western society are no more inclined to go critically into the fundamentals of capitalism than are the media of eastern Europe to question the justice underlying their forms of economy and society. Hall's own contribution to the theory has been to suggest that a view supportive of the capitalist order is 'encoded' or built into many media messages, in order to indicate a 'preferred reading' or interpretation which is not easy to resist.

An additional element in the theory of conservative ideological formation by the media lies in the observation that the media define certain kinds of behaviours and groups as both deviant from, and dangerous to, society. Apart from the obviously criminal, these include groups such as teenage gangs, drugtakers, 'football hooligans', and some sexual deviants. It has been argued that attention by the media often demonstrably exaggerates the real danger and significance of such groups and their activities (Cohen and Young, 1973) and tends to the creation of 'moral panics' (Cohen, 1972). The effect is to provide society with scapegoats and objects of indignation, to divert attention from real evils with causes lying in the institutions of society and to rally support for the agencies of law and order.

It has also been suggested that the media tend to widen the scope of their disapprobation to associate together quite different kinds of behaviour threatening to society. In the pattern of coverage, the activities of some kinds of terrorism, rioting or political violence help to provide a symbolic bridge between the clearly delinquent and those engaged in non-institutionalized forms of political behaviour like demonstrations or the spreading of strikes for political reasons. In some kinds of popular press treatment, according to Hall et al. (1978), it is hard to distinguish the criminal outsider from the political 'extremist'. Within the category of antisocial elements those who rely on welfare may also come to be included under the label of 'welfare scroungers' (Golding and Middleton, 1982) and the same can happen to immigrants. The process has been called 'blaming the victim' and is a familiar feature of collective opinion-forming to which the media can obviously make a contribution.

It is almost impossible to give any useful assessment of the degree to which the effects posited by this body of theory and research actually occur. First, the evidence of content is incomplete, relating only to some media in some places. Secondly, it has not really been demonstrated that the media in any western country offer a very consistent ideology, even if there are significant elements of consistency both of direction and of ideology. Thirdly, we have to accept that many of the processes, especially those of selective use and perception, by which people resist or ignore propaganda apply here as well as in campaign situations, even if it is less easy to opt for what is not there.

The historical evidence since the later 1960s, when theories of powerful mass media began to be revived, seems, nevertheless, to support the contention that something, if not the media, has been working to maintain the stability of capitalist societies in the face of economic crises which might have been expected to cause disaffection and delegitimation. The elements of society which seem inclined to disaffection are not the 'masses' or the 'workers' but the intellectuals and other marginal categories who do not rely on the mass media for their world view. It remains equally plausible, however, that fundamental forces in society helping to maintain the existing order are reflected and expressed in the media in response to a deeply conservative public opinion.

Nevertheless, it would be very difficult to argue that the media are, on balance, a force for major change in society, or to deny that a large part of what is most attended to is generally conformist in tendency. It is also difficult to avoid the conclusion that, insofar as media capture attention, occupy time and disseminate images of reality and of potential alternatives, they fail to provide favourable conditions for the formation of a consciousness and identity among the less advantaged sectors of society and for the organization of opposition, both of which have been found necessary in the past for radical social reform. It should not be lost sight of that the media are mainly owned and controlled either by (often large) business interests or (however indirectly) the state — thus the interests which do have political and economic power.

Bagdikian (1983) has documented the concentration of media power in the United States, showing for instance that fifty corporations control 87 percent of press circulation and 1 percent of owners control 34 percent of daily papers sold. In many European countries very large sections of print media are also in the hands of very few enterprises (true at least of Britain, Germany, and France). Dreier (1982) concluded that the two main elite papers in the US were also the most integrated into the capitalist system and most inclined to adopt a 'corporate-liberal' perspective — an attitude of 'responsible capitalism'. He regarded this level of control to be more significant for power than any tendency to bias selection at newsroom level.

There is a good deal of prima facie evidence that such controlling power over the media is valued beyond its immediate economic yield. In any case, it is no secret that most media most of the time do not see it as their task to promote fundamental change in the social system. They work within the arrangements that exist, often sharing the consensual goal of gradual social improvement. Gans' judgement (1979, p. 68) that 'news is not so much conservative or liberal as it is reformist' probably applies very widely. The media are committed by their own ideology to serving as a carrier for messages (e.g. about scandals, crises, social ills) which could be an impulse to change, even of a quite fundamental kind. They probably do stimulate much activity, agitation and anxiety which disturb the existing order, within the limits of systems which have some capacity for generating change. Ultimately, the questions involved turn on how dynamic societies are and on the division of social power within them and these take us well beyond the scope of media-centred theory.

Effects on other social institutions

As the media have developed, they have, incontrovertibly, achieved two things: diverted time and attention from other activities; and become a channel for reaching more people with more information than was available under 'pre-mass media' conditions. These facts have implications for any other institution which requires allocation of people's time, attention and which has to communicate information, especially to large numbers and in large quantities. The media compete with other institutions and they offer new ways of reaching permanent institutional objectives. It is this which is responsible for the process of institutional effects. Other institutions are under pressure to adapt or respond in some way, or to make their own use of the mass media. In doing so, they are likely to alter. Because this is a slow process, occurring along with other kinds of social change, the specific contribution of the mass media cannot be accounted for with any certainty.

The case of politics, as conducted in those societies with a broadly liberal-democratic basis, provides evidence of adaptation to the circumstances created by the rise of mass media, especially the fact that the media have become a (if not the) main source of information for the public (see Seymour-Ure, 1974; Paletz and Entman, 1981; Blumler, 1970; Robinson and Levy, 1986). The modern mass media inherited from the press and retained an established political function as the voice of the public and of interest groups and as the source of information on which choices and decisions could be made by a mass electorate and by politicians. We can see an interaction between a profound change in media institutions as a result of broadcasting and a response by an established political system which was inclined to resist any profound change in its ways of doing things. There are many examples of established political institutions adapting to the possibilities, but also of new kinds of political initiative being shaped from the start by, and somewhat dependent on, established mass communication. An example of the latter is offered by the case of the newly instituted (transnational) direct elections to the European Parliament, which were obliged to rely on media assistance, which was often only available to a limited degree (Blumler, 1983).

The challenge to politics from mass media institutions has taken several forms, but has been particularly strong because the press was already involved in political processes and because the introduction of broadcasting was a political act. The diversion of time from political activity was less important than the diversion of attention from partisan sources of information and ideology to sources which were more accessible and efficient, often more attractive as well as authoritative, and which embodied the rather novel political values of objectivity and independent 'expert' adjudication. As we have seen, it has increasingly seemed as if it is the mass media which set the 'agenda' and define the problems on a continuous, day-to-day basis while political parties and politicians increasingly respond to a consensus view of what should be done.

Recurring ideas about the effects of media change on political institutions include the following: that personalitites (leaders) have become relatively more important; that attention has been diverted from the local and regional to the national stage; that face-to-face political campaigning has declined; that partisanship and ideology are less important than finding pragmatic solutions to agreed problems; that opinion polls have gained in influence; that electorates have become more volatile (more inclined to change allegiance); that general news values have influenced the attention-gaining activities of political parties; that internal party channels of communication have been attenuated; that media tend more to determine terms of access for politicians; that media logic becomes more important than party logic in selection and presentation. As always, it is hard to separate out the effects of media change from broad changes in society working both on the media and on political institutions and there is much room for dispute about what is the real cause of a given effect.

Event outcomes

The argument for studying the role of the media in the outcome of significant societal events has been eloquently put by Lang and Lang (1981) and they applied their own advice by studying the Watergate affair and the downfall of President Nixon (Lang and Lang, 1983). Other researchers (Kraus, Davis et al., 1975) have made out a similar case for studying what they term 'critical events', mainly elections. There is certainly strong reason for ceasing to treat the effects of mass media as either causal outcomes of a single independent variable on dependent variables, whether in the short or the long term. The lesson of common sense and everyday observation, as well as of research, should tell us that mass media constitute a public institution which may rarely initiate change independently, but which does provide the channels, the means and an arena for the playing-out of society-wide processes in which many actors and interests are involved, often in competition. The primary object of influence may not even be the general media public itself, but other specific organized interest groups, elites, influentials, etc.

The media provide horizontal channels (especially between elites) as well as vertical channels and they can convey information *up* these vertical channels as well as *down*. The Langs note, for instance, that the media 'present political actors with a "looking-glass image" of how they appear to outsiders'. What they call the 'bystander public' (referring to the general media public) provides a significant reference group for political actors, and for whom they are inclined to frame many of their actions in public. This is a part of a process of 'coalition-building'.

This is not the place to detail examples or give a full account of relevant theory. But one can point to some desiderata for research into the role of mass media in events which are at the same time: significant; public; collective in character; long-term; and far-reaching. Ideally, one needs to identify the main actors and agents in the affair (as distinct from media and the general public), examine their motives and the means at their disposal, record their interactions and the sequence of events in which they take part, assess how actors and events are reported in public. No conclusion is likely to be possible until an outcome is arrived at and has entered history. No unambiguous assessment of the precise contribution of mass media can be expected, but no purpose is served by avoiding the task, if the effects of media in society are ever to be understood.

A note on the application of theory

Rather than summarizing general points of theory out of their context, the aim of this section is to bring together some brief implications of theory and research in relation to three areas of applied communication: that of news provision; of advertising; and public information-giving.

News

Main features of the case. This is a very large category of media provision for which there is a widespread, definite and continuous, but generalized, demand. It is usually offered non-purposefully *by the sender* to meet this demand. The news mechanism depends ultimately on receiver interest. Even so, the typical mode of attention to news is of low-involvement and casual attention, and also selective according to perceived relevance. News can be propaganda, misinformation, distortion or non-information but such cases fall outside normal research considerations.

Does it work? There is a curious dearth of evidence on the essential matter of the effectiveness of news (in part due to its lack of purposefulness), but increasingly research is being done (e.g. Robinson and Levy, 1986), especially as competition between news sources increases. The short answer is 'yes', but not very efficiently or effectively. The evidence comes mainly from experiments or surveys on news learning, which show low levels of recall and comprehension and also from general studies of public knowledge about events or matters in the news.

What kinds of effect are involved? Mostly short-term learning of factual information, but also (probably) longer-term reshaping of images of the world and society and frameworks for the interpretation of events. News, as noted, is also normative in tendency and designed or used to form or reinforce values and beliefs.

What mechanisms of effect are involved? The bases of learning from news, its power to inform, lie in personal rewards expected from having useful or interesting information and in the expertise attributed to news sources. Rewards include enhanced possibilities of social participation and reductions in uncertainty. Associated conditions of effect are: adequacy of an accessible supply; communication competence (including prior knowledge); interpersonal support for knowledge; engaging in discussion of public affairs.

Lessons for policy? Aside from matters to do with institutional provision and the quality of news, the main lessons from research seem to concern: the need for it to be relevant and of practical use to receivers; the continued higher performance of print media over television in conveying news information; the potential conflict between production and presentation values and the goals of learning and comprehension (Robinson and Levy, 1986; Clarke and Fredin, 1978).

Advertising and public relations

Main features of the case? Again, the offer is enormous, motivated undisguisedly by the interests of sender rather than receivers. It is always planned and purposeful, but also extremely diverse in its aims. The relevant mode is mainly that of 'display-attention' and audience orientation is usually one of low-involvement (Krugman, 1965).

Does it work? Again, the answer seems to be yes, although also inefficiently and with a good deal of uncertainty about how and why in any given case (and why not). The evidence, even when systematically acquired, is often only correlational and circumstantial and the difficulty of answering the question clearly (more so than in the case of news) lies to a large extent in the problem of isolating the advertising message (except experimentally) from the whole marketing and distribution operation in which advertising campaigns are usually embedded.

What kinds of effect? Mostly short-term behavioural effects (consumption) but also the longer-term formation of (favourable) images of products, brands, firms, etc, and reinforcement of long-term habits. Unplanned side-effects have been postulated — e.g. socialization into consumption (Ward et al., 1977) and, less demonstrated, such matters as consumerism, materialism, high expectations. A possible long-term effect is the control or management of a particular consumer market.

What mechanisms of effect? Expectations of personal rewards from products is probably the primary basis of effect, but advertising sometimes uses other bases of appeal: symbolic coercion (appeal to fear or anxiety); referent power (endorsement by stars, etc); authority (use of experts). There are also sometimes appeals to deeper psychological motivations. The balance between processes of cognition, attitude formation and behaviour change is very variable, as is the sequence in which these processes may occur (Ray, 1973).

Effects of advertising seem to depend primarily on the frequency and relative predominance of exposure to the message, with attention sometimes a sufficient as well as always a necessary condition of effect. Associated conditions of effect are likely to be found mainly in the characteristics of source, channel and message rather than in the receiver (as is the case with news). However, it seems that social contact network can make a positive or negative contribution and low involvement *is* more likely to be helpful than not. Possibility of acting on the message is a necessary condition.

Policy suggestions: There has been no shortage of input from research to advertisers on how to improve their effectiveness. If, as indicated, advertising does have effects in gaining planned objectives there is justification for taking possible side-effects seriously.

Public information campaigns

Main features of the case. This, like advertising, belongs to the category of planned communication. It differs in being, ostensibly at least, designed with the interests of the receiver in mind rather than those of the sender. There is also much less of it in the media. It can usually be categorized according to the kind of target group as follows: intended for everyone (e.g. universally relevant information for citizens); aimed at special sub-groups (e.g. an age group, occupational category); or designed for a minority which is hard to locate or identify (e.g. drivers who drink, tax-avoiders, drugtakers, etc). Many conditions of the case vary accordingly.

Does it work? Both theory and research evidence produce the same answer: sometimes yes, sometimes no. The main reasons have already been given above.

What kind of effects are involved? Virtually all kinds can be involved — learning attitude change, short- or long-term behaviour, etc.

What are the mechanisms of effect? These overlap to a large degree with those applicable in advertising, although there is a bias towards appeals from authority or expert knowledge and cognition usually plays a larger part than association and image. Associated conditions of effect are also numerous, but special attention has to be given to: reaching an appropriate target group; being relevant to receiver needs and interests; offering opportunities to act on the message.

Lessons for policy. There are considerable obstacles to more extensive use of media for purposes of public information, persuasion or activation, aside from questions of cost. These include especially: the potential inconsistency between media aims and spirit (non-purposeful, free time) and what might be seen as official propaganda, however well-intentioned; ethical difficulties for sponsors of such campaigns; risk of counter-productivity if campaigners are over-used and are seen as manipulative.

CHAPTER 10

MASS COMMUNICATION THEORY: A NOTE ON ITS FUTURE

On communication theory and media theory: towards a communication science?

The study of mass media has a somewhat ambiguous position in the social sciences. On the one hand, mass communication can be viewed as a special case of the much broader phenomenon of human communication, while at the same time aspects of it may be claimed as an object of interest by several academic disciplines, including sociology, political science, social psychology and also the humanities. Even if it is viewed primarily as *communication*, the uncertainty of disciplinary location is not removed, since communication is itself too broad to belong to any one existing social science discipline. At the very simplest, we are faced with the choice of defining the subject matter in terms either of social structure, or of social and behavioural processes of varying complexity, or as a matter for cultural analysis, since the production of mass communication now contributes a major component to the culture of societies, however defined.

There are increasing pressures to find some resolution of these ambiguities and some framework within which to relate alternative perspectives. One source of pressure is the growth of research and theory in all departments of the study of communication, which is connected itself with the trend towards 'informatization' of societies and many activities in society. Another pressure stems from the requirements of the research and teaching institution, which has not escaped from the need to have lines of demarcation for fields of enquiry. Labelling and identification are inescapable in handling profuse quantities of information; the development of specialist professional activities still calls for the identification of different kinds of expertise; progress in enquiry is dependent on the possibility of being able to inter-relate research findings and theoretical advances within some framework. Lastly, and more specifically for the study of mass communication, it is increasingly difficult to identify the relevant field of study in terms of the technologies of mass dissemination, around which media institutions happen to have developed.

It has been argued, at several points in this overview of theory, that specific technologies of production, storage and transmission of messages no longer clearly differentiate events or classes of events in the field of communication. Technologies once largely confined to the control and use of bounded public media organizations are increasingly used in other contexts; once typical mass media contents are similarly no longer exclusive to the media institutions; the lines of flow of communication using newer technologies are crossing different boundaries and forming diverse patterns not properly envisaged in most of the media theory inherited from a generation ago or from the founding era of the field of study of mass communications, from which many of the theories cited above stem.

There are active attempts under way to redraw the map of the study of communication and to find a broadly acceptable framework for a communication science, a term which has been in use for at least a quarter of a century to deal with problems raised by mass communication (Schramm, 1963). It is impossible here to enter into the details of such attempts, although we can refer to the work of Berger and Chaffee (1987) in finding an accommodation and interrelation between the study of communication at the different 'levels' of communication process which were signalled on p. 6 above. It may also be helpful to cite their definition of communication science as follows. 'Communication science seeks to understand the production, processing, and effects of symbol and signal systems by developing testable theories, containing lawful generalizations, that explain phenomena associated with production, processing and effects.'

The same authors point out, even so, that such a definition (with its stress on traditional 'scientistic' criteria) tends to leave out of direct account the activities of several categories of persons engaged in relevant enquiry into mass communication in particular, namely: intellectuals who criticize the symbolic output of the media according to social or aesthetic criteria; those primarily concerned with making ethical or moral judgements about communicative conduct of individuals or institutions; reformists trying to change public policies for communications; students of individual communication events in their own terms.

No doubt more categories could be added, but we can draw two broad conclusions at least: first, that the drawing of a line in a meaningful way around some activities to demarcate a 'science' necessarily involves leaving some related activities outside that line; secondly, that mass communication in particular, because of its wider involvement in political, normative and cultural processes of society, is especially in need of the work of some of the 'excluded' categories of scholar. The body of theory brought together in this volume owes its selection, if not a lot of its specific content, in part to such 'non-scientific' intellectual activity, since judgements of value and relevance have been involved.

It is undesirable to leave the question of movement towards a communication science in such an indeterminate way. If one is guided only by specific changes occurring in and around the media institutions and their technologies, it is possible at least to identify those territories adjacent to the traditional area of concern of mass communication theory which can no longer be ignored. The scheme presented in Figure 28 shows one way in which this can be done — by distinguishing between the 'sender' and 'receiver' in communication processes and introducing the distinction between public and private activities. The customary identification of the subject matter for mass communication theory has been in terms of *public* messages received by *publics* and belonging to the sphere of the *public*. The essence of technological and associated social changes has been to blur the lines between public and private and between senders and receivers. Not only are lines of demarcation blurred, but lines of communication are open to reversal of direction, creating new kinds of 'communication events' and of communication situations.

Figure 28
A typology of communication events

		SENDER Public	Sender
R E C E I V E R	Public	I	II
	Private	IV	III

The four categories of communication events (and situations) can be described as follows:

I. *Public Sender — Public Receiver.* This identifies most traditional mass communication processes and relations as dealt with in this book. The collective informational and cultural property of a society are sent and received and play their part in democratic politics, processes of social life and cultural expression and change. Questions of social integration are also indicated by this type of event.

II.   *Private Sender — Public Receiver.* This identifies a set of particular uses of what are usually public and open mass media. Among these are advertising, advocacy and the expression of individual or group opinion to a wider public. This category of event also includes other communication activities which originate within organizations or enclosed institutions directed at a wider public. These may be contacts with actual or potential clients by organizations of many kinds and also public relations or 'image-building' activities and information or persuasion campaigns mounted by charities, pressure groups, government departments or other voluntary bodies. In general, the events identified adapt the institutional channels of mass media to particular ends of advocacy or information, but they can include uses of other communication technologies, for instance direct mail or telephone.

III.   *Private Sender — Private Receiver.* Two main (and large) categories of events are covered: interpersonal communication in many different settings and for many different purposes; and intra-organizational communication. By definition, the use of established mass media is rarely involved (though it happens), although for some purposes, adapted forms and technologies of mass media may be used (for instance, in-house newspapers, closed-circuit television and computer networks, computer-videotex systems, computer mail, etc).

IV.   *Public Sender — Private Receiver.* In one sense, mass communication is normally always open to private reception, based on personal choice or relevant message. Nevertheless, the multiplication and diversification of channels of all kinds may be thought to have decreased the public (and collective) nature of reception. More significant, such developments as videotex systems and associated data bases, subscription cable television and software provision to personal computers have established what are arguably qualitatively new kinds of relationship between senders and receivers and a different concept of what is public. Culture and information offered for choice are often items of private property which have to be paid for and are not considered free public goods as with the original conception of the content of the traditional mass media. Of course, book publishing offers a precedent, but it, significantly, has never been given due attention in mass communication theory, partly because of the diminished sense in which it constituted a public offer.

It may be noted in passing that this scheme also identifies much the same categories of 'information traffic' as in Figure 7 in chapter 2. Type I at least can also correspond largely to 'allocution', type III to 'exchange' and type IV to 'search'. The reasons why this should be so are not hard to account for, but the classification offered here has a wider purpose in identifying different but adjacent fields of interest for the study of communication. It should be clear, from the brief descriptions of the types, why it is increasingly difficult to maintain the boundaries and confine attention only to one type at a time. For instance, much of the content, as well as financial and institutional support for mass communication (type I), now comes from private or particular interest operating according to the second type of concern. The new electronic media, in particular, are being used for events falling under all four types. The category of 'private' receiver is being enlarged through developments of communication technology, as already noted. The main point of this discussion is to emphasize that, quite apart from any developments in the body of knowledge which could comprise a communication science, we can no longer separate one set of concerns so indicated from any of the others, in the empirical reality of what is going on in society.

This comment on the redrawing of boundaries and the possible emergence of something like a 'communication science' does not pre-empt or replace the earlier discussion of possible convergence between 'critical researchers' and others (pp. 103–5), but it does have further implications for that discussion. We can suppose, at least, that any new framework of theory and research concerned with communication would have room within it for theorists and researchers of different persuasions in terms of their social purposes and their priorities. This would mean some measure of acceptance of much the same set of concepts and methods. It is quite likely that those who have discerned signs of convergence are in fact observing some effects of the maturing of a science, which can only advance by co-operation and conflict. Without the common framework of terms and methods and an identification of problems in a shared social and conceptual space, co-operation or conflict are neither very likely to occur nor to have fruitful results.

Main themes of current mass media theory

What follows is not a complete and itemized summary of the many theories, concepts and fragments of theory which have been recounted. Despite the volume of theory and ideas which is now available, media theory is still very provisional and incomplete. In place of clear statements about the degree and direction of various media tendencies or about interactions between media and society, we can only make a number of tentative observations, often entailing alternative positions. As a result, the body of mass media theory available appears sometimes as a set of options or unresolved disagreements. There is no single reason for this state of affairs, but it stems from the insufficiency of evidence, the variations of circumstances, the essential ambiguity and duality of many of the phenomena involved and the lack of integration of media theory in any wider body of communication theory. While separate themes have been distinguished, it will be apparent that they often overlap and sometimes recur. While it is unlikely, given the changes under way in media institutions and society, that definitive answers to the questions posed can be expected, it is equally unlikely that, in the foreseeable future, the issues raised will cease to be relevant.

Media as either socially fragmenting or unifying

The impact of the media on the quality or 'health' of social life has been a recurrent preoccupation of media theorists and the results of their work are as mixed and divided as are conceptions of what does constitute a 'healthy' social formation. On the one hand, the media are associated historically with the break-up of communal, close-knit forms of social life and with the development of more open, calculative and less intense forms of attachment. Media culture has developed as one which is metropolitan and universalistic rather than local or particularistic. As such, the media have opened up wider areas of the life of society to public surveillance and control, but have also tended to increase freedom by offering cultural and informational alternatives over and above those otherwise available, even if the alternatives offered tend everywhere to be much the same.

The central issue has to do with whether the media act as a centralizing and unifying force or one which is decentralizing and fragmenting. Beyond that, the question arises as to whether the given tendency has negative or positive implications. Thus 'unifying' can denote nation-building, modernization, political strength, social integration, group solidarity and a capacity for mobilization for common ends. Or it can be associated with homogenization, manipulation and oppression. Decentralization and fragmentation may be associated with atomization, loneliness or privatization, but can also, in their positive aspects, denote diversity, freedom, choice, change and more opportunity for personal development. Modern societies can, in any case, be loosely integrated as nations, but with well-integrated primary groups and associations, to which mass media can make a contribution. Thus theory does not point unambiguously to either a positive or a negative effect from mass communication, but sets out rather divergent possibilities.

The non-centrality and dependence of the media

The distinction implied here is between a view of media as an independent driving force or initiator in society, either through their technology or dominant messages and one which sees them as essentially dependent, reactive to other primary forces and subordinate to power exercised elsewhere in society. In the theory as summarized in this book, rather more weight is attached to the second position, for several reasons: because the subordination of the media to the state is generally institutionalized and they usually draw on, or defer to, sources of legitimate authority or actual power; because they seem to respond and react to demands and expectations from their audiences, rather than seem to shape them; because media use seems to be shaped, and messages interpreted, according to the dispositions of receivers and according to collective influences from culture and social group; because, however useful and valued, the media do not seem, for most people, to be the object of strong sentiments of attachment — they are widely, but not deeply, valued.

These various reasons for positing dependency on the part of the media are not all consistent with each other, nor do they square with notions of dependency *on* media, for which there is also theoretical support. The inconsistency lies in the argument that media, in their intermediate and mediating position in society, seem to defer both to 'superior' power in society and to their audiences. It is simply that, for most of the time, in pursuing their own predominant objectives, they do tend to find a modus vivendi between the various pressures. It does not rule out possibilities of use for pursuing ends chosen by special publics or instances where media publicly express the popular will or 'public interest' in opposition to power-holders. However, these are not typical situations, any more than it is typical for the media to be directly used as instruments of power.

While there are good grounds for asserting the marginality and dependence of media in general in relation to society, there are also reasons why this situation could change. These have to do with the greater centrality of the media in an 'information society', the growing economic importance of media-related industries and the extension of functions into spheres of 'private' activities in society, as indicated above. It may eventually be necessary to abandon notions of both media subordination and media determinism and treat media as an 'open system', not clearly separable from society or other institutions.

The media as an object of social and cultural definition

Media acquire definitions which are composed of a mixture of observed fact, 'image', valuation, prescription and the results of inbuilt communicative properties. They are sets of ideas about what the media actually do and what they ought to do, which guide expectations and also set limits to their activities. Such definitions are established early in the history of a given medium and are often adaptations of ideas relating to pre-existing media and communication forms. They are not easy to manipulate and have features that are often rather arbitrarily derived from the historical circumstances of their origins. The importance of such definitions lies mainly in their influence on ideas of what is appropriate as media content and media functions in given circumstances. They can thus informally regulate and limit the purposes for which media can be used. They are resistant to revision and tend to discourage 'deviant forms' which are sometimes envisaged in plans and policies to use media for objectives other than those stemming naturally from their origins and use. It is not easy, consequently, to legislate for the coming of newer media according to logical blueprints or to use older media for ends not built into their definitions, for instance to use entertainment media as means of public instruction or cultural advance.

The ambiguity and multiplicity of media purpose and message

The discussion of theory has, at various points, highlighted the fact that media can and do, simultaneously, serve not only many, but even divergent, purposes. These purposes are a mixture of the sacred and the profane, material and spiritual, the enduring and the ephemeral. The media are also inextricably tied in with questions of social control and order and with processes of social change. Sometimes they are about nothing in particular, in the sense of lacking any particular 'message' or communicative purpose. This is especially true where purpose is defined as gaining and keeping attention and where 'ratings' have become an end in themselves or a means to some end other than the ostensible ones of entertaining, informing or uniting in cultural experience.

The media are open to use by different interests, groups and sectors of society for quite different ends. While such objectives do not need to be in conflict or mutually inconsistent, there are usually considerable elements of unresolved contradiction and latent tension in media activity taken as a whole.

Together with multiplicity of purpose goes ambiguity of meaning. Attempts to 'decode' the meaning of content and to use the result as a criterion of evaluation or a means of prediction have found no sure scientific foundation. There is as yet no agreed way of 'reading' in an objective way what is offered by the media. It is not clear what media content can tell us about its own producers, about society, or about its audiences. This is not problematic for the normal media user, who is provided with conventions for distinguishing degrees of reality and objectivity. However, the message of media theory seems to be that we might better regard media content as a unique cultural form, a 'media culture', fashioned according to its own conventions and codes and forming a more or less independent component of the social reality. Thus, even where media act as carriers for other institutions, they tend to alter the substance, adjust the message, to conform to the demands of the 'media culture' or the 'media logic'.

Media freedom and independence

Despite what has already been written about the dependence of the media on society and public, the idea that media are independent and do have a right to operate as free and legitimate agents within a sphere defined as belonging to their professional competence is very much alive. Such a view is embedded in public definitions of the media; it is institutionalized in some normative theories of the press; it comes to light in studies of media organizations and occupations; it is extremely important to most journalists and creative media workers. This expectation of autonomy has some specific implications for mass communication which have been highlighted by theory.

First, media seem to protect or enlarge their autonomy in relation to sources of ultimate political and economic power, by developing an objective, open, neutral, balancing stance which establishes a 'distance' from power and a lack of involvement in conflict. Secondly, efforts to control the circumstances of work within media organizations lead also to some degree of routinization, standardization and loss of creativity. Thirdly, attempts to limit or manage the demands of the audience lead to a measure of detachment from the public and are often accompanied by a stereotyping of the wishes and capacities of the audiences.

Media theory has tended to emphasize the resulting distancing and disengagement of modern mass media from the societies in which they operate. It is sometimes suggested, at the same time, that media find it harder to maintain a genuine detachment from the power pressures of society than from demands or needs of their audiences. The nature of media systems and institutions favours the ideal of independence, but leaves media more scope for detachment from the audience than from state, clients, sources and owners. Media organizations can and do define their own purposes, but often purpose is given from outside and such outside sources are more likely to be found in other powerful institutions than in the public or community which the media are ostensibly supposed to serve.

Media and power

The concept of media power can be formulated in a variety of ways and the lessons of media theory, in this case, as with others, are fragmentary and sometimes inconsistent. Two main questions are at issue: (1) the effectiveness of media as instruments for achieving given power ends — persuasion, mobilization, information, etc; (2) that concerning *whose* power the media exercise — is it that of society as a whole, of a particular class or interest group, or of individual communicators? An extension of this second question is whether, in general, the media act to increase, sustain or diminish existing inequalities of power in society.

Several relevant points have already been made: the media are, in several senses, themselves very dependent and thus limited in what they can achieve on their own for any purpose; they are also allowed some independence to set and pursue their own objectives as organizations or actors in society. The predominant message from media theory on the latter point is that the media prefer to adopt a neutral stance and do not generally try to challenge existing power-holders. They are vulnerable to pressure, sometimes even to assimilation by external power interests — sometimes they seek openly to support the latter.

Among other, somewhat inconsistent messages from theory and research, are the following. First, within limits set by circumstances of distribution, audience dispositions and other trends in society, effects from mass communication and other longer-term consequences can and do occur. In short, theory supports the view that the media can achieve reasonably delimited objectives and thus can be 'effective', according to their chosen purposes. In effect, this is an answer to the first type of power question posed at the start of this section. Secondly, it seems that media, for many reasons, despite, or even because of, their aspirations to neutrality, more often serve, by action or by omission, to protect or advance the interests of those with greater economic and political power in their own societies, especially where these are organized to use the media for their power ends. This is a brief general answer to the second kind of power question raised above.

This is not to say that the power of the media is only that of a dominant class, but it does assert that whatever wider social power the media possess comes mainly from 'outside'. To be effective, the media require legitimacy, authority and social support which cannot be sufficiently generated by their own resources. This does not exclude the possibility that the media will be available to forces of progressive social change, for the expression of popular demands or for advancing the interests of the public they usually claim to serve. However, the normal operation of media does not seem to favour the initiating of fundamental change and the 'interests of the public' tend to be re-interpreted according to the working needs of the media. In the critical choice between using the mass media for the interests of the senders (society, advocates, communicators, advertisers, the media themselves) or those of receivers (audiences, publics or sub-groups in society), the balance is somewhat tilted towards the former. In effect, this means more likelihood of 'manipulation' than of real 'communication'.

The mixing of normative and objective elements

One recurrent strand of media theory to be mentioned briefly, relates to the difficulty of disentangling what is objective and value-free from that which is normative and value-laden. This difficulty faces the media themselves as well as theorists about the media. Virtually none of the issues just raised can even be formulated, let alone settled, without reference to some or other value position. Media theory is thus inescapably normative, as is social theory. Only within a narrow range, holding constant questions of value and purpose, can one pose and test objective propositions. In so doing, one will have almost certainly crossed a boundary and retreated into a territory governed by the rules of other sciences, whether psychology, economics, information theory, statistics, or whatever.

This circumstance will remain one of the obstacles to developing a 'communication science' of the kind envisaged at the start of this chapter.

Diversity of models and modes of communication

Although mass communication is open to typification as one-way transmission to many, we have also been reminded that it covers a great variety of communication aims and relationships. Especially important to the variation are: whether the transmission is directed and purposive or not; whether reception is similarly motivated and active or not; the kind and strength of relationship between audience and communicator. One recurrent theme has been the central place taken by a model of mass communication as a process of display and attention-gaining, rather than expression, persuasion or information. Such a model does at least capture an important aspect of the reality of mass communication from the point of view of mass communicators and helps us to understand both typical forms of content and patterns of audience formation and response.

The central point of the model is that it represents the activity of a good deal of mass communication as directed in the first instance towards gaining and keeping interest and attention from unknown potential 'spectators'. It helps to account for several aspects of organizational behaviour which have to do with gaining audiences, both as an objective in itself, for gaining revenue and as a criterion of success. It is an essential component in any explanation of news values, presentation values and choices of forms and formats. It contributes a unifying feature to the notion of the audience.

Most significantly, perhaps, attention is both an effect in itself and a necessary condition of most other effects, intended or not. Attention-giving is an effect to be measured in individual time-use and displacement, but is also manifested in large-scale, collective phenomena, such as the involvement in television spectacles (Katz and Dayan, 1986). As a key to other effects it is evidently a condition of agenda-setting, reality-defining, opinion conformism and reinforcement. It has a central part in a wide range of behavioural effects, such as imitation, 'triggering', etc. Attention-giving can have several sources: in the circumstances of society; in people themselves (needs, interests, knowledge, dispositions); in the media's own efforts to gain attention (forms of display). Where all three sources are involved, there is a maximum likelihood of actual attention and actual effect. Aside from these points, which help to bring together considerations of media organization, content, audience and society, we are reminded of the ancestry of mass communication in show business and story telling.

Mass communication in the future and new problems of theory

It is no longer in doubt that mass communication systems will change, perhaps radically, in response to the possibilities and challenges of new technologies for communication in all its phases, from conception to 'delivery'. At several points in this book, incipient changes have been noted and possible trends indicated. The outstanding uncertainties are those always present, over the speed, form and consequence of the changes under way. At the time of writing the mass communication systems established throughout the world in the second half of the present century, based on a balance of functions between print and electronic media, still largely conform to the models underlying the definitions given at the start of this book. We are still, to a large extent, dealing with media of *mass dissemination*.

Even the most developed economies have not yet experienced any great discontinuity as a result of new technologies and, for the most part, these have been used to make existing ways of working and disseminating more efficient and more extensive. Radical change is still largely a matter of (increasingly realistic) speculation, experimentation and marginal adoption. Nevertheless, it is necessary to conclude this book about mass communication theory with another brief look into the future, to assess what implications for theoretical development (whether within the boundaries of a communication science or not) are discernible. These can best be treated under two separate headings, one to do with problems of a (social) science of communication, the other to do with normative, regulative and political aspects of what will remain a deeply institutionalized set of activities and events.

Adaptation of the concepts, models and methods for a communication science

Media institution and organization

In respect of the production of media content, the main changes are likely to be in the direction of *delocating* the site of production and making it *less unitary*. This is partly due to further division of labour and normal economic developments in an expanding and highly labour- and capital-intensive industry. But it also comes from internationalization and from the possibilities of dispersion of communication and control networks which underlie media production. Not unimportant is the fact that at the core of the mass communication industry (it is hard to use any other term now) there still reside individual creators, performers, experts, small teams and groups of creative workers, who have always had a degree of resistance to bureaucratization. In a sense, therefore, the emerging circumstances affecting mass communication are already recognizable and to that extent not new.

It is more a case of the ruling concepts and units of analysis deployed in the study of mass communication being themselves somewhat dated as the reality moves further forward. This problem was discussed in chapter 6 in commenting on the somewhat fictional view of media as bounded units of organization within fairly clear lines of institutional demarcation. To recognize the problem is not to find the solution, and neither is unique to the case of mass communication. However, in general, the study of production of media content does become more difficult, the more it is fragmented as a process and further separated from the process of distribution and reception.

The audience

Most of the problems of dealing with newer kinds of audiences have already been discussed in the relevant chapter, but they boil down to another kind of fragmentation and individualizing of reception. The changes likely to be caused by greater availability of content are accompanied by probable changes in the *relation* between receivers and senders. To a certain extent these developments can still be handled by the concepts already in use which deal with degrees and kinds of attachment to sources and with new types of information traffic (as shown in Figure 7). Nevertheless, the predominant images of the audience, as either a large aggregate of passive spectators or as an active and self-conscious public, will gradually capture less and less of the reality. The change of balance towards a view of 'audience behaviour' as individual acts of purchase or consumption, or acts of consultation will have to be better recognized in the tools of audience research.

This is likely to involve, among other things, more use of a variety of functionalist theory as developed in uses and gratifications research. The 'expectancy value' theory described already (p. 235) seems, for example, to offer one model of analysis of audience behaviour in the new situation where units of content offered are likely to be chosen or avoided on the basis of evaluations (which the media will seek to manage) and subjected to assessments in terms of satisfactions obtained, which will guide future choice of channels in competitive situations. The break-up of audiences, previously more socially and culturally homogeneous, will also seem to open up more scope and need for 'reception analysis' of various kinds, to chart the range of meanings acquired and to play a part in research on satisfaction and information transfer.

Communication effects

Effect research will probably remain, as now, suitably equipped with concepts, models and methods, since it is hard to envisage effects which have not been broadly conceived in existing theory and a vast ingenuity has already been devoted to investigating almost any imaginable kind of effect. However, the balance of attention is likely to change, with relatively more weight to cognitive effects from mass media channels and to structural effects on the distribution of knowledge in society. More weight will also have to be given to factors relating to attention-giving, especially motivation and prior knowledge and interest. What may well have to change, however, is the broad definition of effect as it was conceived in the 1930s, to admit more readily as categories of effect, matters such as time-use and amount and degree of attention given to message stimuli. These are not new ideas, but they come more to the fore as the significance of the whole system of society-wide communication changes.

Content as information

It can be argued that the study of mass communication will have to converge on the study of information (part of the case for a science of communication), but this will require some developments of concept and method. A central problem is that of finding appropriate units of measurement and analysis for measuring flow in comparable ways across different media channels and different social systems. Tied in with this is the problem of qualitative differentiation between units of information. If information is being increasingly offered and demanded as a commodity, it may have to be treated much as other things handled in different kinds of exchange and production systems. This can be done fairly simply if one closes one's eyes to qualitative differences in general and to the real problem of treating as a commodity something which may not have a material form and which can be used over and over again without loss of value. Most available theory relating to commodities or services with an economic value does not have to face these problems, which are acute for the formal analysis of communication flows and uses.

It has been found possible to measure quantities of flow and use of information in terms of time, cost of energy use (e.g. Pool et al., 1984) and also to differentiate between channels and conventional functions of communication (e.g. between private and business correspondence or telephone calls, etc). Sometimes refined and flexible classification systems have been applied to the subject matter of complex forms of media content (as by Gould et al., 1984). The task of assigning qualitative weightings to units of 'information', in the broadest sense, is still at an early stage and will still involve solving further theoretical problems, since there are numerous dimensions of quality which have to be taken into account.

Nevertheless, certain useful principles have already been established for evaluating the products of 'information work', aside from taking account of differential investment in time and money. For instance, it is widely recognized that: some information products have uniqueness or rarity value; some have an 'aura' which cannot be reproduced (as with antiques or original works of art); some have a depth and rich ambiguity of meaning (as with poems or other art objects); some a high storage or re-use value (e.g. musical scores, computer programs, maps); some are given an arbitrary (but recorded) value by society (as with sacred texts, founding documents etc), and so on. The theoretical problems to be solved involve turning these basic principles into systematic forms of measurement or classification. In general, we can say at least that information units do have a differential 'added value' over and above their 'uncertainty reduction' capacity according to dimensions which can often be stated.

It is arguable that the study of information and culture (conceived as information) in terms of its production, flow, reception and application could now begin to develop more rapidly, especially with the computer as an aid to multi-dimensional classification and measurement. The more the flow of information is mediated by computers, the more feasible will such a project become.

Emerging issues for normative theory of mass communication

The close interconnection between the theory of the working of mass communication in society and several potent and essentially normative issues in social and political theory has already been remarked on. Even if a communication science of the kind envisaged at the start of this chapter does develop, it will not be able to escape from the questions, choices and dilemmas which are faced by those who participate in communication institutions. One of the tasks of theory appropriate to communication science will be to provide concepts and formulations for handling normative questions. Much of what we already have in the way of normative theory will remain relevant and it is impossible to predict the future well enough to say what will become less relevant or what must be added. Nevertheless it is hard to see how we can ever escape from fundamental questions of power, freedom, control, equality and solidarity, and we do have enough idea of the problems posed by current developments of communication to suggest some of the issues which will need attention.

New technology as ideology

New media and new and expanded uses of communication technology are being widely advocated on the basis of an implied theory of media technology determinism, which is also often a normative theory, giving positive weighting to the maximization of communication possibilities, especially in interactive forms. There is relatively little that is new in the theory, but it is being offered on the back of a vision of economic and industrial opportunities, which does have some qualitative novelty about it. Its normative implications (where not made explicit) lie in the general value placed on change, novelty, variety, mobility and individualism. Social progress is assumed to follow and be caused by the expansion of communication of all kinds and to take the form of greater individual freedom and satisfaction. One of the tasks for the normative branch of a communication science will be to formulate such propositions clearly and provide a framework for putting such theories to the test, under the conditions of information societies which do actually emerge.

Freedom and control

Mass communication theory already has to deal with an institution which varies very much in terms of the degree of regulation and control which is either exerted in practice or justified by a reigning social and political theory. The variation can range from a strongly-enforced authoritarian theory to total libertarianism. But within societies there are also variations between the amount of control applied to different media and different kinds of content. In countries with a liberal media theory, broadcasting and film have almost always been subject to more limitations and controls than press media. The justifications for control generally offered, mainly on technical grounds, have never been fully convincing, and are being increasingly undermined. It was in the interests of most states to control the early electronic media and they proved easier to control than did print media, partly because they escaped established political definitions. Both factors are declining in their force: the wish to stimulate the use of new technology for industrial-economic reasons has become more widespread and has outweighed the fear of subversion; and it is simply becoming harder to police the air- and cable-ways. In addition, the ostensible grounds for the original control are no longer so valid or convincing.

Social–cultural problems versus economic–commercial goals

This provides the background to another set of issues of theoretical interest and practical consequence for the media institution. Decisions about communication were formerly taken largely on grounds of social, political and cultural considerations. Now economic and commercial factors play at least as much of a part, to judge from developments in Europe at least (McQuail and Siune, 1986). The potential conflict between the two obliges one to be much more clear about the objectives and the means of communication policy, both in their 'economic-technological' and their 'cultural' varieties. A normative theory for communication policy should be able to offer guidance on: the objectives of a social-cultural policy; the threats posed by an unrestrained economic-technological policy; and the possible forms which social control could, or which intervention should, take.

On the first of these, what is called for is some reformulation of the concept of the public interest in communication and what kinds of things should be regarded as deserving protection (Ferguson, 1986). While many current goals of 'communication welfare' (of the kind discussed in chapter 5) will remain, there is likely to be some shift in the balance of priorities of public communication policy. In the past, the major priorities have been: to secure universal distribution and maximum potential to receive; to establish a sphere of public communication in the service of both democratic and capitalistic institutions; the preservation of good order and the security of the state.

In the future, problems are likely to be posed by growing 'gaps' in society and globally in terms of access to information and cultural goods. There will be 'relative deprivation' in access and capacity to use information and such deprivation will be structured by and reinforce social-economic inequality (Golding and Murdock, 1986). There will also be a relatively greater demand for access to the new channels as 'senders' or 'suppliers' of information, in the widest sense. The somewhat conflicting demands for rights of access to information on the one hand and protection of privacy on the other are also likely to attract more attention within normative theory.

Cui bono

Accompanying the search for new criteria for establishing priorities, will be fresh attention to the question of *who* should benefit from intervention or regulation of communication provision (hardware or software). The main ostensible beneficiaries of communication policy in the past have tended to be one or more of the following: the nation state; society at large; minorities of one kind or another; cultural elites; media business interests. It is not that many new kinds of beneficiary can be envisaged, but the relative strength of alternative claims will have to be reassessed under conditions of change. It may, for instance, seem desirable to shift subsidies away from producers and senders (as with public broadcasting) and to receivers, to increase their potential to use information and cultural services made available in the information market as a whole.

Future of communication policy

Something similar can be said of the means and forms for implementing communication policies. The range of possibilities exemplified at present is already very wide, but the dominant forms are: public monopoly control; limitations on private monopoly; various kinds of legal regulation; various kinds of financial support; international agreements on technical and cultural matters. These are usually practical devices for achieving some specific objective, but a critical understanding of how they do or might work under changing conditions will call for a considerable elaboration of theory. Currently, it is often difficult even to describe the logic of the institutional devices which have proliferated in the sphere of public communication. Although the spirit of the times and the logic of new communication technology both seem opposed to any extension of control over communication, there seems to be no reduction in the amount of planning and regulation, however facilitatory in intention, of communication matters. Hence, theory of communication in the service of communication policy, broadly conceived, is likely to be needed well into the future.

REFERENCES

Adorno, T. and Horkheimer, M. (1972) 'The Culture Industry: Enlightenment as Mass Deception', in *The Dialectics of Enlightenment*. New York: Herder and Herder.

Alexander, J.C. (1981) 'The News Media in Systemic, Historical and Comparative Perspective', in E. Katz and T. Szecsko (eds), *Mass Media and Social Change*, pp. 17–51. Beverly Hills and London: Sage Publications.

Allen, I.L. (1977) 'Social Integration as an Organizing Principle', in G. Gerbner (ed), *Mass Media Policies in Changing Cultures*, pp. 235–50. New York: Wiley.

Altheide, D.L. (1974) *Creating Reality*. Beverly Hills and London: Sage Publications.

Altheide, D.L. (1985) *Media Power*. Beverly Hills and London: Sage Publications.

Altheide, D.L. and Snow, R.P. (1979) *Media Logic*. Beverly Hills and London: Sage Publications.

Althusser, L. (1971) 'Ideology and Ideological State Apparatuses', in *Lenin and Philosophy and Other Essays*. London: New Left Books.

Altschull, J.H. (1984) *Agents of Power: the Role of the News Media in Human Affairs*. New York: Longman.

Andrew, D. (1984) *Concepts in Film Theory*. New York: Oxford University Press.

Ang, I. (1985) *Watching Dallas: Soap Opera and the Melodramatic Imagination*. London: Methuen.

Baehr, H. (1980) *Women and the Media*. London: Pergamon.

Bagdikian, B. (1983) *The Media Monopoly*. Boston: Beacon Press.

Baker, R.K. and Ball, S. (eds) (1969) *Violence and the Media*. Washington DC: GPO.

Ball-Rokeach, S. and DeFleur, M.L. (1976) 'A Dependency Model of Mass Media Effects', *Communication Research* 3: 3–21.

Ball-Rokeach, S.J. (1985) 'The Origins of Individual Media-System Dependency', *Communication Research* 12(4): 485–510.

Barthes, R. (1967) *Elements of Semiology*. London: Jonathan Cape.

Barthes, R. (1972) *Mythologies*. London: Jonathan Cape.

Barthes, R. (1977) *Image, Music, Text: Essays*. Selected and translated by Stephen Heath. London: Fontana.

Barwise, T.P., Ehrenberg, A.S.C. and Goodhart, G.J. (1982) 'Glued to the Box? Patterns of TV Repeat Viewing', *Journal of Communication* 32(4): 22–9.

Bass, A.Z. (1969) 'Refining the Gatekeeper Concept', *Journalism Quarterly* 46: 69–72.

Bauer, R.A. (1958) 'The Communicator and the Audience', *Journal of Conflict Resolution* 2(1): 67–77. Also in L.A. Dexter and D.M. White, *People, Society and Mass Communication*, pp. 125–39. New York: Free Press.

Bauer, R.A. (1964) 'The Obstinate Audience', *American Psychologist* 19: 319–28.

Bauer, R.A. and Bauer, A. (1960) 'America, Mass Society and Mass Media', *Journal of Social Issues* 10(3): 3–66.

Bauman, Z. (1972) ' A Note on Mass Culture: On Infrastructure', in D. McQuail (ed), *Sociology of Mass Communication*, pp. 61–74. Harmondsworth: Penguin.

Becker, L. (1982) 'The Mass Media and Citizen Assessment of Issue Importance', in Whitney et al., *Mass Communication Review Year Book*, pp. 521–36. Beverly Hills: Sage Publications.

Beharrell, B. and Philo, G. (eds) (1977) *Trade Unions and the Media*. London: Macmillan.

Behr, R.L. and Iyengar, S. (1985) 'TV News, Real World Cues and Changes in the Public Agenda', *Public Opinion Quarterly* 49(1): 38–57.

Bell, D. (1961) *The End of Ideology*. New York: Collier Books.

Bell, D. (1973) *The Coming of Post-Industrial Society*. New York: Basic Books.

Bell, D.V.J. (1975) *Power, Influence and Authority*. London and Toronto: Oxford University Press.

Belson, W.A. (1967) *The Impact of Television*. London: Crosby Lockwood.

Benet, J. (1970) 'Interpretation and Objectivity in Journalism', in A.K. Daniels and C. Kahn-Hut (eds), *Academics on the Line*. San Francisco: Jossey-Bass.

Benjamin, W. (1977) 'The Work of Art in an Age of Mechanical Reproduction', in J. Curran et al., *Mass Communication and Society*, pp. 384–408. London: Edward Arnold.

Berelson, B. (1949) 'What Missing the Newspaper Means', in P.F. Lazarsfeld and F.M. Stanton, *Communication Research 1948–9*, pp. 111–29. New York: Duell, Sloan and Pearce.

Berelson, B. (1952) *Content Analysis in Communication Research*. Glencoe, Ill: Free Press.

Berelson, B. (1959) 'The State of Communication Research', *Public Opinion Quarterly* 23(1): 1–6.

Berelson, B. and Salter P.J. (1946) 'Majority and Minority Americans: An Analysis of Magazine Fiction', *Public Opinion Quarterly* 10: 168–190.

Berezhnoi, A.F. (1978) 'The Objective Laws of the Press', *Democratic Journalist* 7–8: 10–19.

Berger, C.R. and Chaffee, S.H. (1987) 'The Study of Communication as a Science', in C.R. Berger and S.H. Chaffee (eds), *Handbook of Communication Science*. Beverly Hills and London: Sage Publications.

Blau, P. and Scott, W. (1963) *Formal Organizations*. London: Routledge and Kegan Paul.

Blumer, H. (1933) *Movies and Conduct*. New York: Macmillan.

Blumer, H. (1939) 'The Mass, the Public and Public Opinion', in A.M. Lee (ed), *New Outlines of the Principles of Sociology*. New York: Barnes and Noble.

Blumer, H. and Hauser, P.M. (1933) *Movies, Delinquency and Crime*. New York: Macmillan.

Blumler, J.G. (1964) 'British Television: The Outline of a Research Strategy', *British Journal of Sociology* 15(3): 223–33.

Blumler, J.G. (1970) 'The Political Effects of Television', in J.D. Halloran, *The Effects of Mass Communication*, pp. 69–104. Leicester: Leicester University Press.

Blumler, J.G. (1979) 'Looking at Media Abundance', *Communications* 5: 125–58.

Blumler, J.G. (ed) (1983) *Communicating to Voters: The Role of Television in the 1979 European Election*. Beverly Hills and London: Sage Publications.

Blumler, J.G. (1985) 'The Social Character of Media Gratifications', in K.E. Rosengren et al., *Media Gratification Research: Current Perspectives*, pp. 41–59. Beverly Hills and London: Sage Publications.

Blumler, J.G. and Katz, E. (eds) (1974) *The Uses of Mass Communications*. Beverly Hills and London: Sage Publications.

Blumler, J.G. and McQuail, D. (1968) *Television in Politics: Its Uses and Influence*. London: Faber.

Blumler, J.G., Brynin, M. and Nossiter, T.J. (1986) 'Broadcasting Finance and Programme Quality: An International Review', *European Journal of Communication* 1(3): 343–64.

Boorstin, D. (1961) *The Image: A Guide to Pseudo-Events in America*. New York: Athenaeum.

Bordewijk, J.L. and van Kaam, B. (1986) 'Towards a New Classification of Tele-Information Services', *Intermedia* 14(1): 16–21. Originally published in *Allocutie* (1982). Baarn, Bosch and Keuning.

Bourdieu, P. (1986) 'The Aristocracy of Culture', in R. Collins, J. Curran, N. Garnham, P. Scannell, P. Schlesinger and C. Sparks (eds), *Media Culture and Society*. London and Beverly Hills: Sage Publications.

Boyd-Barrett, O. (1977) 'Media Imperialism', in J. Curran et al. (eds), *Mass Communication and Society*, pp. 116–35. London: Edward Arnold.

Boyd-Barrett, O. (1982) 'Cultural Dependency and the Mass Media', in M. Gurevitch et al. (eds), *Culture, Society and the Media*, pp. 174–95. London: Methuen.

Bramson, L. (1961) *The Political Context of Sociology*. Princeton: Princeton University Press.

Breed, W. (1955) 'Social Control in the Newsroom: a Functional Analysis', *Social Forces* 33: 326–55.

Breed, W. (1956) 'Analysing News: Some Questions for Research', *Journalism Quarterly* 33: 467–77.

Breed, W. (1958) 'Mass Communication and Socio-Cultural Integration', *Social Forces* 37: 109–16.

Brown, J.R. (ed) (1976) *Children and Television*. London: Collier-Macmillan.

Brown, J.R. and Linné, O. (1976) 'The Family as a Mediator of Television's Effects', in J.R. Brown (ed), 184–98. *Children and Television,* London: Collier Macmillan.

Burgelin, O. (1972) 'Structural Analysis and Mass Communication', in D. McQuail, *Sociology of Mass Communication*, pp. 313–28. Harmondsworth: Penguin.

Burgelman, J.–C. (1986) 'The Future of Public Service Broadcasting: A Case Study for a "New" Communications Policy', *European Journal of Communication* 1(2): 173–202.

Burns, T. (1969) 'Public Service and Private World', in P. Halmos, *The Sociology of Mass Media Communicators*, pp. 53–73. Keele: University of Keele.

Burns, T. (1977) *The BBC: Public Institution and Private World*. London: Macmillan.

Burrell, G. and Morgan, G. (1979) *Sociological Paradigms and Organizational Analysis*. London: Heinemann.

Cantor, M. (1971) *The Hollywood Television Producers*. New York: Basic Books.

Cantor, M. (1980) *Prime Time Television*. Beverly Hills and London: Sage Publications.

Cantor, M. (1982) 'Audience Control', in H. Newcomb (ed), *Television: The Critical View*, pp. 311–34. New York: Oxford University Press.

Cantril, H., Gaudet, H. and Hertzog, H. (1940) *The Invasion from Mars*. Princeton: Princeton University Press.

Carey, J. (1969) 'The Communication Revolution and the Professional Communicator', in P. Halmos, *The Sociology of Mass Media Communicators*, pp. 23–38. Keele: University of Keele.

Carey, J. (1975) 'A Cultural Approach to Communication', *Communication* 2: 1–22.

Carey, J. (1978) 'The Ambiguity of Policy Research', *Journal of Communication*, 28(2): 114–19.

Carlsson, G., Dahlberg, A. and Rosengren, K.E. (1981) 'Mass Media Content, Public Opinion and Social Change', in K. Rosengren (ed), *Advances in Content Analysis*, pp. 227–40. Beverly Hills and London: Sage Publications.

Chaffee, S.H. and Berger, C.R. (eds) (1987) *Handbook of Communication Science*. Beverly Hills and London: Sage Publications, forthcoming.

Chaney, D. (1972) *Processes of Mass Communication*. London: Macmillan.

Chibnall, S. (1974) *Law and Order News*. London: Tavistock.

Clark, T.N. (ed) (1969) *On Communication and Social Influence* (Collected Essays of Gabriel Tarde). Chicago: Chicago University Press.

Clarke, P. and Fredin, E. (1978) 'Newspapers, Television and Political Reasoning', *Public Opinion Quarterly* 43: 143–60.

Clausse, R. (1968) 'The Mass Public at Grips with Mass Communication', *International Social Science Journal* 20(4): 625–43.

Cohen, B. (1963) *The Press and Foreign Policy*. Princeton: Princeton University Press.

Cohen, S. (1972) *Folk Devils and Moral Panics*. London: McGibbon and Kee.

Cohen, S. and Young, J. (eds) (1973) *The Manufacture of News*. London: Constable.

Comstock, G., Chaffee, S., Katzman, N., McCombs, M. and Roberts, D. (1978) *Television and Human Behaviour*. New York: Columbia University Press.

Cooper, E. and Jahoda, M. (1947) 'The Evasion of Propaganda', *Journal of Psychology* 23: 15–25.

Cox, H. and Morgan, D. (1973) *City Politics and the Press*. Cambridge: Cambridge University Press.

Curran, J. (1986) 'The Impact of Advertising on the British Mass Media', in R. Collins et al. (eds), *Media, Culture and Society*, pp. 309–35. Beverly Hills and London: Sage Publications.

Curran, J., Gurevitch, M. and Woollacott, J. (eds) (1977) *Mass Communication and Society*. London: Edward Arnold.

Curran, J., Douglas, A. and Whannel, G. (1981) 'The Political Economy of the Human Interest Story', in A. Smith (ed), *Newspapers and Democracy*, pp. 288–316. Cambridge, Mass: MIT Press.

Curran, J. and Seaton, J. (1985) *Power Without Responsibility* (2nd ed.). London: Fontana.

Dahlgren, P. (1985) 'The Modes of Reception: For a Hermeneutics of Television News', in P. Drummond and R. Patterson (eds), *Television in Transition*, pp. 235–49. London: BFI Publications.

Darnton, R. (1975) 'Writing News and Telling Stories', *Daedalus*, Spring: 175–94.

Davis, D.K. and Robinson, J.P. (1986) 'News Story Attributes and Comprehension', in J. Robinson and M. Levy, *The Main Source*, pp. 179–210. Beverly Hills and London: Sage Publications.

Davis, F. (1981) 'Contemporary Nostalgia and the Mass Media', in E. Katz and T. Szecsko (eds), *Mass Media and Social Change*, pp. 219–29. Beverly Hills and London: Sage Publications.

Dawson, R.E. and Prewitt, K. (1969) *Political Socialization*. Boston: Little Brown.

DeFleur, M.L. (1964) 'Occupational Roles as Portrayed on Television', *Public Opinion Quarterly* 28: 57–74.

DeFleur, M.L. (1970) *Theories of Mass Communication* (2nd ed.). New York: David McKay.

Dennis, J. (ed) (1973) *Socialization to Politics*. New York: Wiley.

Deutsch, K.W. (1966) *Nationalism and Social Communication* (2nd ed.). Cambridge, Mass: MIT Press.

Dewey, J. (1927) *The Public and Its Problems*. New York: Holt Rinehart.

Dexter, L.A. and White, D.M. (eds) (1964) *People, Society and Mass Communication*. New York: Free Press.

Dimmick, J. and Coit, P. (1982) 'Levels of Analysis in Mass Media Decision-Making', *Communication Research* 9(1): 3–32.

Dominick, J.R. et al., (1975) 'TV Journalism as Show Business: A Content Analysis of Eyewitness News', *Journalism Quarterly* 52: 213–18.

Donohue, G.A., Tichenor, P. and Olien, C.N. (1975) 'Mass Media and the Knowledge Gap', *Communication Research* 2: 3–23.

Donsbach, W. (1983) 'Journalists' Conception of Their Role', *Gazette* 32(1): 19–36.

Doob, A. and McDonald, G.E. (1979) 'Television Viewing and the Fear of Victimization: Is the Relationship Causal?', *Journal of Social Psychology and Personality* 37: 170–9. Reprinted in G.C. Wilhoit and H. de Bock, *Mass Communication Review Year Book*, pp. 479–88. Beverly Hills and London: Sage Publications.

Dreier, P. (1982) 'The Position of the Press in the US Power Structure', *Social Problems* 29(3): 298–310.

Eco, U. (1977) *A Theory of Semiotics*. London: Macmillan.

Edelman, M.J. (1967) *The Symbolic Uses of Politics*. Urbana, Ill: University of Illinois Press.

Eisenstein, E. (1978) *The Printing Press as an Agent of Change* (2 vols). New York: Cambridge University Press.

Elliott, P. (1972) *The Making of a Television Series — a Case Study in the Production of Culture*. London: Constable.

Elliott, P. (1974) 'Uses and Gratifications Research: a Critique and a Sociological Alternative', in J.G. Blumler and E. Katz, *The Uses of Mass Communication*, pp. 249–68. Beverly Hills and London: Sage Publications.

Elliott, P. (1977) 'Media Organizations and Occupations — An Overview' in J. Curran et al.: 142–73.

Elliott, P. (1982) 'Intellectuals, The "Information Society" and the Disappearance of the Public Sphere', *Media Culture and Society* 4: 243–53.

Ellis, J. (1982) *Visible Fictions*. London: Routledge and Kegan Paul.

Ellis, T. and Child, J. (1973) 'Placing Stereotypes of the Manager into Perspective', *Journal of Management Studies* 10: 233–55.

Engwall, L. (1978) *Newspapers as Organizations*. Farnborough, Hants: Saxon House.

Ennis, P. (1961) 'The Social Structure of Communication Systems: a Theoretical Proposal', *Studies in Public Communication* 3 (University of Chicago): 120–44.

Enzensberger, H.M. (1970) 'Constituents of a Theory of the Media', *New Left Review* 64: 13–36. Also in D. McQuail, 1972: 99–116.

Espé, H. and Seiwert, M. (1986) 'European Television Viewer Types: A Six-Nation Classification by Programme Interests', *European Journal of Communication* 1(3): 301–25.

Ettema, J.S. and Whitney, D.C. (eds) (1982) *Individuals in Mass Media Organizations*. Beverly Hills and London: Sage Publications.

Etzioni, A. (1961) *Complex Organizations*. Glencoe, Ill: Free Press.

Febvre, L. and Martin, H.J. (1984) *The Coming of the Book*. London: Verso Edition.

Fedler, F. (1973) 'The Media and Minority Groups: A Study of Access', *Journalism Quarterly* 50: 109–17.

Ferguson, M. (1983) *Forever Feminine: Women's Magazines and the Cult of Femininity*. London: Heinemann.

Ferguson, M. (1986) 'The Challenge of Neo-Technological Determinism for Communication Systems of Industry and Culture', pp. 52–70, in M. Ferguson (ed), *New Communication Technologies and the Public Interest*.

Ferguson, M. (ed) (1986) *New Communication Technologies and the Public Interest*. London and Beverly Hills: Sage Publications.

Festinger, L.A. (1957) *A Theory of Cognitive Dissonance*. New York: Row Peterson.

Findahl, O. and Höijer, B. (1981) 'Studies of News from the Perspective of Human Comprehension', in G.C. Wilhoit and H. de Bock, *Mass Communication Review Year Book*, pp. 393–403. Beverly Hills and London: Sage Publications.

Firsov, B. (1979) 'Social-Cultural Characteristics of Soviet Mass Media', *Democratic Journalist* 1: 12–14.

Fishman, M. (1982) 'News and Non-events: Making the Visible Invisible', in J.S. Ettema and D.C. Whitney, *Individuals in Mass Media Organizations*, pp. 219–40. Beverly Hills and London. Sage Publications.

Fiske, J. (1982) *Introduction to Communication Studies*. London: Methuen.

Fiske, J. and Hartley, J. (1978) *Reading Television*. London: Methuen.

Fjaestad, B. and Holmlov, P.G. (1976) 'The Journalist's View', *Journal of Communication* 2: 108–14.

Frank, A.G. (1971) *Capitalism and Underdevelopment*. Harmondsworth: Penguin.

Frank, R.S. (1973) *Message Dimensions of Television News*. Lexington, Mass: Lexington Books.

French, J.R.P. and Raven, B.H. (1953) 'The Bases of Social Power', in D. Cartwright and A. Zander (eds), *Group Dynamics*. London: Tavistock.

Friedson, E. (1953) 'Communications Research and the Concept of the Mass', *American Sociological Review* 18(3): 313–17.

Galtung, J. and Ruge, M. (1965) 'The Structure of Foreign News', *Journal of Peace Research* 1: 64–90. Also in J.Tunstall (ed), *Media Sociology*. London: Constable.

Gans, H.J. (1957) 'The Creator-Audience Relationship in the Mass Media', in B. Rosenberg and D.M. White (eds) *Mass Culture*. New York: Free Press.

Gans, H.J. (1979) *Deciding What's News*. New York: Vintage Books.

Garnham, N. (1979) 'Contribution to a Political Economy of Mass Communication', *Media, Culture and Society* 1(2): 123–46.

Gaziano, C. (1983) 'The "Knowledge Gap": an Analytical Review of Media Effects', *Communication Research* 10(4): 447–86.

Geiger, K. and Sokol, R. (1959) 'Social Norms in Watching Television', *American Journal of Sociology* 65(3): 178–81.

Gerbner, G. (1964) 'Ideological Perspectives and Political Tendencies in News Reporting', *Journalism Quarterly* 41: 495–506.

Gerbner, G. (1969) 'Institutional Pressures on Mass Communicators', in P. Halmos, *The Sociology of*

Mass Media Communicators, pp. 205–48. Keele: University of Keele.

Gerbner, G. (1973) 'Cultural Indicators — the Third Voice', in G Gerbner, L. Gross and W. Melody (eds), *Communications Technology and Social Policy*, pp. 553–73. New York: Wiley.

Gerbner, G. (1977) 'Comparative Cultural Indicators', in G. Gerbner (ed), *Mass Media Policies in Changing Cultures*. New York: Wiley.

Gerbner, G. and Gross, L.P. (1976) 'Living With Television: The Violence Profile', *Journal of Communication* 26(2): 173–99.

Gerbner, G. and Marvanyi, G. (1977) 'The Many Worlds of the World's Press', *Journal of Communication* 27(1): 52–66.

Gerbner, G., Gross, L., Morgan, M. and Signorelli, N. (1980) 'The Mainstreaming of America: Violence Profile No.11', *Journal of Communication* 30: 10–27.

Gerbner, G., Gross, L., Morgan, M. and Signorelli, N. (1984) 'The Political Correlates of TV Viewing', *Public Opinion Quarterly* 48: 283–300.

Gieber, W. (1956) 'Across the Desk: A Study of 16 Telegraph Editors', *Journalism Quarterly* 33: 423–33.

Gieber, W. and Johnson, W. (1961) 'The City Hall Beat: a Study of Reporter and Source Roles', *Journalism Quarterly* 38: 289–97.

Giner, S. (1976) *Mass Society*. London: Martin Robertson.

Gitlin, T. (1978) 'Media Sociology: The Dominant Paradigm', *Theory and Society* 6: 205–253. Reprinted in G.C. Wilhoit and H. de Bock, *Mass Communication Review Year Book*, pp. 73–122. Beverly Hills and London: Sage Publications.

Gitlin, T. (1981) *The Whole World is Watching — Mass Media in the Making and Unmaking of the New Left*. Berkeley: University of California Press.

Glasgow Media Group (1976) *Bad News*. London: Routledge and Kegan Paul.

Glasgow Media Group (1980) *More Bad News*. London: Routledge and Kegan Paul.

Glasgow Media Group (1985) *War and Peace News*. London: Routledge and Kegan Paul.

Golding, P. (1977) 'Media Professionalism in the Third World: the Transfer of an Ideology', in J. Curran et al., *Mass Communication and Society*, pp. 291–308. London: Edward Arnold.

Golding, P. (1981) 'The Missing Dimension — News Media and the Management of Social Change', in E. Katz and T. Szescko, *Mass Media and Social Change*, pp. 63–81. Beverly Hills and London: Sage Publications.

Golding, P. and Elliott, P. (1979) *Making the News*. London: Longman.

Golding, P. and Middleton, S. (1982) *Images of Welfare — Press and Public Attitudes to Poverty*. Oxford: Basil Blackwell and Martin Robertson.

Golding, P. and Murdock, G. (1986) 'Unequal Information: Access and Exclusion in the New Communication Marketplace', in M. Ferguson, *New Communication Technologies and the Public Interest*, pp. 71–83. Beverly Hills and London: Sage Publications.

Goodhart, G.J., Ehrenberg, A.S.C. and Collins, M.A. (1975) *The Television Audience: Patterns of Viewing*. Farnborough, Hants: Saxon House. (Second edition with updating, 1986.)

Gould, P., Johnson, J. and Chapman, G. (1984) *The Structure of Television*. London: Pion.

Gouldner, A. (1976) *The Dialectic of Ideology and Technology*. London: Macmillan.

Graber, D. (1976) *Verbal Behavior and Politics*. Urbana, Ill: University of Illinois Press.

Graber, D. (1980) *Crime News and the Public*. New York: Praeger.

Graber, D. (1981) 'Political Language', in D.D. Nimmo and D. Sanders, *Handbook of Political Communication*, pp. 195–224. Beverly Hills and London: Sage Publications.

Gramsci, A. (1971) *Selections From the Prison Notebooks*. London: Lawrence and Wishart.

Greenberg, B.S. (1964) 'Person-to-Person Communication in the Diffusion of a News Event', *Journalism Quarterly* 41: 489–94.

Gross, L.P. (1977) 'Television as a Trojan Horse', *School Media Quarterly*, Spring: 175–80.

Grossman, M.B. and Kumar, M.J. (1981) *Portraying the President*. Baltimore: Johns Hopkins University Press.

Gurevitch, M., Bennet, T., Curran, J. and Woollacott, J. (1982) (eds) *Culture, Society and the Media*. London: Methuen.

Gurevitch, M. and Levy, M. (1986) 'Information and Meaning: Audience Explanations of Social Issues', in J. Robinson and M. Levy, *The Main Source*, pp. 159–75. Beverly Hills and London: Sage Publications.

Hackett, R.A. (1984) 'Decline of a Paradigm? Bias and Objectivity in News Media Studies', *Critical Studies in Mass Communication* 1: 229–59.

Hagen, E. (1962) *On the Theory of Social Change*. Homewood, Ill: Dorsey Press.

Haight, T. (1983) 'The Critical Research Dilemma', *Journal of Communication* 33(3): 226–36.

Hall, S. (1973a) 'The Determination of News Photographs', in S. Cohen and J. Young, *The Manufacture of News*, pp. 176–90. London: Constable.

Hall, S. (1973b) 'Coding and Encoding in the Television Discourse', in S. Hall et al., (eds), *Culture, Media, Language*. London: Hutchinson.

Hall, S. (1977) 'Culture, the Media and the Ideological Effect', in J. Curran et al., *Mass Communication and Society*, pp. 315–48. London: Edward Arnold.

Hall, S. (1982) 'The Rediscovery of Ideology: Return of the Repressed in Media Studies', in M. Gurevitch et al., *Culture, Society and the Media*, pp. 56–90. London: Methuen.

Hall, S. and Jefferson, T. (1975) *Resistance Through Rituals*. London: Hutchinson.

Hall, S., Clarke, J., Critcher, C., Jefferson, T. and Roberts, B. (1978) *Policing the Crisis*. London: Macmillan.

Hall, S., Hobson, D., Lowe, A. and Willis, P. (1980) *Culture, Media, Language*. London: Hutchinson.

Hallin, D.C. and Mancini, P. (1984) 'Political Structure and Representational Form in US and Italian TV News', *Theory and Society* 13(40): 829–50.

Halloran, J.D. (1965) *The Effects of Mass Communication*. Leicester: Leicester University Press.

Halloran, J.D. (ed) (1970) *The Effects of Television*. London: Grenada.

Halloran, J.D., Brown, R.L. and Chaney, D. (1970) *Television and Delinquency*. Leicester: Leicester University Press.

Halloran, J.D., Elliott, P. and Murdock, G. (1970) *Communications and Demonstrations*. Harmondsworth: Penguin.

Halmos, P. (ed) (1969) *The Sociology of Mass Media Communicators, Sociological Review Monographs* 13. University of Keele.

Hardt, H. (1979) *Social Theories of the Press: Early German and American Perspectives*. Beverly Hills and London: Sage Publications.

Harrison, S. (1974) *Poor Men's Guardians*. London: Lawrence and Wishart.

Hartman, P. and Husband, C. (1974) *Racism and Mass Media*. London: Davis Poynter.

Hawkes, T. (1977) *Structuralism and Semiology*. London: Methuen.

Hawkins, R. and Pingree, S. (1980) 'Some Processes in the Cultivation Effect', *Communication Research* 7: 193–226.

Hedinsson, E. (1981) *Television, Family and Society — The Social Origins and Effects of Adolescent TV Use*. Stockholm: Almquist and Wiksel.

Hemánus, P. (1976) 'Objectivity in News Transmission', *Communication Research* 26: 102–7.

Hessler, R.C. and Stipp, H. (1985) 'The Impact of Fictional Suicide Stories on US Fatalities: a Replication', *American Journal of Sociology* 90(1): 151–67.

Hetherington, A. (1985) *News, Newspapers and Television*. London: Macmillan.

Himmelweit, H.T., Vince, P. and Oppenheim, A.N. (1958) *Television and the Child*. London: Oxford University Press.

Himmelweit, H.T and Swift, T. (1976) 'Continuities and Discontinuities in Media Taste', *Journal of Social Issues* 32(6): 133–56.

Hirsch, F. and Gordon, D. (1975) *Newspaper Money*. London: Hutchinson.

Hirsch, P.M. (1973) 'Processing Fads and Fashions: an Organization-set Analysis of Culture Industry Systems', *American Journal of Sociology* 77: 639–59.

Hirsch, P.M. (1977) 'Occupational, Organizational and Institutional Models in Mass Communication', in P.M. Hirsch et al., *Strategies for Communication Research*, pp. 13–42. Beverly Hills and London: Sage Publications.

Hirsch, P.M. (1980) 'The "Scary World" of the Non-Viewer and Other Anomalies — a Re-analysis of Gerbner et al.'s Findings in Cultivation Analysis, Part I', *Communication Research* 7(4): 403–56.

Hirsch. P.M. (1981) 'On Not Learning From One's Mistakes, Part II', *Communication Research* 8(1): 3–38.

Hirsch, P.M., Miller, P.V. and Kline, F.G. (eds) (1977) *Strategies for Communication Research*. Beverly Hills and London: Sage Publications.

Holden, R.T. (1986) 'The Contagiousness of Aircraft Hijacking', *American Journal of Sociology* 91(4): 876–904.

Hopkins, M. (1970) *Mass Media in the Soviet Union*. New York: Pegasus.

Horton, D. and Wohl, R.R. (1956) 'Mass Communication and Para-Social Interaction', *Psychiatry* 19: 215–29.

Hovland, C.I., Lumsdaine, A.A. and Sheffield, F.D. (1949) *Experiments in Mass Communication*. Princeton: Princeton University Press.

Howitt, D. and Cumberbatch, G. (1975) *Mass Media, Violence and Society*. New York: John Wiley.

Huaco, G.A. (1963) *The Sociology of Film Art*. New York: Basic Books.

Hughes, H.M. (1940) *News and the Human Interest Story*. Chicago: University of Chicago Press.

Hughes, M. (1980) 'The Fruits of Cultivation Analysis: A Re-examination of Some Effects of TV Viewing', *Public Opinion Quarterly* 44(3): 287–302.

Hutchins, R. (1974) 'Commission on Freedom of the Press', *A Free and Responsible Press*. Chicago: University of Chicago Press.

Hyman, H. and Sheatsley, P. (1947) 'Some Reasons Why Information Campaigns Fail', *Public Opinion Quarterly* 11: 412–23.

Innis, H. (1950) *Empire and Communication*. Oxford: Clarendon Press.

Innis, H. (1951) *The Bias of Communication*. Toronto: University of Toronto Press.

Ito, Y. (1981) 'The "Johoka Shakai" Approach to the Study of Communication in Japan', in G.C. Wilhoit and H. de Bock, *Mass Communication Review Year Book*. Beverly Hills and London: Sage Publications.

Jackson, I. (1971) *The Provincial Press and the Community*. Manchester: Manchester University Press.

Janowitz, M. (1952) *The Community Press in an Urban Setting*. Glencoe, Ill: Free Press.

Janowitz, M. (1975) 'Professional Models in Journalism: the Gatekeeper and Advocate', *Journalism Quarterly* 52(4): 618–26.

Janowitz, M. (1981) 'Mass Media: Institutional Trends and Their Consequences', pp. 303–21, in M. Janowitz and P.M. Hirsch (eds), *Reader in Public Opinion and Mass Communication* (3rd ed.). New York: Free Press.

Jay, M. (1973) *The Dialectical Imagination*. London: Heinemann.

Johns-Heine, P. and Gerth, H. (1949) 'Values in Mass Periodical Fiction 1921-1940', *Public Opinion Quarterly* 13: 105–13.

Johnstone, J.W.L., Slawski, E.J. and Bowman, W.W. (1976) *The News People*. Urbana, Ill: University of Illinois Press.

Jowett, G. and Linton, J.M. (1980) *Movies as Mass Communication*. Beverly Hills and London: Sage Publications.

Katz, D. (1960) 'The Functional Approach to the Study of Attitudes', *Public Opinion Quarterly* 24: 163–204.

Katz, E. (1977) *Social Research and Broadcasting: Proposals for Further Development*. London: BBC.

Katz, E. (1983) 'Publicity and Pluralistic Ignorance: Notes on the Spiral of Silence', in Wartella et al.: 89–99.

Katz, E. and Lazarsfeld, P.F. (1955) *Personal Influence*. Glencoe, Ill: Free Press.

Katz, E., Lewin, M.L. and Hamilton, H. (1963) 'Traditions of Research on the Diffusion of Innovations', *American Sociological Review* 28: 237–52.

Katz, E., Gurevitch, M. and Haas, H. (1973) 'On the Use of Mass Media for Important Things', *American Sociological Review* 38: 164–81.

Katz, E., Blumler, J.G. and Gurevitch, M. (1974) 'Utilization of Mass Communication by the Individual', in J.G. Blumler and E. Katz, *The Uses of Mass Communication*, pp. 19–32. London: Faber.

Katz, E. and Dayan, D. (1986) 'Contents, Conquests and Coronations: Media Events and their Heroes', in C.F. Graumann and S. Moscovici (eds) *Changing Conceptions of Leadership*.

Katz, E. and Szecsko, T. (eds) (1981) *Mass Media and Social Change*. Beverly Hills and London: Sage Publications.

Kelman, H. (1961) 'Processes of Opinion Change', *Public Opinion Quarterly* 25: 57–78.

Kerner, O. et al. (1968) *Report on the National Advisory Committee on Civil Disorders*. Washington DC: GPO.

Key, V.O. (1961) *Public Opinion and American Democracy*. New York: Alfred Knopf.

Kingsbury, S.M. and Hart, M. (1937) *Newspapers and the News*. New York: Putnams.

Klapper, J. (1960) *The Effects of Mass Communication*. New York: Free Press.

Kleinsteuber, H.J., McQuail, D. and Siune, K. (eds) (1986) *Electronic Media and Politics in Western Europe: Euromedia Group Handbook of National Systems*. Frankfurt: Campus.

Köcher, R. (1986) 'Bloodhounds or Missionaries: Role Definitions of German and British

Journalists', *European Journal of Communication* 1(1): 43–64.

Kornhauser, W. (1959) *The Politics of Mass Society*. New York: Free Press.

Kornhauser, W. (1968) 'The Theory of Mass Society', in *International Encyclopedia of the Social Sciences* Vol. 10, pp. 58–64. New York: Macmillan and Free Press.

Kracauer, S. (1949) 'National Types as Hollywood Represents Them', *Public Opinion Quarterly* 13: 53–72.

Kraus, S., Davis, D.K., Lang, G.E. and Lang, K. (1975) 'Critical Events Analysis', in S.H. Chaffee (ed), *Political Communication Research*, pp. 195–216. Beverly Hills and London: Sage Publications.

Kraus, S. and Davis D.K. (1976) *The Effects of Mass Communication on Political Behavior*. University Park: Pennsylvania State University Press.

Krippendorf, K. (1980) *Content Analysis*. Beverly Hills and London: Sage Publications.

Krugman, H.E. (1965) 'The Impact of Television Advertising: Learning Without Involvement', *Public Opinion Quarterly* 29: 349–56.

Kumar, C. (1975) 'Holding the Middle Ground', *Sociology* 9(3): 67–88. Reprinted in J. Curran et al., *Mass Communication and Society*, pp. 231–248. London: Edward Arnold.

Lang, K. and Lang, G.E. (1953) 'The Unique Perspective of Television and its Effect', *American Sociological Review* 18(1): 103–12.

Lang, K and Lang, G.E. (1959) 'The Mass Media and Voting', in E.J. Burdick and A.J. Brodbeck (eds), *American Voting Behavior*. New York: Free Press.

Lang, G. and Lang, K. (1981) 'Mass Communication and Public Opinion: Strategies for Research', in M. Rosenberg, and R.H. Turner (eds), *Social Psychology: Sociological Perspectives*, pp. 653–82. New York: Basic Books.

Lang, G. and Lang, K. (1983) *The Battle for Public Opinion*. New York: Columbia University Press.

Lasswell, H. (1948) 'The Structure and Function of Communication in Society', in L. Bryson (ed) *The Communication of Ideas*. New York: Harper.

Laswell, H., Lerner, D. and Pool, I. de Sola (1952) *The Comparative Study of Symbols*. Stanford: Stanford University Press.

Lazarsfeld, P.F. (1941) 'Administrative and Critical Communications Research', *Studies in Philosophy and Social Science* 9.

Lazarsfeld, P.F., Berelson, B. and Gaudet, H. (1944) *The People's Choice*. New York: Duell, Sloan and Pearce.

Lazarsfeld, P.F. and Stanton, F.M. (1949) *Communication Research 1948–9*. New York: Harper and Brothers.

Lemert, J.B. (1974) 'Content Duplication by the Networks in Competing Evening Newscasts', *Journalism Quarterly* 51: 238–44.

Lerner, D. (1958) *The Passing of Traditional Society*. New York: Free Press.

Levy, M. (1977) 'Experiencing Television News', *Journal of Communication* 27: 112–17.

Levy, M. and Windahl, S. (1985) 'The Concept of Audience Activity', in Rosengren et al., *Media Gratification Research*, pp. 109–22. Beverly Hills and London: Sage Publications.

Lewis, G.H. (1980) 'Taste Cultures and Their Composition: Towards a New Theoretical Perspective', in E. Katz and T. Szecsko: 201–17.

Liebes, T. and Katz, E. (1986) 'Patterns of Involvement in Television Fiction: A Comparative Analysis', *European Journal of Communication* 1(2): 151–72.

Lippman, W. (1922) *Public Opinion*. New York: Harcourt Brace.

Lowenthal, L. (1961) *Literature, Popular Culture and Society*. Englewood Cliffs, NJ: Prentice-Hall.

Lull, J. (1982) 'The Social Uses of Television', in D.C. Whitney et al., *Mass Communication Review Yearbook*, pp. 397–409. Beverly Hills and London: Sage Publications.

McBride, S. et al. (1980) *Many Voices, One World*. Report by the International Commission for the Study of Communication Problems. Paris: Unesco; London: Kogan Page.

Maccoby, E. (1954) 'Why Do Children Watch TV?', *Public Opinion Quarterly* 18: 239–44.

McCombs, M.E. and Shaw, D.L. (1972) 'The Agenda-Setting Function of the Press', *Public Opinion Quarterly* 36: 176–87.

McCormack, T. (1961) 'Social Theory and the Mass Media', *Canadian Journal of Economics and Political Science* 4: 479–89.

McCormack, T. (1981) 'Revolution. Communication and the Sense of History', in E. Katz and T. Szescko, *Mass Media and Social Change*, pp. 167–85. Beverly Hills and London: Sage Publications.

McCron, R. (1976) 'Changing Perspectives in the Study of Mass Media and Socialization', in J. Halloran (ed), *Mass Media and Socialization*, pp. 13–44. Leicester: IAMCR.

McGinnis, J. (1969) *The Selling of the President*. New York: Trident Press.

McGanahan, D.V. and Wayne, L. (1948) 'German and American Traits Reflected in Popular Drama', *Human Relations* 1(4): 429–55.

McGuire, W.J. (1973) 'Persuasion, Resistance and Attitude Change', in I. de Sola Pool et al. (eds), *Handbook of Communication*, pp. 216–52. Chicago: Rand McNally.

McLelland, D.W. (1961) *The Achieving Society*. Princeton, NJ: Van Nostrand.

McLeod, M.J., Ward, L.S. and Tancill, K. (1965) 'Alienation and Uses of Mass Media', *Public Opinion Quarterly* 29: 583–94.

McLuhan, M. (1962) *The Gutenberg Galaxy*. Toronto: Toronto University Press.

McLuhan, M. (1964) *Understanding Media*. London: Routledge and Kegan Paul.

McQuail, D. (1969) *Towards a Sociology of Mass Communication*. London: Collier Macmillan.

McQuail, D. (ed) (1972) *Sociology of Mass Communications*. Harmondsworth: Penguin.

McQuail, D. (1977) *Analysis of Newspaper Content*. Royal Commission on the Press, Research Series 4: HMSO.

McQuail, D. (1984) 'With the Benefit of Hindsight: Reflections on Uses and Gratifications Research', *Critical Studies in Mass Communication* 1: 177–93.

McQuail, D. (1985a) 'Gratifications Research and Media Theory: Four Models or One?', in K.E. Rosengren et al., *Media Gratification Research: Current Perspectives*, pp. 149–67. Beverly Hills and London: Sage Publications.

McQuail D. (1985b) 'The Communicative Capacity of Different Media', *Massacommunicatie* 12(4): 138–51.

McQuail, D. (1986a) 'Is Media Theory Adequate to the Challenge of the New Communications Technologies?', in M. Ferguson (ed), *New Communication Technologies and the Public Interest*, pp. 1–17. Beverly Hills and London: Sage Publications.

McQuail, D. (1986b) 'From Bias to Objectivity and Back: Concepts of News Performance and a Pluralistic Alternative', in T. McCormack (ed), *Studies in Communication (3)*. Greenwich, Connecticut: JAI Press.

McQuail, D. (1987) 'The Functions of Communication: a Non-functionalist Overview' in C.R. Berger and S.H. Chaffee, *Handbook of Communication Science*. Beverly Hills and London: Sage Publications.

McQuail, D., Blumler, J.G. and Brown, J. (1972) 'The Television Audience: A Revised Perspective', in D. McQuail, *Sociology of Mass Communication*, pp. 135–65. Harmondsworth: Penguin.

McQuail, D. and Gurevitch, M. (1974) 'Explaining Audience Behaviour', in J.G. Blumler and E. Katz, *The Uses of Mass Communication*, pp. 287–306. Beverly Hills and London: Sage Publications.

McQuail, D. and Windahl, S. (1982) *Communication Models*. London: Longman.

McQuail, D. and van Cuilenburg, J.J. (1983) 'Diversity as a Media Policy Goal: a Strategy of Evaluative Research and a Netherlands Case Study', *Gazette* 31(3): 145–62.

McQuail, D. and Siune, K. (eds) (1986) 'Euromedia Research Group', *New Media Politics*. London: Sage Publications.

Marcuse, H. (1964) *One Dimensional Man*. London: Routledge and Kegan Paul.

Martel, M.U. and McCall, G.J. (1964) 'Reality-Orientation and the Pleasure Principle', in L.A. Dexter and D.M. White, *People, Society and Mass Communication*, pp. 283–333. New York: Free Press.

Martin, L.J. (1981) 'Government and News Media', in D.D. Nimmo and D. Sanders, *Handbook of Political Communication*, pp. 445–65. Beverly Hills and London: Sage Publications.

Mattelart, A. (1979) *Multinational Corporations and the Control of Culture*. Brighton: Harvester Press.

Mazzoleni, G. (1987) 'Media Logic and Party Logic in Campaign Coverage: The Italian General Election of 1983', *European Journal of Communication* 2(1).

Melischek, G., Rosengren, K.E. and Stappers, J. (eds) (1984) *Cultural Indicators: An International Symposium*. Vienna: Royal Academy of Science.

Mendlesohn, H. (1964) 'Listening to Radio', in L.A. Dexter and D.M. White (eds), *People, Society and Mass Communication*, pp. 239–48. New York: Free Press.

Mendelsohn, H. (1966) *Mass Entertainment*. New Haven, Conn: College and University Press.

Mendelsohn, H. (1973) 'Some Reasons Why Information Campaigns can Succeed', *Public Opinion Quarterly* 37: 50–61.

Merton, R.K. (1949) 'Patterns of Influence', in R. Merton, *Social Theory and Social Structure*, pp. 387–470. Glencoe: Free Press.

Merton, R.K. (1957) *Social Theory and Social Structure*. Glencoe, Ill: Free Press.

Metz, C. (1974) *Language and Cinema*. The Hague: Mouton.

Meyerson, R. (1968) 'Television and the Rest of Leisure', *Public Opinion Quarterly* 32(1): 102–12.

Meyrowitz, J. (1985) *No Sense of Place*. New York: Oxford University Press.

Mickiewicz, E.P. (1981) *Media and the Russian Public*. New York: Praeger.

Miliband, R. (1969) *The State in Capitalist Society*. London: Weidenfeld and Nicolson.

Mills, C.W. (1951) *White Collar*. New York: Oxford University Press.

Mills, C.W. (1956) *The Power Elite*. New York: Oxford University Press.

Moles, A. (1973) 'Television Organizations and Audience Influence — the Typology of Feedback', in *Broadcasters and Their Audiences*. Rome: Edizioni RAI.

Molotch, H.L. and Lester, M.J. (1974) 'News as Purposive Behavior', *American Sociological Review* 39: 101–12.

Monaco, J. (1981) *How To Read a Film*. New York: Oxford University Press.

Morin, E. (1962) *L'Esprit du Temps: Essai sur la culture de masse*. Paris: Grasset.

Morin, V. (1976) 'Televised Current Events Sequences or a Rhetoric of Ambiguity', in *News and Current Events on TV*. Rome: Edizioni, RAI.

Murdock, G. and Golding, P. (1977) 'Capitalism, Communication and Class Relations', in J. Curran et al. (eds), *Mass Communication and Society*, pp. 12–43. London: Edward Arnold.

Murdock, G. and Golding, P. (1978) 'Theories of Communication and Theories of Society', in *Communication Research* 5(3): 390–56.

Murdock, G. and Phelps, G. (1973) *Mass Media and the Secondary School*. London: Constable.

Murphy, D. (1976) *The Silent Watchdog*. London: Constable.

Neumann, W.R. (1982) 'Television and American Culture: The Mass Media and the Pluralistic Audience', *Public Opinion Quarterly* 46: 471–87.

Newcomb, H. (1978) 'Assessing the Violence Profile on Gerbner and Gross: A Humanistic Critique and Suggestion', *Communication Research* 5(3): 264–82.

Nimmo, D.D. and Sanders, D. (eds) (1981) *Handbook of Political Communication*. Beverly Hills and London: Sage Publications.

Noble, G. (1975) *Children in Front of the Small Screen*. London: Constable.

Noelle-Neumann, E. (1973) 'Return to the Concept of Powerful Mass Media', *Studies of Broadcasting* 9: 66–112.

Nordenstreng, K. (1974) *Informational Mass Communication*. Helsinki: Tammi.

Novak, K. (1977) 'From Information Gaps to Communication Potential' in M. Berg et al. (eds), *Current Theories in Scandinavian Mass Communication*. Grenaa, Denmark: GMT.

Ogden, C.K. and Richards, I.A. (1923) *The Meaning of Meaning* (reprinted 1985). London: Routledge and Kegan Paul.

Padioleau, J. (1985) *Le Monde et le Washington Post*. Paris: PUF.

Paletz, D.L. and Dunn, R. (1969) 'Press Coverage of Civil Disorders: a Case-Study of Winston-Salem', *Public Opinion Quarterly* 33: 328–45.

Paletz, D.L. and Entman, R. (1981) *Media, Power, Politics*. New York: Free Press.

Palmgreen, P. and Rayburn, J.D. (1985) 'An Expectancy-Value Approach to Media Gratifications', in K.E. Rosengren et al., *Media Gratification Research*, pp. 61–72. Beverly Hills and London: Sage Publications.

Park, R. (1940) 'News as a Form of Knowledge', in R.H. Turner (ed), *On Social Control and Collective Behavior*, pp. 32–52. Chicago: Chicago University Press, 1967.

Pearlin, L. (1959) 'Social and Personal Stress and Escape Television Viewing', *Public Opinion Quarterly* 23: 255–9.

Peirce, C.S. (1931–35) *Collected Papers*. (eds C. Harteshorne and P. Weiss. Cambridge, Mass: Harvard University Press. Vols II and V.)

Peters, A.K. and Cantor, M.G. (1982) 'Screen Acting as Work', in J.S. Ettema and D.C. Whitney, *Individuals in Mass Media Organizations*, pp. 53–68. Beverly Hills and London: Sage Publications.

Peterson, R.C. and Thurstone, L.L. (1933) *Motion Pictures and Social Attitudes*. New York: Macmillan.

Peterson, T., Jensen, J.W. and Rivers, W.L. (1965) *The Mass Media and Modern Society*. New York: Holt, Rinehart and Winston.

Phillips, D.P. (1980) 'Airplane Accidents, Murder and the Mass Media', *Social Forces* 58(4): 1001–24.

Phillips, D.P. (1982) 'The Impact of Fictional TV Stories in Adult Programming on Adult Fatalities', *American Journal of Sociology* 87: 1346–59.

Phillips, E.B. (1977) 'Approaches to Objectivity', in P.M. Hirsch et al., *Strategies for Communication Research*, pp. 63–77. Beverly Hills and London: Sage Publications.

Pool, I. de Sola (1959) 'Newsmens' Fantasies, Audiences and Newswriting', *Public Opinion Quarterly* 23(2): 145–58.

Pool, I. de Sola (1973) 'Newsmen and Statesmen — Adversaries or Cronies', in W.L. Rivers and N.J. Nyhan (eds), *Aspen Papers on Government and Media*. London: Allen and Unwin.

Pool, I. de Sola (1983) *Technologies of Freedom*. Cambridge, Mass: Belknap Press of Harvard University Press.

Pool, I. de Sola., Inose, H., Takasaki, N. and Hurwitz, R. (1984) *Communication Flows: A Census in the US and Japan*. Amsterdam: North Holland Press.

Poulantzas, N. (1975) *Classes in Contemporary Society*. London: New Left Books.

Pye, L.W. (1963) *Communications and Political Development*. Princeton: Princeton University Press.

Radway, J. (1984) *Reading the Romance*. Chapel Hill: University of North Carolina Press.

Ray, M.L. (1973) 'Marketing Communication and the Hierarchy of Effects', in P. Clarke (ed), *New Models for Communication Research*, pp. 147–76. Beverly Hills and London: Sage Publications.

Rayburn, J.D. and Palmgreen, P. (1984) 'Merging Uses and Gratifications and Expectancy-Value Theory', *Communication Research* 11: 537–62.

Rice, R.E. and Paisley, W.J. (eds) (1981) *Public Communication Campaigns*. Beverly Hills and London: Sage Publications.

Richardson, K. and Corner, J. (1986) 'Reading Reception: Mediation and Transference in Viewers' Accounts of a TV Programme', *Media Culture and Society* 8(4): 485–508.

Rikardsson, G. (1981) 'Newspaper Opinion and Public Opinion', in K.E. Rosengren, *Advances in Content Analysis*, pp. 215–26. Beverly Hills and London: Sage Publications.

Riley, M.W. and Riley, J.W. (1951) 'A Sociological Approach to Communications Research' *Public Opinion Quarterly* 15(3): 445–60.

Rivers, W.L., Schramm, W. and Christians, G.C. (1980) *Responsibility in Mass Communications*. New York: Harper and Row.

Robinson, J.P. (1972) 'Mass Communication and Information Diffusion', in F.G. Kline and P.J. Tichenor (eds), *Current Perspectives in Mass Communication Research*. Beverly Hills and London: Sage Publications.

Robinson, J.P. (1976) 'Interpersonal Influence in Election Campaigns: 2-Step Flow Hypotheses', *Public Opinion Quarterly* 40: 304–19.

Robinson, J. and Levy, M. (1986) *The Main Source*. Beverly Hills and London: Sage Publications.

Rogers, E.M. (1962) *The Diffusion of Innovations*. Glencoe, Ill: Free Press.

Rogers, E.M. (1976) 'Communication and Development: The Passing of a Dominant Paradigm', *Communication Research* 3: 213–40.

Rogers, E.M. (1986) *Communication Technology*. New York: Free Press.

Rogers, E. and Shoemaker, F. (1973) *Communication of Innovations*. New York: Free Press.

Rosenberg, B. and White, D.M. (eds) (1957) *Mass Culture*. New York: Free Press.

Rosengren, K.E. (1973) 'News Diffusion: an Overview', *Journalism Quarterly* 50: 83–91.
Rosengren, K.E. (1974) 'International News: Methods, Data, Theory', *Journal of Peace Research* 11: 45–56.
Rosengren, K.E. (1976) 'The Barseback "Panic"', Lund University.
Rosengren, K.E. (1981a) 'Mass Media and Social Change: Some Current Approaches', in E. Katz and T. Szecsko, *Mass Media and Social Change*, pp. 247–63. Beverly Hills and London: Sage Publications.
Rosengren, K.E. (ed) (1981b) *Advances in Content Analysis*. Beverly Hills and London: Sage Publications.
Rosengren, K.E. (1983) 'Communication Research: One Paradigm or Four?', *Journal of Communication* 33(3): 185–207.
Rosengren, K.E. (1985) 'Culture, Media and Society', *Massacommunicatie* 13(3–4): 126–44.
Rosengren, K.E. (1987) 'The Comparative Study of News Diffusion', *European Journal of Communication* 2(2):forthcoming.
Rosengren, K.E. and Windahl, S. (1972) 'Mass Media Consumption as a Functional Alternative', in D. McQuail, *Sociology of Mass Communication*, pp. 166–94. Harmondsworth: Penguin.
Rosengren, K.E., Palmgreen, P. and Wenner, L. (eds) (1985) *Media Gratification Research: Current Perspectives*. Beverly Hills and London: Sage Publications.
Roshco, B. (1975) *Newsmaking*. Chicago: University of Chicago Press.
Roshier, R.J. (1973) 'The Selection of Crime News by the Press', in Cohen and Young, 1973: 28–39.
Rositi, F. (1976) 'The Television News Programme: Fragmentation and Recomposition of Our Image of Society', in *News and Current Events on TV*. Rome: Edizioni RAI.
Rosten, L.C. (1937) *The Washington Correspondents*. New York: Harcourt Brace.
Rosten, L.C. (1941) *Hollywood: the Movie Colony, the Movie Makers*. New York: Harcourt Brace.
Ryan, J. and Peterson, R.A. (1982) 'The Product Image: the Fate of Creativity in Country Music Song Writing', in J.S. Ettema and D.C. Whitney, 1982: 11–32.
Salvaggio, J.L. (1985) 'Information Technology and Social Problems: Four International Models', in B.D. Ruben, *Information and Behavior Vol. 1*, pp. 428–54. Rutgers, NJ: Transaction Books.
de Saussure, F. (1915) *Course in General Linguistics*. (English trans. London: Peter Owen, 1960).
Schiller, H. (1969) *Mass Communication and American Empire*. New York: Augustus M. Kelly.
Schlesinger, P. (1978) *Putting 'Reality' Together: BBC News*. London: Constable.
Schlesinger, P., Murdock, G. and Elliott, P. (1983) *Televising Terrorism*. London: Comedia.
Schmid, A.P. and de Graaf, J. (1982) *Violence as Communication*. Beverly Hills and London: Sage Publications.
Schramm, W. (1963) *The Science of Communication*. Urbana: University of Illinois Press.
Schramm, W. (1964) *Mass Media and National Development*. Stanford: Stanford University Press.
Schramm, W., Lyle, J. and Parker, E. (1961) *Television in the Lives of Our Children*. Stanford: Stanford University Press.
Schroder, K.C. (1987) 'Convergence of Antagonistic Traditions?', *European Journal of Communication* 2, forthcoming.
Schudson, M. (1978) *Discovering the News*. New York: Basic Books.

Seggar, T. and Wheeler, P. (1973) 'The World of Work on TV: Ethnic and Sex Representation in TV Drama', *Journal of Broadcasting* 17: 201–14.

Seymour-Ure, C. (1974) *The Political Impact of the Mass Media*. London: Constable.

Shibutani, T. (1966) *Improvised News*. New York: Bobbs Merrill.

Shoemaker, P.J. (1984) 'Media Treatment of Deviant Political Groups', *Journalism Quarterly* 61(1): 66–75, 82.

Siebert, F., Peterson, T. and Schramm, W. (1956) *Four Theories of the Press*. Urbana, Ill: University of Illinois Press.

Sigal, L.V. (1973) *Reporters and Officials*. Lexington, Mass: Lexington Books.

Sigelman, L. (1973) 'Reporting the News: an Organizational Analysis', *American Journal of Sociology* 79: 132–51.

Sigman, S.J. and Fry, D.L. (1985) 'Differential Ideology and Language Use: Readers' Reconstruction and Description of News Events', *Critical Studies in Mass Communication* 2(4): 307–22.

Singer, B.D. (1970) 'Mass Media and Communications Processes in the Detroit Riots of 1967', *Public Opinion Quarterly* 34: 236–45.

Singer, B.D. (1973) *Feedback and Society*. Lexington, Mass: Lexington Books.

Siune, K. (1981) 'Broadcast Election Campaigns in a Multiparty System', in K.E. Rosengren, *Advances in Content Analysis*, pp. 177–96. Beverly Hills and London: Sage Publications.

Smith, A. (1973) *The Shadow in the Cave*. London: Allen and Unwin.

Smith, A. (1977) *Subsidies and the Press in Europe*. London: PEP.

Smythe, D.W. (1977) 'Communications: Blindspot of Western Marxism', *Canadian Journal of Political and Social Theory* 1: 120–7.

Snow, R.P. (1983) *Creating Media Culture*. Beverly Hills and London: Sage Publications.

Snow, R.P. (1984) *Media Power*. Beverly Hills and London: Sage Publications.

Spilerman, S. (1976) 'Structural Characteristics and Severity of Racial Disorders', *American Sociological Review* 41: 771–92.

Sreberny-Mohammadi, A. (1984) 'The "World of the News" Study', *Journal of Communication* 34(1): 121–34.

Stamm, K.R. (1985) *Newspaper Use and Community Ties: Towards a Dynamic Theory*. Norwood, NJ: Ablex.

Star, S.A. and Hughes, H.M. (1950) 'Report on an Education Campaign: the Cincinatti Plan for the UN', *American Sociological Review* 41: 771–92.

Steiner, G. (1963) *The People Look at Television*. New York: Alfred Knopf.

Surgeon General's Scientific Advisory Committee (1972) *Television and Growing Up: the Impact of Televised Violence*. Washington DC: GPO.

Szpocinski, A. (1987) 'Evolution of Value Systems in Radio Plays on Historical Subjects', *European Journal of Communication* 2,1: forthcoming.

Tannenbaum, P.H. (ed) (1981) *The Entertainment Functions of Television*. Hillside, NJ: LEA.

Tannenbaum, P.H. and Lynch, M.D. (1960) 'Sensationalism: the Concept and its Measurement', *Journalism Quarterly* 30: 381–93.

Taylor, D.G. (1982) 'Pluralistic Ignorance and the Spiral of Silence', *Public Opinion Quarterly* 46:311–55.

Teheranian, M. (1979) 'Iran: Communication, Alienation, Revolution', *Intermedia* 7(2): 6–12.

Thompson, E.P. (1963) *The Making of the English Working Class*. London: Gollancz.

Thrift, R.R. (1977) 'How Chain Ownership Affects Editorial Vigor of Newspapers', *Journalism Quarterly* 54: 327–31.

Tichenor, P.J., Donohue, G.A. and Olien, C.N. (1970) 'Mass Media and the Differential Growth in Knowledge', *Public Opinion Quarterly* 34: 158–70.

Trenaman, J.S.M. (1967) *Communication and Comprehension*. London: Longman.

Trenaman, J.S.M. and McQuail, D. (1961) *Television and the Political Image*. London: Methuen.

Tuchman, G. (1973–74) 'Making News by Doing Work: Routinizing the Unexpected', *American Journal of Sociology* 79: 110–31.

Tuchman, G. (1978) *Making News: A Study in the Construction of Reality*. New York: Free Press.

Tuchman, G., Daniels, A.K. and Benet, J. (eds) (1978) *Hearth and Home: Images of Women in Mass Media*. New York: Oxford University Press.

Tunstall, J. (1970) *The Westminster Lobby Correspondents*. London: Routledge and Kegan Paul.

Tunstall, J. (1971) *Journalists at Work*. London: Constable.

Tunstall, J. (1977) *The Media are American*. London: Constable.

Tunstall, J. (1982) 'The British Press in an Age of Television', in D.C. Whitney et al., *Mass Communication Yearbook*, pp. 463–79. Beverly Hills and London: Sage Publications.

Turow, J. (1982) 'Unconventional Programs on Commercial Television: an Organizational Perspective', in J.S. Ettema and D.C. Whitney, *Individuals in Mass Media Organizations*, pp. 107–29. Beverly Hills and London: Sage Publications.

van Cuilenberg, J.J. (1987) 'The Information Society: Some Trends and Implications', *European Journal of Communication* 2(1):105–21.

Van Dijk, T. (1983) 'Discourse Analysis: Its Development and Application to the Structure of News', *Journal of Communication* 33(3): 20–43.

Varis, T. (1984) 'The International Flow of Television Programs', *Journal of Communication* 34(1): 143–52.

Vidmar, N. and Rokeach, M. (1974) 'Archie Bunker's Bigotry: a Study of Selective Perception and Exposure', *Journal of Communication* 24: 36–47.

Wagenberg, R.M. and Soderlund, W.C. (1975) 'The Influence of Chain Ownership on Editorial Comment in Canada', *Journalism Quarterly* 52: 93–8.

Ward, S., Wackman, D.B. and Wartella, E. (1977) *How Children Learn to Buy*. Beverly Hills and London: Sage Publications.

Wartella, E. et al. (1983) *Mass Communication Review Yearbook*. Beverly Hills and London: Sage Publications.

Weaver, D.H. (1981) 'Media Agenda-Setting and Media Manipulation', *Massacommunicatie* 9(5): 213–29. Reprinted in D.C. Whitney et al., *Mass Communication Yearbook*, pp. 537–54. Beverly Hills and London: Sage Publications.

Weaver, D. and Wilhoit, C.G. (1986) *The American Journalist*. Bloomington: University of Indiana Press.

Weber, M. (1948) 'Politics as a Vocation', in H. Gerth and C.W. Mills (eds), *Max Weber Essays*. London: Routledge and Kegan Paul.

Wells, A. (1972) *Picture Tube Imperialism? The Impact of US TV in Latin America*. New York: Orbis.

Westergaard, J. (1977) 'Power, Class and the Media', in J. Curran et al. (eds), *Mass Communication and Society*. London: Edward Arnold.

Westerstahl, J. (1983) 'Objective News Reporting', *Communication Research* 10(3): 403–24.

Westley, B. and MacLean, M. (1957) 'A Conceptual Model for Mass Communication Research', *Journalism Quarterly* 34: 31–8.

Whale, J. (1969) *The Half-Shut Eye*. London: Macmillan.

White, D.M. (1950) 'The Gatekeeper: a Case-Study in the Selection of News', *Journalism Quarterly* 27: 383–90.

Whitney, D.C., Wartella, E. and Windahl, S. (eds) (1982) *Mass Communication Review Yearbook, Vol.3*. Beverly Hills and London: Sage Publications.

Wilensky, H.L. (1964) 'Mass Society and Mass Culture: Interdependence or Independence?', *American Sociological Review* 29(2): 173–97.

Wilhoit, G.C. and de Bock, H. (eds) (1980 and 1981) *Mass Communication Review Yearbook, Vols. 1 and 2*. Beverly Hills: Sage Publications.

Williams, R. (1958) *The Long Revolution*. London: Chatto and Windus.

Williams, R. (1961) *Culture and Society*. Harmondsworth: Penguin.

Williams, R. (1973) 'Base and Superstructure', *New Left Review* 82.

Williams, R. (1975) *Television, Technology and Cultural Form*. London: Fontana.

Wintour, C. (1973) *Pressures on the Press*. London: Andre Deutsch.

Wobor, J.M. (1978) 'Televised Violence and the Paranoid Perception: the View from Great Britain', *Public Opinion Quarterly* 42: 315–21.

Wolfe, K.M. and Fiske, M. (1949) 'Why They Read Comics' in P.F. Lazarsfeld and F.M. Stanton, *Communication Research 1948–9*, pp. 3–50. New York: Harper and Brothers.

Wolfenstein, M. and Leites, N. (1947) 'An Analysis of Themes and Plots in Motion Pictures', *Annals of the American Academy of Political and Social Sciences* 254: 41–8.

Womack, B. (1981) 'Attention Maps of Ten Major Newspapers', *Journalism Quarterly* 58(2): 260–5.

Wright, C.R. (1960) 'Functional Analysis and Mass Communication', *Public Opinion Quarterly* 24: 606–20.

Wright, C.R. (1974) 'Functional Analysis and Mass Communication Revisited', in J.G. Blumler and E. Katz, *The Uses of Mass Communications*, pp. 197–212. Beverly Hills and London: Sage Publications.

Zassoursky, Y. (1974) 'The Role of the Soviet Means of Mass Information in the Growth of Scientific and Communist Class Consciousness', Proceedings of IAMCR Congress, Liepzig.

Zillman, D. (1980) 'The Anatomy of Suspense', in P.H. Tannenbaum, *The Entertainment Functions of Television*, pp. 133–63. Hillsdale, NJ: LEA.

Zillman, D. (1985) 'The Experimental Explorations of Gratifications from Media Entertainment', in D. Zillman and J. Bryant (eds) *Selective Exposure to Communication*, pp. 225–39. Hillsdale, NJ: LEA.

Zillman, D. and Bryant, J. (eds) (1985) *Selective Exposure to Communication*. Hillsdale, NJ: LEA.

INDEX